Published by ARTSCROLL / SHAAR PRESS
4401 Second Avenue / Brooklyn, NY 11232 / (718) 921-9000
www.artscroll.com • www.kosherbydesign.com

Distributed in Israel by SIFRIATI / A. GITLER
6 Hayarkon Street / Bnei Brak 51127 / Israel

Distributed in Europe by LEHMANNS
Unit E, Viking Business Park, Rolling Mill Road
Jarrow, Tyne and Wear, NE32 3DP / England

Distributed in Australia and New Zealand by GOLDS WORLD OF JUDAICA
3-13 William Street / Balaclava, Melbourne 3183, Victoria / Australia

Distributed in South Africa by KOLLEL BOOKSHOP
Ivy Common / 105 William Road / Norwood 2192 / Johannesburg, South Africa

ISBN: 1-57819-447-4
ISBN 13: 978-1-57819-447-6

Printed in the USA by Noble Book Press

# kosher by design Entertains

*"To invite a person to your house is to take charge of his happiness as long as he is beneath your roof".*

–Jean Anthelme Brillat-Savarin
(18th-century gourmand)

Welcome to *Kosher by Design Entertains*. This book is about entertaining the way we really want to, in our homes, surrounded by our family and friends. It is about opening our homes to bring people together. It is about having the intention of your heart reflected on your table. It is about overcoming desires to have the caterer on speed-dial or to move celebrations to a restaurant. It is intended to provide inspiration.

In the two years since *Kosher By Design* was released, I have had the incredible privilege of being invited into many varied Jewish communities. While I have loved giving demonstrations and classes in large arenas, the most special ones to me were when I was treated like an honored guest and invited into people's homes. It was great getting to know so many different types of people. Hearing the devotion and extreme interest people have in preparing for special family events and milestones led me to the theme of this book.

The photo spreads are comprised of nine different parties, each a different occasion, but, more importantly, each a different party format. Along with my creative team, we have set a mood, set a table, accessorized it, and given you the ideas for inspiration. You may select a buffet format for a birthday while we showed it for a house-warming. The point is for you to choose and tailor the details to your needs. These are just party strategies that will allow your creativity to soar.

The whole book is comprised of carefully tested recipes that are simple yet elegant enough for any Shabbat, any holiday, or really any day. The menus work well as written but you can prepare as many or as few dishes as suit your needs. Use the menus as guidelines, pick apart the entertaining ideas, and personalize them for your parties. Have fun creating new dishes that thrill your guests and wonderful feasts that bring your loved ones together.

I am often asked for my opinion on how to make a party special. More important than any menu, more memorable than any party favor, is you being there, enjoying, bringing your own sense of personal spirit and style to the events of your life. Savor your most special moments with your most special people.

*Susie Fishbein*

# parties

table of

# recipes

contents

# Thank You

## Kalman
*For standing by me in the kitchen, at the computer and in life. Your intelligence, unending patience and overwhelming love enrich our family. Everything is better with you by my side.*

## Kate, Danielle, Jodi, and Eli
*You are the most important guests at my table and you make every day a celebration. Without even knowing it, your attitudes and excitement during every step of this book really encouraged me. I love you and I am so proud of each of you.*

## Mom and Dad
*Remembering all the special holidays and events when you entertained with a full heart in our home were an inspiration to me in creating this book.*

## Muth
*Your ideas and creativity were always ahead of your time.*

## Gedaliah
*Working with you has been that rare experience where each day brings a new level of respect and admiration. I am grateful for the opportunities you and your father have given me.*

### To my creative team:

## Renee Erreich & Larry Sexton
*You made every day we spent together a real party. I can't imagine working with a better team of people who love what they do as much as you.*

## John Uher, Bob Piazza, Melanie Dubberley, & Robin L. Kerr
*A recipe for success: Assemble a diverse talented group. Add thirteen-hour work days and good kosher lunches. Mix in some camaraderie and laughter. Yield: exquisitely styled and photographed food.*

## Tzini Fruchthandler
*For selfish reasons, I am glad your baby waited until I had the chance to almost wrap this book up. Thank you to Esty Lebovits*

*for crossing the finish line with it. To Eli Kroen, Hershy Feuerwerker, and Charlotte Friedland, thanks for putting the finishing touches on this project.*

## Paula Shoyer
*Your dedication, incredible focus, attention to detail, and talent made you a dream to work with. Your love for what you do comes through in every conversation.*

## Chef Damian Sansonetti, Chef Alex Petard & Chef Jean Chin
*What I learned from you in our kitchen sessions together equals the culinary education of a lifetime. Your skills and exuberance for creating recipes with me will surely stand out on these pages.*

### Thank you to the following people who gave to this book in so many ways:

## Atlas Florist
*Your flowers added style and beauty that were just the right crowning touch to our parties.*

## Nico Sumas & ShopRite
*Like many people, my day is not complete without my daily run. However, my destination is not the track, it is the Livingston ShopRite. Thanks for your support and for running such an unbelievable supermarket.*

## Michael Kane & Park East
*As we say in my home, "Park East, like Porsche, there is no substitute." Thank you for your generosity.*

## Miriam Morgenstern and McCabe's Wine & Spirits
*Thanks for adding "spirit" to our parties.*

### Thank you to these people who shared their favorite recipes and their friendship:

*Shari Alter, Iris Altschuler, Estee Berman, Atara Blumenthal, Limor Decter, Beth Eidman, Sarah Epstein, Steven Epstein, Marcia Feldman, Karen Finkelstein, Myrna Fishbein, Karen Friedman, Rina Fuchs, Elisa Greenbaum, Phyllis Greenstein, Aline Grossman, Elisa Karash, Ellie Langer, Betty Makovsky, Naomi Nachman, Janet Pernick, Jessica Spector, Lenny Spector, Marisa Stadtmauer*

### To the following people who welcomed our crew into their spectacular homes:

*Shelly & Elliot Atlas
Larry Sexton*

*Robin & Ted Withington
Joanne Rose*

*Maida & Mickey Perlmutter
Phyllis & Jack Gross*

*Lauren & Mitchell Presser
Shira & Leslie Westreich*

# engagement party
## cocktail party format

## Menu

❧

Shooters of
Roasted Tomato Bread Soup
page 61

~

Thai Beef in Cucumber Cups
page 19

~

Mandarin Chicken Salad
page 103

~

Lamb Kabobs on Eggplant Purée
page 40

~

Mini Chicken Wellingtons
page 37

~

Two-Tone Potato Skewers
with Pesto Sauce
page 212

~

Champagne Green Beans
page 225

~

Stained-Glass Cookies
page 282

~

Chocolate Berry Tarts
page 269

Engagement, the promise of a new couple beginning their journey to marriage. The coming together of two families. There are so many things to celebrate at this special time.

Open your home; invite your friends and neighbors to come drink a *L'Chaim* and bring their best wishes.

For this event I chose the cocktail party format. This easy setup requires no seating or tables and very little in the way of cleanup. When your front door is open to dozens of people, this is the most practical of solutions. Guests come and go, platters are replenished over and over, and you are free to mingle.

The menu is made up of finger foods. You can showcase a wide range of foods and flavors. Recipes that normally have sauces, have their sauces left behind out of respect to our furniture. Fun drinks are served. Silverware is not necessary, but lots of napkins are mandatory. Make sure there are plenty of trash receptacles spread throughout the house. This will ensure that no untidy toothpicks will be left lying around. This is the kind of party where lively interaction and loud conversations flow.

The food is set up in various stations around the house. The Roasted Tomato Bread Soup, usually served hot, is just as tasty at room temperature. Stack servings in a pyramid of 2-ounce shooters, no spoons necessary.

A bamboo rug serves as the tablecloth while large tropical leaves, such as Thai leaves, Papyrus, and Kaladium are a wonderful backdrop and serve as disposable platters for hors d'oeuvres. Skewers in various materials and sizes add to the appeal of the finger foods. Keep the portions small, 2-3 bites-worth are easiest to handle while balancing your food without a plate. Keep this in mind for any recipes that you adapt to be bite-sized: just cut cooking time and keep the portions small enough so that they don't need to be cut. We've even skewered our Champagne Roasted Green Beans for ease of serving and eating! Edible containers, like the Eggroll Wrappers Cups holding the Mandarin Chicken Salad, help you avoid plates, and can be made days in advance.

Clockwise top to bottom:

▸ Mandarin Chicken Salad in Eggroll Wrapper Cups

▸ Champagne Green Beans

▸ Mini Chicken Wellingtons

An engagement party is the right time and place to raise a glass with a *L'Chaim*. We've set out three beautifully colored drinks: Purple Passions, Caramel Green Apple Martinis, and Sea Breezes. Keep each in a unique glass with a special garnish. As an ice-breaker, let your guests play bartender. Set out the ingredients, place pretty photo frames with the recipes on the bar, and allow your guests to mix the drinks themselves. Don't forget the makings for great garnishes.

### Purple Passion:

1½ ounces vodka

3 ounces grape juice

ginger ale or club soda

Wet the rims of tall collins glasses and dip into purple sugar. Add vodka, grape juice, and ice cubes. Fill with ginger ale or soda. Stir.

### Caramel Green Apple Martini:

¾-ounce butterscotch schnapps

½ ounce sour apple pucker

1 ounce vodka

Combine all ingredients and pour into a martini glass. Garnish with a cinnamon stick and green apple slices.

### Sea Breeze:

3 ounces vodka

3 ounces ruby red grapefruit juice

3 ounces cranberry juice

Mix all with cracked ice in a shaker and pour into a highball glass. Garnish with candied grapefruit slices.

The dessert is simple and should be plentiful. Stained-Glass Cookies, each embellished with the names of the new couple, are tied together and piled high on a three-tiered platter. An assortment of mini Chocolate Berry Tarts add color to the table.

This fun party is a great way to start the new couple off with good wishes — and in style!

# salmon mousse with horseradish aïoli

*Looking for a great alternative to gefilte fish? This beautiful, easy, and elegant dish is your answer.*
*A blender will yield a creamier result, a food processor more of a paté consistency. Leftover aïoli will go great on a turkey, roast beef, or grilled tuna sandwich.*

**Salmon Mousse:**

16 ounces salmon fillet

fine sea salt

freshly ground black pepper

¼ cup chopped flat leaf parsley

¼ cup chopped chives

¼ cup soy milk

juice of ½ lemon

⅛ teaspoon liquid smoke, can be hickory seasoning liquid smoke

frisée lettuce

**Horseradish Aïoli:**

1 cup mayonnaise

¼ cup white bottled horseradish, drained

fine sea salt

freshly ground black pepper

juice of ½ lemon

toast points or crackers

1. Preheat oven to 375°F.

2. Place the salmon on a parchment-lined baking tray. Generously season with salt and pepper. Place in oven and roast for 15 minutes, or until done. Remove from oven and let cool.

3. When cool, separate the flesh from the skin: Using a fork, flake off the salmon. Discard the skin. Place the salmon in a blender or food processor. Add the parsley, chives, soy milk, lemon juice, and liquid smoke. Pulse until completely smooth, reaching a mousse consistency. Refrigerate for at least 1 hour before serving.

4. Prepare the aïoli: In a small bowl, using a spoon, combine the mayonnaise, horseradish, salt, pepper, and lemon juice. Stir until smooth. Set aside.

5. For each serving: Place a handful of frisée in the center of each plate. Use two tablespoons to form oval quenelles and place 2 on lettuce, or use a small ice-cream scoop to place 2 scoops of salmon on the lettuce. Put 3 toast points around plate. Drizzle the plate with aïoli sauce.

*Yield: 4-6 servings*

# barbecue buffalo wings

*The barbecue sauce for this recipe is fabulous. Make a big batch and use it on everything from burgers to steak to chicken breasts. Go heavier on the hot sauce for a spicier version.*

## Chicken Wings:

16 chicken wings, cleaned

freshly ground black pepper

crushed red pepper flakes

1 clove fresh garlic, smashed with the side of your knife blade
to release the flavor

fine sea salt

1 bay leaf

## Barbecue Sauce:

1 cup bottled ketchup

1 teaspoon liquid smoke

1 tablespoon prepared hot espresso or strong coffee

2 cloves fresh garlic, minced

1 teaspoon fish-free Worcestershire sauce

1-2 drops Tabasco or other hot sauce

canola or peanut oil

1. Place the chicken wings into a pot and cover with water. Season the water with red pepper flakes, smashed garlic clove, salt, pepper, and bay leaf. Bring to a boil. Cover, reduce to medium-low, and cook for 10-12 minutes.

2. Preheat oven to 425°F.

3. Prepare the sauce: In the bowl of a food processor fitted with a metal blade, or with an immersion blender in a tall container, combine the ketchup, liquid smoke, espresso, garlic, Worcestershire sauce, and hot sauce. Add a sprinkle of black pepper, salt, and red pepper flakes. Blend until it forms a thick red sauce.

4. Remove the chicken wings from the pot and pat with a paper towel.

5. Heat oil in a deep fryer or large pot to 375°F. Drop the wings in and fry for 2-3 minutes until golden. Drain on paper towels.

6. Lay the wings on a baking sheet in a single layer. Brush both sides of the wings with the prepared barbecue sauce. Roast 10-15 minutes, until sauce starts to caramelize, basting often; watch to make sure they don't burn.

*Yield: 4 servings*

A note about Worcestershire sauce: Most Worcestershire sauce contains anchovies. If the kosher certification mark stands alone, then the percentage of anchovies is less than 1.6% of the whole product. Many rabbinical authorities say that this is okay to use with meat. If the kosher certification on the label has a fish notation next to it, the level exceeds 1.6% and you should refrain from using it in meat dishes.

# steak and green beans with wasabi cream sauce

*This dish can also be made using London broil or minute steak fillets. These steaks are not as salty as skirt steak or hanger steak, so there is no need to soak them. When you season with pepper, also season with salt.*

*If you are making this dish in advance, with any of the cuts, make sure not to overcook the steaks. Keep the steaks whole until right before serving.*

2 teaspoons wasabi powder

2 tablespoons cold water, divided

⅓ cup nondairy sour cream, such as Sour Supreme

⅓ cup nondairy cream cheese, such as Tofutti brand

1 tablespoon chopped fresh chives

½ tablespoon chopped fresh parsley

1 teaspoon apple-cider vinegar

fine sea salt

freshly ground black pepper

4 hanger or skirt steaks steaks (1½ pounds total), soaked in water for at least 1 hour or longer to remove saltiness; pat dry

1 tablespoon olive oil

¾ pound green beans, ends trimmed

1½ tablespoons teriyaki sauce

1. In a medium bowl, whisk the wasabi powder with 1 tablespoon cold water. Add the non-dairy sour cream and cream cheese, chives, parsley, and vinegar. Season with salt and pepper. Cover and refrigerate until ready to serve; can be done in advance.

2. Season both sides of the steaks with pepper.

3. Heat the olive oil in a heavy skillet over medium heat. Add the steaks and sear on each side, about 8 minutes per side for medium.

4. Remove steaks from pan; add the green beans, teriyaki, and remaining tablespoon water. Sauté for 3-4 minutes, scraping up the browned bits. The green beans should be shiny and a bright green color.

5. When ready to serve, slice steak into ¼-½ inch slices on an angle.

6. Serve with the green beans in the center of the plate, the slices of steak fanned around the bottom, and a small dollop of wasabi sauce at the top where the ends of the steak meet.

*Yield: 6-8 servings*

# thai beef in cucumber cups

*The components of this recipe can be prepared in advance. Just keep the cucumbers refrigerated, covered with a damp paper towel.*

## Marinade:

1-inch fresh ginger, peeled, thinly sliced

¾ cup low-sodium soy sauce

¾ cup water

2 tablespoons light brown sugar

1 teaspoon roasted or toasted sesame oil

1 pound London broil

2 tablespoons olive oil

2-3 large English hothouse cucumbers (seedless)

handful of baby sprouts

2 red radishes, unpeeled, sliced into matchsticks

## Dressing:

juice of 2 fresh limes

1½ tablespoons roasted or toasted sesame oil

½ jalapeño pepper, seeds discarded, cut into matchsticks, then minced

2 tablespoons water

3 tablespoons rice vinegar

1 clove fresh garlic, minced

1½ tablespoons soy sauce

2 pinches of cayenne pepper

black sesame seeds, for garnish

1. Mix the sliced ginger, soy sauce, water, light brown sugar, and sesame oil in a bowl. Cut the London broil into 4 large chunks. Add these chunks to the marinade. Let it marinate 2-3 hours or up to overnight.

2. Remove meat from marinade. Dry it with a paper towel; the marinade will burn otherwise. Heat a frying pan over medium heat. Add 2 tablespoons of olive oil. Sear the meat and cook through, about 9-10 minutes per side. Remove from pan. Slice meat into thin matchstick strips.

3. Prepare the dressing: Place the lime juice, sesame oil, jalapeño pepper, water, rice vinegar, garlic, soy sauce, and cayenne in a medium bowl and whisk.

4. Cut the ends off the cucumbers. Peel the ends, chop into ¼-inch pieces and mix with the meat, sprouts, and radishes. Cut the remaining cucumbers into 1-inch pieces. To create the wells, scoop out pulp and some flesh with a melon baller or a ¼-teaspoon measuring spoon. Leave a base on the bottom. Loosely stuff the meat mixture into each well. It is okay if some meat falls onto the plate or over the sides of the cucumber well.

5. Drizzle with the dressing. Garnish with black sesame seeds. Drizzle extra dressing around the plate.

*Yield: 10-12 servings*

# mushroom ravioli with sage cream sauce

Dairy or Parve

*The ravioli can also be used in clear chicken soup as a dumpling. You can make the ravioli and freeze them in a single layer before being cooked. When ready to use, drop into boiling salted water right from freezer.*

*Clean mushrooms with a damp towel or brush. Mushrooms are about 80% water, so if you drown them in water they will soak it up like sponges and lose flavor.*

## Mushroom Ravioli:

3 tablespoons olive oil

3 large or 4 medium shallots, finely minced

12 crimini mushrooms, finely chopped

2 tablespoons fresh thyme leaves, finely chopped

¼ cup fresh sage leaves, finely minced

36 round dumpling wrappers or square wonton wrappers

fine sea salt

freshly ground black pepper

water as needed

## Sage Cream Sauce:

2 tablespoons olive oil

4 shallots, finely minced

⅓ cup fresh sage leaves, finely chopped

2½ cups light cream or soy milk

6 tablespoons sour cream or nondairy sour cream, such as Sour Supreme

1. Place olive oil into a large sauté pan. Over medium heat, sauté the shallots until translucent, about 7-8 minutes. Add the mushrooms; add a drop more oil if necessary. Let the mushrooms release their moisture and then dry or they will make the pasta dough mushy. If shallots start to burn, lower the heat. Add the thyme and sage. Season with salt and pepper. Remove to a bowl and place in the refrigerator to cool.

2. Meanwhile prepare the sauce: In a medium pot heat olive oil over low heat. Add the shallots. Sauté until just translucent, 5-6 minutes. Add the sage leaves and light cream or soy milk. Bring to a low simmer. Whisk in the sour cream. Cook for 1 minute. If sauce becomes too thick, thin with a little more cream or soy milk. Don't allow the sauce to come to a boil or it will separate. Remove from heat.

3. Remove filling from refrigerator.

4. Partially fill a large pot with water, add salt, and bring to a boil. Lay out 1 dumpling or wonton wrapper. Using a rounded measuring spoon, place 1 scant tablespoon of filling in the center of wrapper. With a wet finger, dampen the edges of the wrapper. Cover with second wrapper. Cupping the mound of filling with one hand, press down the edges of the ravioli to seal. Do this with all 18. Drop into water for 2-3 minutes. Drain a few at a time or the ravioli will stick together. Place the ravioli on plates. Ladle the sauce over each portion.

*Yield: 18 ravioli*

# orecchiette pasta with salmon in cream sauce

*When making this dish dairy, there is no need to thicken the sauce with flour at the end.*

2 (6-ounce) salmon fillets

fine sea salt

freshly ground black pepper

1 (16-ounce) box orecchiette or medium shell pasta

2 tablespoons olive oil

4 shallots, minced

3 cups light cream or soy milk

1 (8-ounce) container sour cream or nondairy sour cream, such as Sour Supreme

juice of 1 fresh lemon

⅔ cup chopped fresh dill, plus extra for garnish

2 tablespoons Wondra flour or sifted all-purpose flour

2 cups frozen peas

1. Preheat oven to 375°F.

2. Place the salmon fillets on a baking pan. Season with salt and black pepper.

3. Bake, uncovered, for 15-20 minutes, until no longer translucent in the center. While fish is baking, cook the pasta al denté, according to package directions. Remove salmon from oven. Using a fork, flake the salmon into bite-size pieces. Discard skin. Set salmon aside.

4. In a medium pot, heat 2 tablespoons olive oil. Add the shallots and sauté 5-6 minutes on medium-low heat. Add the cream or soy milk. Bring to a simmer. Whisk in the sour cream. Add the lemon juice. Season with salt and pepper. Add the dill and mix. Whisk in the Wondra or flour. Mix in the peas. Add the cooked pasta and coat with the sauce. Mix in the salmon pieces. Place in serving bowl. Garnish with fresh dill.

*Yield: 10 servings*

# chicken guacamole in flour tortillas

*If you can't find the schwarma spice mix in your neighborhood, mix 1 teaspoon ground cumin, 1 teaspoon allspice, 1 teaspoon paprika, 1 teaspoon onion powder, 1 teaspoon garlic powder, 1 teaspoon dried cilantro, dash salt, pinch of pepper. This mix will keep in a small covered jar for up to 6 months.*

4 boneless, skinless chicken breasts

fine sea salt

freshly ground black pepper

2 cloves fresh garlic, minced, divided

1 tablespoon olive oil

1 tablespoon schwarma spice mix, such as Pereg brand

2 medium Hass avocados, peeled, diced

2 small plum tomatoes, seeds and ribs discarded, diced

3-4 fresh cilantro leaves, lightly chopped

1 shallot, minced

1 teaspoon jalapeño or serrano pepper, seeded, minced

juice of ½ lemon

large flour tortillas

mesclun greens

1. Wash the chicken breasts and pat dry. Season with salt and pepper. Mix the garlic, oil, and schwarma spice in a small bowl to form a paste. Rub into each cutlet. Refrigerate for a few hours or overnight.

2. Cook the chicken on a grill, or indoors in a grill pan or broiled in an oven, about 6 minutes per side. Remove from heat and set aside to cool. When cool, cut into ½-inch dice.

3. Combine the chicken, avocado, tomato, cilantro, shallot, garlic, jalapeño pepper, and lemon juice. Mix together gently; you do not want to turn the mixture into a mush. Season to taste with salt and pepper.

4. Heat each flour tortilla briefly in a large frying pan or on a grill.

5. Place a long mound of the chicken guacamole at the end of the tortilla. Fold the sides in 1-inch and then roll up like a burrito. With a very sharp knife, slice each tortilla on the diagonal into 4 pieces and place on a bed of greens.

*Yield: 6-8 servings*

22    ぷ    KOSHER BY DESIGN ENTERTAINS

# chicken dumplings in ginger broth

*The filling for these dumplings makes a fabulous and healthy chicken burger. Just whip up a batch of the filling, form patties, and sauté in a pan in a drop of olive oil. Serve on a bun or over greens. In fact, when I plan a dinner that includes the chicken dumplings, I always put chicken burgers on my menu for the next night's dinner and make a double batch of the filling.*

*These dumplings freeze well; just keep them in a single layer.*

## Chicken Dumplings:

2 teaspoons olive oil, divided

¾-inch fresh ginger, peeled, minced

6-8 ounces shiitake mushrooms, stems removed, finely chopped

1 tablespoon soy sauce

1 tablespoon dry sherry

3 scallions, finely minced

¼-½ teaspoon fine sea salt

¼-½ teaspoon freshly ground black pepper

1 teaspoon roasted or toasted sesame oil

1 large egg white

½ pound ground chicken

24 wonton wrappers

## Ginger Broth:

8 cups chicken stock

4-5 (2-inch) chunks ginger, peeled

## Garnish:

4 shiitake mushroom caps, thinly sliced

2 scallions, cut on the bias into long, thin strips

roasted or toasted sesame oil

1. Place 1 teaspoon oil in a skillet over medium heat. Add the minced ginger. Sauté 1 minute. Add the mushrooms and remaining teaspoon olive oil. Cook for 2 minutes. Add the soy sauce and sherry. Let the liquid cook out. Add the scallions and sauté 1 minute longer. Remove from heat. Add salt and pepper to taste. Let the mixture cool; refrigerate if necessary to hasten the cooling.

2. Add 1 teaspoon sesame oil and the egg white to the mushroom mixture. Fold in the ground chicken. Mix to combine.

3. Heat the chicken broth in a pot. Add the chunks of ginger. Simmer for 10 minutes. While the broth is simmering, prepare the dumplings.

4. Prepare the dumplings: Place 1 teaspoon chicken mixture into the center of each wonton wrapper. With a wet finger, dampen the edges of the wonton wrapper and gather it up to form a purse shape, enclosing the filling. Remove the chunks of ginger from the broth and discard. Add the dumplings to the broth and simmer for 7-8 minutes. Remove the dumplings.

5. Add the sliced shiitake caps to the broth and cook for 2 minutes. Pour the broth into the serving bowls. Add 3 dumplings to each bowl. Garnish with the sliced scallions.

6. Drizzle each bowl with sesame oil.

*Yield: 8 servings*

# tuna tartare

*Bluefin Toro tuna is very expensive, but due to the high fat content it is the moistest, best quality tuna you can buy. It literally melts in your mouth. It can be difficult to find, so use the freshest, highest sushi-grade ahi tuna available. If you are serving this dish as an hors d'oeuvres, mound 1 tablespoon on each of 25 flatbread squares and garnish each with a small cilanto leaf. Arrange on a platter or tray.*

4 (4-ounce) fresh raw Toro tuna steaks, sliced into strips, cut into tiny squares

1 tomato, seeded, chopped

sesame seeds

freshly ground black pepper

pinch of fine sea salt

1 clove fresh garlic, finely minced

1 teaspoon fresh ginger, minced

1 shallot, finely minced

2 teaspoons soy sauce

½ teaspoon roasted or toasted sesame oil

1 teaspoon fresh lemon juice

2 teaspoons fresh lime juice

2 cilantro leaves, minced

extra cilantro leaves, for garnish

small crackers, for garnish

1. In a medium bowl, mix the tuna, tomato, sesame seeds, black pepper, salt, garlic, ginger, shallot, soy sauce, sesame oil, lemon juice, lime juice, and cilantro. Toss to combine; try not to mix too much. Allow the tuna to absorb the flavors for 15 minutes or up to 2 hours, covered, in the refrigerator.

2. Wet 4 small rounded espresso or tea cups; shake out extra water. Line each with plastic wrap, letting extra hang over the sides. Place ⅓ cup mixture into each tea cup. Press with the back of a spoon to compress. Bring the excess plastic wrap into the center of the cup and push in to close the packet and further compress the tartare. Place in refrigerator for 15-20 minutes.

3. Open the plastic wrap. Invert each packet onto a plate. Garnish with a fresh cilantro leaf and small crackers placed upright against the side of the mound.

*Yield: 4 servings*

# meat croustade

*This simple meat tart looks so elegant in its phyllo dough crust.*

2 tablespoons olive oil

1 medium onion,
cut into ¼-inch dice

2 cloves fresh garlic,
coarsely chopped

1 pound ground beef

1 (15-ounce) jar favorite
marinara sauce

nonstick cooking spray

10 sheets phyllo dough,
thawed

6 tablespoons margarine,
melted

2 plum tomatoes,
cut into ¼-inch slices

1. Preheat oven to 350°F.

2. Heat the olive oil in a large sauté pan over medium heat. Add the onion and garlic and sauté until translucent and golden, about 6 minutes.

3. Add the meat, breaking it up with a fork, and sauté until brown. Drain off any fat. Add the marinara. Cook until all the liquid evaporates, about 7-8 minutes. Tilt the pan to be sure no liquid remains.

4. Meanwhile, lightly spray a 9-inch springform pan with nonstick spray. Open up the phyllo sheets. Lightly brush the first sheet with some of the melted margarine. Fold the sheet in half lengthwise. Brush top with margarine. Place one end of the folded sheet in the center of the springform pan, let the rest hang over the side. Repeat with remaining phyllo and margarine, arranging the strips in a spoke-like fashion evenly around the pan. Make sure the whole bottom surface of the pan is covered with phyllo.

5. Spoon the meat mixture into the bottom of the phyllo crust. Cover the center of the meat with overlapping layers of tomatoes.

6. Starting with the last phyllo strip placed in the pan, lift the end of the strip and bring it toward the center of the filling. Holding the end, twist the end several times; coil and tuck the end under to form a rosette. Lay the rosette over the filling.

7. Repeat with remaining phyllo strips in the reverse order in which they were placed into the pan, leaving a 3-inch circle in the center where the filling is visible. Drizzle any remaining margarine over all.

8. Bake for 30 minutes.

*Yield: 10 servings*

# edamame with dipping sauce

*Move over tofu — the new buzz on soy is all about edamame. Americans have just discovered what the Japanese have known for centuries. Edamame are soybeans. They pack a powerhouse of protein, only half-a-cup provides 16 grams of protein. They contain 8 amino acids, as well as calcium, fiber, zinc, and B vitamins. Not bad for a funny-looking little green bean! They are a delicious fat-free appetizer. Sushi restaurants offer them on the table the way steak restaurants offer bread. The Japanese eat them with beer, the way we snack on nuts. When I am watching TV, I like to have them around in place of pretzels, chips, or other snacks. My kids love popping them into their mouths right out of the pod. I use extra in salads, stir fries, and soups.*

*You can find them in any Asian market and at upscale organic markets like Whole Foods and Trader Joes, fresh and in their freezer sections.*

*The way to eat them is right from the pod. Simply squeeze the pod and pop the beans right in your mouth, discarding the pod.*

## Edamame:

½ tablespoon coarse sea salt
or kosher salt

1 (1-pound) bag fresh or
frozen edamame (soybeans
in the pod)

bowl of ice water

## Dipping Sauce:

2 tablespoons low-sodium
soy sauce

2 tablespoons rice-wine vinegar

½ teaspoon roasted
or toasted sesame oil

1 teaspoon honey

1 clove fresh garlic, minced

1 tablespoon chopped scallions

1. Place the salt into a small ungreased skillet. Place over medium heat and cook until tan, about 6-7 minutes; toss as it cooks. Set aside.

2. Place the edamame into a pot of boiling water and cook until tender, 4 minutes. You want to cook out the raw taste but don't want them to get mushy. Immediately transfer with a slotted spoon to a bowl of ice water to stop the cooking. Drain and pat dry. Toss with the prepared salt.

3. Prepare the dipping sauce: In a small bowl, whisk the soy sauce, vinegar, sesame oil, honey, garlic, and scallions. Serve in small dipping bowls with the edamame.

*Yield: 4 servings*

# garlic knots with olive tapenade

*These garlic knots are crowd-pleasers. They are so simple and add so much to a bowl of soup or pasta. My family is happy to see them at any meal. They are easy enough that I make them quite often. I usually buy the dough at my local pizza shop. I have also found great frozen parve pizza dough at some supermarkets. Just thaw and proceed with the recipe.*

*The tapenade is a wonderful spread that has so many uses. Use as a spread for challah or sandwiches. Add it to a salad or grilled vegetables. Toss some into your pasta or over a grilled fish fillet.*

*At a recent party, I took small Mission figs, lightly brushed with olive oil, and broiled them for 6-8 minutes, turning once. Using a sharp knife, I cut X's into the stem ends and spread them open to look like flowers. I combined some goat cheese with the tapenade and, using a pastry bag fitted with a star tip, piped the mixture into the figs. They were the perfect size for passing on trays and my guests were not left holding a toothpick or small plate.*

## Olive Tapenade:

1 cup Kalamata or other brine-cured black olives, such as Niçoise or Gaeta, pitted

2 oil-packed anchovy fillets, rinsed

1 tablespoon bottled capers, rinsed and drained

2 large cloves fresh garlic

½ teaspoon fresh thyme

½ teaspoon fresh rosemary

1 tablespoon fresh lemon juice

¼ cup good-quality extra-virgin olive oil

freshly ground black pepper, to taste

## Garlic Knots:

4 tablespoons margarine, melted

2 tablespoons fresh parsley, minced

4 cloves fresh garlic, minced

1 pound store-bought pizza dough, cut into 10-12 strips

1. Prepare the tapenade: Place the olives, anchovies, capers, garlic, thyme, rosemary, and lemon juice into the bowl of a food processor fitted with a metal blade. Pulse a few times until finely chopped, allowing it to retain some texture; don't overprocess. Add the olive oil and pulse until incorporated. Season with pepper as needed. Let the tapenade refrigerate overnight to allow the flavors to mature.

2. Prepare the garlic knots: Preheat oven to 375°F.

3. In a small bowl, whisk the margarine, parsley, and garlic.

4. On a flat surface, roll the strips of dough into 8-inch ropes. Brush each strip with the garlic mixture. Tie each strip into a loose knot. Place on a parchment-lined or ungreased baking sheet, allowing room for the knots to spread. Brush the knots again with the garlic mixture. Bake for 20-25 minutes, or until golden brown. Serve warm. If you are going to re-warm, undercook them slightly, until just beginning to brown.

*Yield: 10-12 garlic knots*

*1¼ cups tapenade*

# mexican gefilte fish

*A spicy and fabulous alternative to the traditional.*

water as needed

1 (1.25-ounce) packet taco seasoning

1 (22-ounce) roll frozen gefilte fish, not defrosted

2 teaspoons canola oil

1 large onion, chopped

2 cups shredded carrots, or 2 carrots, peeled, sliced

1 clove fresh garlic, chopped

1 medium chili pepper or jalapeño pepper, seeds and ribs discarded, minced

1 (16-ounce) can tomato sauce

3 tablespoons sugar

2 teaspoons water

1. Bring a medium pot of water to boil. Add the taco seasoning to the water. Place the gefilte fish in its paper wrapper into the boiling water. Make sure there is enough water to cover or add water as needed. Turn heat down; simmer for 1½ hours.

2. In a medium pan, heat the oil on medium heat. Add the onion and sauté for 3-4 minutes, until shiny. Add the carrots, garlic, and chili pepper. Sauté for an additional 3 minutes.

3. Add the tomato sauce, sugar, and water. Bring to a boil. Remove from heat and set aside.

4. Preheat oven to 350°F.

5. When fish is done, remove it from the pot, discarding the water. When cool enough to handle, unwrap and discard the paper. Slice the fish and place into a baking dish. Pour the sauce over, and place, covered, into the oven. Bake for 1½ hours. Allow to cool. Best if done one day in advance and kept in refrigerator. Serve cold.

*Yield: 10 servings*

---

## Measurement Chart:

When you are cooking for a party, this chart may help you to multiply ingredients:

| | | | | |
|---|---|---|---|---|
| 3 teaspoons | = 1 tablespoon | | ¼ cup butter | = 4 tablespoons or ½ stick |
| 4 tablespoons | = ¼ cup = 2 fluid ounces | | ⅓ cup butter | = 5⅓ tablespoons |
| 8 tablespoons | = ½ cup | | ½ cup butter | = 8 tablespoons or 1 stick |
| 16 tablespoons | = 1 cup = 8 fluid ounces | | 1 cup butter | = 16 tablespoons or 2 sticks |
| ⅔ cup | = ½ cup plus 2⅔ tablespoons | | 4 sticks butter | = 2 cups |

Eggs:

2 medium eggs = ⅓ cup
2 large eggs  = ½ cup

# stuffed tomatoes

*Acini di pepe is the Italian for peppercorns. These tiny balls of pasta resemble peppercorns in size and shape.*

6 beefsteak tomatoes

fine sea salt

freshly ground black pepper

olive oil, for drizzling

8 ounces acini di pepe, cooked in salted water until al denté, according to package directions

1 tablespoon canola oil

1 onion, cut into ¼-inch dice

½ cup chopped button mushrooms

½ small zucchini, unpeeled, cut into ¼-inch dice

¼ teaspoon dried oregano

½ small yellow squash, unpeeled, cut into ¼-inch dice

10 grape tomatoes, quartered

Dressing:

¼ cup red wine vinegar

1 tablespoon balsamic vinegar

5 tablespoons olive oil

¼ teaspoon dry mustard powder

2 cloves fresh garlic, minced

1 tablespoon fresh oregano, chopped

fine sea salt

freshly ground black pepper

1. Preheat oven to 375°F.

2. Cut off the crown of each tomato and reserve. Using a spoon, remove the pulp and seeds and discard. Season the inside of each tomato with salt and pepper. Season the lid with salt and pepper. Place the tomatoes into a baking dish. Arrange the lids in the pan as well. Drizzle all with olive oil. Bake 10-12 minutes, until soft but still holding their shape. Remove from oven, set aside.

3. Place the cooked, drained pasta into a large bowl. Set aside.

4. Heat the canola oil in a large skillet over medium heat. Add the onion, sauté for 3 minutes. Add the mushrooms, zucchini, and dried oregano. Sauté for 4 minutes. Add the yellow squash and grape tomatoes. Sauté 3 minutes longer.

5. Prepare the dressing: In a medium bowl, with an immersion blender or whisk, combine the red wine vinegar, balsamic vinegar, olive oil, mustard powder, garlic, oregano, pinch of salt, and pinch of pepper. Blend or whisk until emulsified. Pour the dressing into the pan and mix with the vegetables. Add the pasta into the pan, tossing to combine. Scoop into the tomato shells, setting a lid on each stuffed tomato.

*Yield: 6 servings*

# coconut chicken strips with two dipping sauces

Chicken Strips:

6 boneless, skinless chicken breasts

fine sea salt

freshly ground black pepper

¼ cup all-purpose flour

¼ teaspoon garlic powder

¼ teaspoon cayenne pepper

2 eggs, lightly beaten

½ cup panko (see resource guide, p. 317) or cornflake crumbs

1 cup sweetened flaked coconut

honey

Mango Sauce:

1 fresh mango

¼ cup soy milk

2 tablespoons dry white wine

2 teaspoons honey mustard

Apricot Sauce:

6 ounces apricot preserves

2 teaspoons yellow mustard (not Dijon)

2 tablespoons teriyaki sauce

3 tablespoons chopped hazelnuts, for garnish

1. Preheat oven to 350°F.

2. Remove the tenders from the chicken. Cut each breast into long ½-inch thin strips, trimming the ends to make rectangles. Trim the tenders as well. Season the strips with salt and pepper.

3. Place the flour into a shallow dish. Add some salt and pepper to the flour. Add the garlic powder and cayenne. Toss to combine. Place the beaten egg into a second shallow dish. Mix the panko or cornflake crumbs and coconut in a third dish.

4. Lightly coat the chicken strips with flour, shaking off excess. Dip each strip into the egg, shaking off excess. Roll into coconut mixture, pressing the coconut into the chicken to evenly coat.

5. Place the coated strips on a baking sheet. Lightly drizzle with honey. Bake 20 minutes, turning the strips halfway through.

6. Meanwhile, prepare the mango sauce: Place the mango into a blender or the bowl of a food processor fitted with a metal blade. Purée. Add the soy milk, wine, and mustard. Pulse 2-3 times. Set aside.

7. Prepare the apricot sauce: Combine apricot preserves, yellow mustard, and teriyaki sauce. Stir to combine.

8. To serve, place 3-4 chicken strips on each plate with two small bowls, one with the mango sauce and the other with the apricot sauce. Garnish mango sauce wtih chopped hazelnuts

*Yield: 8-10 servings*

# mini chicken wellingtons

## Mini Chicken Wellingtons:

3 boneless, skinless chicken breasts, pounded to an even thickness

fine sea salt

freshly ground black pepper

3 tablespoons olive oil, divided

⅓ cup chopped crimini mushrooms

⅓ cup chopped shiitake mushroom caps

⅓ cup chopped oyster mushrooms or other wild mushrooms

1 shallot, very finely minced

1 clove fresh garlic, minced

3 sheets puff pastry (from 2 17.5-ounce boxes)

24 baby spinach leaves

1 egg, lightly beaten

## Raspberry Sauce:

1 (10-ounce) box frozen raspberries in light syrup

zest and juice of 1 fresh lime

10 chives, finely chopped

1 tablespoon fresh parsley leaves, chopped

1. Preheat oven to 400°F. Line a jelly-roll pan or cookie sheet with parchment paper. Set aside.

2. Remove tenders from chicken if they are attached. Set aside for another use. Cut each breast in half lengthwise. Cut each strip in half widthwise. You will end up with 12 square pieces. Season both sides of each piece of chicken with salt and pepper.

3. In a medium saucepan, heat 2 tablespoons olive oil over medium heat. Add the chicken and sear each side for 1-2 minutes. Don't overcook or the chicken will dry out when it bakes in the oven. Remove the chicken from the pan and set aside. To the same pan, add the cremini, shiitake, and oyster mushrooms. Add the shallot and garlic. Season with salt and pepper. Drizzle with remaining tablespoon olive oil. Sauté for 4-6 minutes, until soft and fragrant. Remove from heat and set aside to cool. Refrigerate if necessary to hasten the cooling.

4. Cut each of the two sheets of puff pastry into 6 equal squares, totaling 12 squares. Season the puff pastry with salt and pepper. Lay 1 spinach leaf in the center of each square. Top with 1/12 of the cooled mushroom mixture. Top with a second baby spinach leaf. Place a square of chicken on top of the spinach leaf. Wrap the puff pastry around the mound, sealing it on the bottom and tucking the ends underneath. Place, seamside down, on prepared baking sheet.

5. Using a mini cookie cutter, cut leaves or flowers from the third puff pastry sheet. Place 1 leaf or flower on top of each mini wellington. Brush the whole packet with the beaten egg. Bake for 15-20 minutes, until pastry is golden brown.

6. Meanwhile, prepare raspberry sauce: Pour the frozen raspberries and syrup into a small pot. Add the zest and juice of the lime. Bring to a boil. Reduce to a simmer for 5 minutes. In the bowl of a food processor fitted with a metal blade or with an immersion blender in the pot, purée the raspberries. Strain though a fine mesh strainer and discard the seeds. Mix in the chives and parsley. Adjust seasoning with salt and pepper. Serve the sauce warm or at room temperature with mini wellingtons.

*Yield: 12 servings*

# roasted pepper, artichoke, and caramelized onion frittata

Parve

*Frittata are great big baked omelettes. Many people think of them as strictly a brunch item, but I have served frittata as a Shabbos appetizer in the warmer weather. We tend to eat lighter in the hot weather and this dish is colorful and delightful. It fills us up without weighing us down.*

1 tablespoon olive oil

1 small onion, thinly sliced

fine sea salt

freshly ground black pepper

½ cup canned artichokes, quartered, or ½ cup sliced canned hearts of palm

½ cup (or 2 halves) jarred roasted red pepper, cut into ¼-inch pieces (don't get the kind that is preserved in vinegar and oil)

4 large eggs

¼ cup soy milk

4 sprigs fresh flat leaf parsley, leaves finely chopped, stems discarded

1. Preheat oven to 350°F.

2. Place the olive oil into an 8–10-inch ovenproof frying pan. If the pan has a plastic handle, triple-wrap the handle with aluminum foil. Heat the oil over medium heat. Add the onion. Season with salt and pepper. Allow to cook for 15 minutes, until caramelized, shaking the pan every 5 minutes. Add the artichokes or hearts of palm and chopped peppers. Sauté 3 minutes.

3. In a medium bowl, whisk the eggs with the soy milk. Season with salt and pepper. Add the parsley leaves. Whisk to combine.

4. Add the eggs to the pan with the onions. Stir once. Turn heat to high and cook until beginning to set around the edges of the pan.

5. Place the pan into the preheated oven for 5-10 minutes, until eggs are set. Remove from oven, run a spatula around the outside of the pan to loosen the edges, making sure the bottom is loosened as well. Place a plate over the pan and flip the frittata out on to the plate.

6. Serve warm or at room temperature. Can be made a day in advance.

*Yield: 4 servings*

# moussaka

*For Simchat Torah my family invades the home of our friends, Rina and Moshe Fuchs. The fun and friendship we share with them is enhanced by Rina's generous hospitality, especially at mealtime.*

*By dinner time on the last night of the holiday, just when my husband thought it was safe to take a snooze and that none of us could even look at food for at least a week, out came this moussaka. When he awoke, only 20 minutes later, and jokingly asked if he had missed a meal, we pointed to the empty moussaka dish. Well, you snooze — you lose. Some dishes can't be missed.*

nonstick cooking spray

1 large eggplant, (about 1½ pounds), peeled or unpeeled, cut into ½-inch round slices

fine sea salt

2 tablespoons olive oil

1 medium onion, chopped

1 pound ground beef

2 tablespoons tomato paste

3 tablespoons red wine

1 (15-ounce) can tomato sauce

2 tablespoons fresh parsley, chopped

1 teaspoon dried oregano

¼ teaspoon ground cinnamon

½ teaspoon garlic powder

freshly ground black pepper

3 tablespoons margarine

2 tablespoons all-purpose flour or Wondra flour

2 cups soy milk

3 large eggs, whisked

2 beefsteak tomatoes, evenly cut into ½-inch slices

⅛ cup bread crumbs

1. Preheat oven to 350°F.

2. Spray a 9-by 9-inch square baking pan with nonstick cooking spray. Set aside.

3. Place the eggplant slices on a piece of paper towel. Sprinkle with salt. Top with a piece of paper towel. Place a pan or other weight on top. Leave for 20 minutes. This salting will draw the bitterness from the eggplant and the salt will be drawn out with it. Rinse after 20 minutes and pat dry.

4. Meanwhile, heat the olive oil in a large skillet. Add the chopped onion. Sauté for 4-5 minutes, until beginning to soften. Add the ground beef, breaking it up with a fork. Sauté for 15 minutes. Add the tomato paste, wine, tomato sauce, parsley, oregano, cinnamon, and garlic powder. Simmer for 15 minutes, until the mixture is almost dry. Season with salt and pepper.

5. Lay half of the eggplant slices in the bottom of the prepared pan. Pour the meat mixture over the eggplant. Top with remaining eggplant slices. Press down to compact.

6. In a small pot, over medium-low heat, melt the margarine. Add the flour, whisking for 1 minute. Add the soy milk, whisking until smooth. Simmer for 2 minutes, whisking constantly. Mix a small amount of the hot liquid into the eggs to temper them so they don't scramble. Add the egg mixture to the pot and bring to a low boil, whisking constantly. As soon as you see small bubbles, remove custard from heat.

7. Pour over the meat. Arrange the tomato slices over the top. Sprinkle with bread crumbs.

8. Cover loosely with foil and bake 1 hour. Uncover and cook for 10 minutes longer, until golden brown and bubbling around the edges.

*Yield: 8 servings*

# lamb kabobs on eggplant purée

*One of the best jobs I ever had was giving cooking demonstrations for Chosen Voyage, a completely glatt kosher luxury cruiseliner. Just imagine, unlimited amounts of gourmet prepared food, it was like a 5-star Grossinger's Hotel at sea. The team of international chefs even prepared their renditions of my Kosher by Design food at the Shabbos buffet. Good manners dictated that I had to try everything at every meal. While there were many amazing dishes, this was one must-have recipe that the chefs graciously shared with me for this book.*

## Lamb Kabobs:

1 medium onion, finely chopped

3 cloves fresh garlic, minced

1 teaspoon dried thyme

¼ cup fresh mint leaves, chopped

¼ cup fresh curly parsley leaves, chopped

¼ teaspoon fine sea salt

¼ teaspoon freshly ground black pepper

¼ teaspoon red pepper flakes

½ teaspoon ground cumin

1 tablespoon paprika

2 teaspoons olive oil

2 pounds boneless lamb cubes

cherry tomatoes

1 medium red onion, cubed

## Eggplant Purée:

2 large purple eggplants

2 cloves fresh garlic

3 tablespoons fresh parsley, chopped

½ teaspoon ground cumin

½ teaspoon ground coriander

3 tablespoons tahini

fine sea salt to taste

1. In a large mixing bowl or ziplock bag, combine the onion, garlic, thyme, mint, parsley, salt, pepper, red pepper flakes, cumin, paprika, and olive oil. Mix to combine. Add the lamb cubes and mix again to evenly distribute the spice mixture on the lamb.

2. Cover or seal and refrigerate several hours or overnight.

3. Meanwhile, prepare the eggplant purée: Preheat oven to 350°F.

4. With the skin intact, cut the eggplants in half lengthwise. Make diamond-shaped slash marks on the cut surface of the eggplants. Place, cut-side-down, on a parchment-lined baking sheet.

5. Bake for about 1 hour or until soft. In the bowl of a food processor fitted with a metal blade, place the garlic, parsley, cumin, coriander, and tahini. When the eggplant is cool enough to handle, use a large spoon to scoop the flesh out of the shells and place into the food processor bowl. Discard the eggplant peel. Purée the mixture. Add salt to taste. The purée can be served at room temperature or warm, so feel free to make it a few days in advance and keep in a sealed container in the refrigerator.

6. Remove lamb from spice mixture, leaving some of the onions and spices adhering to the lamb. Thread the lamb onto skewers, alternating with tomatoes and red onion cubes. If you have wooden skewers, soak skewers in water for ½ hour before using.

7. Place the kabobs on a hot oiled grill or in a hot grill pan lightly coated with olive oil. Grill for a total of 8-10 minutes, turning to cook all sides, until lamb is done. It should still be slightly pink inside. You can broil them in your oven as well, turning every three minutes until done, for a total of 10 minutes.

8. Serve with eggplant purée.

*Yield: 8 servings*

# peking duck wontons with sweet soy sauce

*If you were fortunate enough to dine at The Box Tree Restaurant in NYC when Chef Alex Petard was there, you will recognize this as his signature appetizer. If you did not get a chance to eat there, here is your chance to sample kosher dining at its finest, right in your own home.*

## Sweet Soy Sauce:

½ cup soy sauce

½ cup sugar

1 teaspoon fresh ginger, minced

1 clove fresh garlic, minced

1 teaspoon Jack Daniels or other whiskey

## Duck Wontons:

2 each duck drumsticks and thighs, or ½ duck, cut into pieces

water as needed

½ teaspoon freshly ground black pepper

½ teaspoon crushed red pepper flakes

2 cloves fresh garlic, smashed with the back of a knife

1 bay leaf

2 scallions, chopped

2 teaspoons red onion, minced

1 egg yolk, slightly beaten, optional

1 package 6- by 6-inch eggroll wrappers

peanut oil

1. Place the soy sauce and sugar into a small pot. Bring to a boil. Add the ginger, garlic, and whiskey. Turn down to the lowest heat and simmer for 20 minutes. Pass through a strainer. Set aside. The sauce can be made in advance. Rewarm to make it pourable when ready to serve.

2. Place the duck pieces into a soup pot. Add water to come halfway up the duck. Add the black pepper, red pepper flakes, garlic, and bay leaf. Bring to a boil. Cover and turn the heat down to a low simmer for 1 hour. Add more water as necessary so that it doesn't cook out.

3. Remove duck from pot and let it cool. Remove the skin, setting it aside. Cut the meat off the bones, trimming away any fat. Using a very sharp knife or a food processor, chop the duck meat very well and place into a bowl. Add the scallion and red onion. Mix together. Add 3 teaspoons of the soy sauce mixture.

4. Lay one eggroll wrapper flat. Rub the duck skin around the edge of each wrapper to moisten it. Alternatively, you can use a slightly beaten egg yolk. Place a small mound of filling in the center; a mini ice-cream scoop works well here. Make a purse by pleating and gathering the ends of the dough as you enclose the filling.

5. Bring a pot of peanut or canola oil to 375°F. This can also be done in a deep fryer. Fry for 2-3 minutes.

6. Remove to a paper towel and then place 3 wontons on each plate. Drizzle the plate with extra sauce.

*Yield: 12 wontons*

# cajun sweet potato latkes

*Don't wait for Chanukah to make these fabulous funky latkes.*

2 pounds (about 3 large) sweet potatoes, peeled

3 large eggs

2 tablespoons plus 1 teaspoon Cajun spice blend

⅓ cup chopped cilantro

peanut oil

sour cream or nondairy sour cream, such as Sour Supreme

1. Using the coarse grating disc of a food processor, grate the sweet potatoes. Transfer to a large bowl.

2. In a small bowl, whisk the eggs. Sprinkle the Cajun spice blend into the eggs and whisk. Mix in the cilantro.

3. Add egg mixture to the grated potatoes.

4. In a large skillet, heat the peanut oil until very hot but not smoking. If you are using a thermometer, bring the oil to 375°F.

5. Add the sweet potato mixture, ¼ cup at a time. Fry until golden, flip, and fry until golden on the other side. Drain on paper towels. Repeat until all the potatoes are used.

6. Serve with a dollop of sour cream.

*Yield: 14-18 latkes*

# guacamole latkes

2 pounds Yukon Gold potatoes, unpeeled

2 large eggs

2 teaspoons sea salt

3 avocados, peeled, pitted

½ large red onion, minced

2 small jalapeño peppers, seeded, finely chopped

1½ cups canned black beans, rinsed and drained

peanut oil

store-bought salsa

1. Using the coarse grating disc of a food processor, grate the unpeeled potatoes. Transfer to a large bowl.

2. In a small bowl, whisk the eggs. Add the salt into the eggs.

3. In a medium bowl, mash the avocado with the back of a fork. Add the onions, jalapeño peppers, and beans. Mix to combine.

4. Add the egg mixture and the avocado mixture into the grated potatoes. Gingerly toss to combine.

5. In a large skillet, heat the peanut oil until very hot but not smoking. If you are using a thermometer, bring the oil to 375°F.

6. Add the potato/avocado mixture, ¼ cup at a time. Fry until golden, flip, and fry until golden on the other side. Drain on paper towels. Repeat until all the potatoes are used.

7. Serve with a dollop of salsa.

*Yield: 14-18 latkes*

Steven

just for guys

# just for guys
## family style format

Your husband's birthday is coming and you're not sure how to celebrate. We have the perfect answer: invite a few of his friends over and set up a family-style dinner with a beer tasting that's sure to please.

Family style is for casual or informal entertaining. It's great for small groups of friends or family. The beauty of serving family style is that all the food comes out of the oven at the same time and is served out of platters from the center of the table. That means you can set the table and the stage for a great time — then leave for a night out with *your* friends!

To achieve a homey, masculine look, we covered the tables in brown and black large check cloth and set it with rugged earthenware. Beer mugs and pilsner glasses at each place setting made it easy for the guests to sample a variety of beers. The centerpiece, a simple wooden bowl filled with lemons and miniature Calais, added bright color contrast.

There's nothing like the company of good friends enjoying a hefty, scrumptious meal together. Food that is warm and filling creates a sense of camaraderie that lends itself to sharing reminiscences. So we began this dinner with individual ramekins of hot Shepherd's Pie. We selected English brown ale to go with this traditional English comfort food. This course was followed by Chicken Dumplings in Ginger Broth, paired with a choice of Asian beer or Pilsner Urquell. The main meal of succulent Hazelnut-and-Honey-Crusted Veal Chops was superb with German Bock, and our tangy Chicken Osso Buco was paired with Modelo, a citrusy beer. Carrot and Snap Pea Bundles and down-home Asparagus Shiitake Loaf rounded out this menu.

The hum of conversation stopped suddenly when our Triple Chocolate Explosion cake was brought out of the kitchen. Now here was a serious dessert — a gift to every chocolate lover! Set ablaze for the occasion, and paired with Stout, a traditional Lambic, or Porter, it was the perfect surprise ending to this relaxed, hassle-free celebration.

soups

# cream of corn soup

Meat, Dairy, or Parve

4 ears corn on the cob, discard husk and silks

4 cloves fresh garlic, sliced

1 onion, cut into large chunks

1 cup chicken broth or vegetable stock

4 cups water

¼-½ teaspoon fine sea salt

1 cup light cream or soy milk

¼-½ teaspoon ground white pepper

1. Cut the kernels from the cobs, reserving the kernels. Place the cobs into a medium pot. Add the garlic and onion. Pour in the broth. Add the water. Season with salt.

2. Bring to a boil, then turn down and simmer, covered, for 45 minutes.

3. Discard the cobs and add the corn kernels. Simmer for 15 minutes.

4. With an immersion blender, purée the soup until it is as smooth as possible; there will be some texture from the corn kernels. This step can also be done in a blender.

5. Add the cream or soy milk and ¼ teaspoon white pepper. Simmer for 5 minutes. Add another ¼ teaspoon white pepper if needed.

*Yield: 6-8 servings*

# broccoli and almond bisque

Meat, Dairy, or Parve

1½ cup blanched almonds, divided

1 tablespoon olive oil

2 small onions, chopped

2 heads broccoli, florets cut off, stalks coarsely chopped

2 potatoes, peeled, cut into ½-inch cubes

5 cups chicken or vegetable stock

1 teaspoon dried tarragon

1 teaspoon Dijon mustard

1 cup light cream or soy milk

fine sea salt

freshly ground black pepper

1. Place the almonds into the container of a food processor fitted with a metal blade. Process until finely ground but not pasty. Set aside.

2. Heat the oil in a large pot over medium heat. Add the onions. Sauté until translucent, 4-6 minutes. Add the broccoli, potatoes, stock, tarragon, and 1 cup of the ground almonds. Cover and simmer for 20-25 minutes, until broccoli is tender.

3. Transfer to a blender or food processor and process until smooth. You can also use an immersion blender right in the pot; purée until smooth. Add mustard and light cream or soy milk. Blend.

4. Season with salt and black pepper as needed.

5. Garnish each bowl of soup with a sprinkle of the ground almonds.

*Yield: 6-8 servings*

# yellow split pea vegetable soup

*This was one line of praise for a recipe which I had never heard before. My friend Atara Blumenthal, who'd been allowed kosher food on a sequestered jury, called me one morning to say, "Sue, my soup was the hit of the jury dinner; ya gotta try it!" When I stopped laughing and started cooking, I whipped up a batch and was impressed.*

1 tablespoon canola oil

2 strips flanken or short ribs

12 cups water

1 onion, chopped

4 carrots, peeled, sliced

4 celery stalks, sliced

1 leek, sliced, white and pale green parts only

¼ cup fresh dill, chopped

3 button mushrooms, chopped

1¾ cup dried yellow split peas

⅓ cup pearl barley

2 teaspoons salt

3 chicken bouillon cubes, crumbled; or 3 teaspoons powdered consommé powder

1 cup chicken stock

1. Heat the oil in a large soup pot. Add the meat and sear for 5 minutes on each side.

2. Add the water to the pot. Add the onion, carrots, celery, leek, dill, mushrooms, split peas, barley, salt, bouillon, and stock. Bring to a boil. Cover and simmer for 2 hours. Stir every so often to make sure nothing is sticking to the bottom of the pot. Thin with extra stock if necessary.

*Yield: 10-12 servings*

# sweet and sour cabbage soup

*A hearty meal in a bowl, this soup is even better when allowed to sit a day or two before serving.*

2 tablespoons olive oil

2 large strips flanken or beef short ribs, 2-2½ pounds

2 onions, chopped

3 cloves fresh garlic, chopped

4 cups finely sliced green cabbage, about ½ of a small head of cabbage

1 (28-ounce) can whole tomatoes, finely chopped, with their juices

1 (8-ounce) can tomato sauce

8 cups beef stock (can be made from 8 teaspoons beef consommé powder and 8 cups water)

juice of 2 fresh lemons

½ cup dark brown sugar

½ cup sauerkraut (from jar or can)

½ teaspoon freshly ground black pepper

1. Heat the oil in a large pot over medium heat. Sear the flanken or short ribs on all sides, about 3-5 minutes per side, depending on thickness. Add the onions and garlic. Sauté for 3 minutes.

2. Add the cabbage, tomatoes, tomato sauce, beef stock, lemon juice, brown sugar, sauerkraut, and pepper. Bring to a boil. Stir. Reduce heat to low and cover. Simmer for 3 hours.

*Yield: 8-10 servings*

# root vegetable soup

⅓ cup olive oil

4 carrots, peeled, cut into
½-inch chunks

2 parsnips, peeled, cut into
½-inch chunks

2 plum tomatoes, cut into
1-inch chunks

1 medium turnip or rutabaga,
peeled, cut into ½-inch chunks

2 large onions, peeled, diced

2 leeks, white and pale green
parts only, cleaned, chopped

4 cloves fresh garlic, peeled

2 teaspoons dried basil

1 teaspoon dried thyme

4 tablespoons fresh dill,
chopped, divided

1 bay leaf

8 cups chicken or vegetable
stock

fine sea salt

freshly ground black pepper

dill sprigs, for garnish

crème fraîche, optional,
for dairy meals

1. Heat the oil in a large soup pot over medium heat. Add the carrots, parsnips, tomatoes, turnip or rutabaga, onions, leeks, and garlic. Sauté for 4-6 minutes. Cover and sweat the vegetables over low heat for 15 minutes, stirring occasionally.

2. Add the basil, thyme, 2 tablespoons dill, and bay leaf. Add the stock and bring to a boil. Cover and turn down to a simmer for 20-25 minutes, or until the vegetables are soft. Add remaining dill. Remove and discard bay leaf.

3. Transfer soup to a blender or food processor and process until smooth. You can also use an immersion blender right in the pot; purée until smooth. Season with salt and pepper.

4. Garnish each bowl with a sprig of fresh dill. If using for dairy, add a dollop of crème fraîche to each bowl.

*Yield: 8-10 servings*

# winter white soup

*If ever there was the perfect time to be developing the soup section for this book, it was last winter. As the snow piled up outside, and I was working in the kitchen inside, we had a very meticulous crew doing some remodeling of our home. They took great care in their work but my ability to communicate with them was limited by a language barrier. At lunchtime I was happy to feed them samples from the many different recipes I was working on. We all came to look forward to sharing soup together and they conveyed their thanks through their warm smiles, nods, and punctual appearances in my kitchen.*

*After several days I asked a friend of mine to act as translator. I told her to explain to the guys that I was testing these recipes for my upcoming cookbook and would appreciate their honest feedback. Suddenly the group formed a huddle and were all talking at once. Prepared for accolades, what I got instead was an earful of earnest comments and critiques. Who knew that these were soup connoisseurs disguised as workmen? They recounted soup after soup with comments and suggestions. The soups that made it to the book all passed muster. This, along with the Tomato Bread Soup on page 61, was their favorite and I hope they will be yours as well.*

*The key to this recipe is cooking the leeks over a low heat so that they "sweat" but don't get any color on them, and the same when you add the vegetables. The pesto, either homemade or store-bought, is a great garnish, both visually and in taste.*

2 tablespoons olive oil

1 large leek, white and pale green parts only, sliced

4 medium parsnips, peeled, cut into 1-inch chunks

½ turnip, peeled, cut into 1-inch chunks

½ stalk celery, sliced

5 cups fresh chicken or vegetable stock

1½ cups soy milk

⅛ teaspoon ground white pepper

¼ teaspoon fine sea salt

pesto, store-bought or homemade, (see box on facing page)

1. Place the olive oil into a large pot over medium-low heat. When the oil is hot, add the leek and slowly cook for 4-5 minutes, until it is shiny and soft but not brown.

2. Add the parsnips, turnip, and celery. Sauté for 6-7 minutes longer.

3. Add the stock; turn the heat to medium. Bring to a boil. Reduce heat and simmer, covered, for 15-20 minutes, or until the vegetables are soft. Add the soy milk, white pepper, and salt.

4. Use an immersion blender or transfer in batches to a blender to blend until completely smooth.

5. Ladle into bowls. Garnish with a ½ teaspoon pesto in the center of each bowl. Swirl with the tip of a knife.

*Yield: 6-8 servings*

**Parve Pesto:**

2 cups fresh basil leaves

1 clove fresh garlic

1 tablespoon pine nuts

2 tablespoons walnuts

3 tablespoons good-quality extra-virgin olive oil

fine sea salt

freshly ground black pepper

In the bowl of a food processor fitted with a metal blade, process the basil, garlic, pine nuts and walnuts. Drizzle in the oil. Season with salt and pepper. Can be kept covered in the refrigerator for 1 week. To keep the pesto from changing color, top it off with ½-inch olive oil. Pour off the extra oil and stir before serving.

# roasted cauliflower soup

Meat, Dairy, or Parve

2 heads cauliflower, cut into
1-inch florets

8 cloves fresh garlic, peeled

2 shallots, sliced

½ cup olive oil

5 cups chicken or vegetable
broth, fresh or canned

1 cup water

3 tablespoons fresh dill,
chopped, divided

½ teaspoon fine sea salt

½ teaspoon white pepper

1 cup soy milk or light cream

1. Preheat oven to 300°F.

2. Place cauliflower onto a large parchment-lined baking sheet.
Add the garlic and shallots. Drizzle with the olive oil and toss to
coat. Slowly roast the cauliflower in the oven for 1 hour and 10
minutes, checking every 20 minutes to make sure that it is not
burning. Toss as needed.

3. Place the broth and water into a large pot. Add 1 tablespoon of
chopped dill, salt, and white pepper. When the vegetables are
roasted, add them to the pot. Bring the mixture to a boil. Turn
down to a simmer, and cook, covered, for 30 minutes.

4. Uncover pot and add remaining dill. Using an immersion
blender, purée the soup right in the pot, or alternatively, transfer
in batches to a blender. Add the soy milk, and cook until heated
through. Adjust seasonings as needed.

*Yield: 10 servings*

# porcini celery soup

Meat or Parve

*Celery root or celeriac, the knobby ugly vegetable, tastes a lot better than it looks. It is not the root of a celery plant. It is
sweeter and milder and is wonderful and rich in soups like this one.*

1 large celery root

1 tablespoon olive oil

1 tablespoon margarine

2 cloves fresh garlic, sliced

1 onion, thinly sliced

8 fresh porcini mushrooms,
caps and stems, sliced, or ½
cup dried porcini mushrooms,
soaked in hot water, drained,
chopped

3 sprigs fresh thyme

5 cups chicken or vegetable
stock

½ cup soy milk

1. Peel the celery root and cut into small cubes.

2. Place the oil and margarine into a large pot over a medium-low
heat. Add the celery root and garlic. Cook for 8 minutes. Add
the onion slices. Stir as they soften and try not to let them get
too brown, 5-7 minutes. Add the mushrooms and cook for 8
minutes longer, until soft, fragrant, and brownish in color.

3. Add the leaves from the sprigs of thyme; discard the stems.

4. Add the stock and simmer for 20 minutes. Add the soy milk and
heat through.

5. Use an immersion blender right in the pot or transfer to a
blender to purée until smooth.

*Yield: 6-8 servings*

# yukon gold and caramelized leek soup

3 pounds Yukon Gold potatoes, peeled, cut into large chunks

water as needed, divided

1 teaspoon fine sea salt

3 tablespoons olive oil

3 leeks, white and pale green parts only, cleaned, cut into 1-inch chunks

4 cups chicken or vegetable broth, plus 1 extra cup for thinning the soup

freshly ground black pepper

2 leeks, for garnish

all-purpose flour, for garnish

4 tablespoons canola oil, for garnish

1. Prepare the soup: Place the potatoes into a large pot. Cover with water by 2 inches. Add salt. Bring the water to a boil. When the potatoes are soft, remove from heat and drain.

2. In a second large pot, heat the olive oil over low heat. Add the leeks and sauté until caramelized, about 30 minutes. Add the broth and 2 cups water. Season with salt and pepper. Add the potatoes. Using an immersion blender, purée the soup. Thin with stock as needed.

3. Prepare the garnish: Slice the white and pale green part of two leeks lengthwise. Slice into long thin julienne strips. Lightly dust with flour and then shake off the excess. Fry in batches in hot canola oil over medium heat for just under a minute, until lightly browned. Stir frequently and adjust heat if the leeks start to burn. Sprinkle over the center of each bowl of soup.

*Yield: 8-10 servings*

# roasted tomato bread soup

1 large loaf (about 15 inches long) day-old rustic bread, preferably Portuguese, French, or Italian bread

extra-virgin olive oil

fine sea salt

freshly ground black pepper

5 cloves fresh garlic: 2 cloves minced, 3 cloves sliced

6 whole plum tomatoes

2 medium shallots, sliced

1 (28-ounce) can whole peeled tomatoes

6 cups chicken or vegetable broth

1 tablespoon chopped chives

1 tablespoon Italian flat leaf parsley, cut into thin ribbons

1. Preheat oven to 350°F.

2. Using a serrated knife, trim the crusts from the bread. Cut the bread into 1-inch cubes. Place cubes onto a baking sheet. Drizzle with ¼ cup olive oil. Season with salt, pepper, and the minced garlic. Toss to coat evenly.

3. Toast the bread until it is hard and crunchy, like croutons; about 20 minutes, stirring every 5 minutes so that all sides are toasted. Remove from oven and set aside.

4. Turn the oven to broil.

5. Cut the plum tomatoes in half. Scoop out and discard the seeds. Place the tomato halves, cut-side-down, on a baking sheet. Broil until blackened and the skin is blistered, about 8-10 minutes.

6. Meanwhile, heat a tablespoon of olive oil in a medium or large soup pot. Add the sliced garlic and shallots. Sauté over medium heat until shiny, about 4-5 minutes. Add the canned tomatoes with their liquid. Break the tomatoes with the back of your spoon. Add half the toasted bread cubes. Simmer for 10 minutes.

7. Remove and discard the blackened tomato skins. Add the roasted tomatoes to the pot. Add the broth and simmer for 5 minutes. Add the chives and parsley.

8. Purée the soup using an immersion blender in the pot, or transfer in batches to a blender. Purée for 3-4 full minutes, until completely smooth.

9. Serve with remaining croutons. Season with salt and pepper.

*Yield: 8-10 servings*

# carrot and spinach soup

2 tablespoons olive oil

2 cloves fresh garlic, chopped

1 small onion, chopped

4 cups canned or fresh chicken or vegetable broth

2 cups water

1 pound carrots, peeled, cut into 1-inch chunks

1 cinnamon stick

1 bay leaf

¼ teaspoon freshly ground black pepper

½ teaspoon fine sea salt

1 tablespoon fresh dill, chopped

1 sweet potato, peeled, cooked or microwaved for 7-8 minutes, or ½ cup canned sweet potatoes, drained

2 cups fresh baby spinach leaves

1. Heat the olive oil in a large pot. Add the garlic and onion. Cook for 5 minutes over low heat, making sure not to brown the onions, just soften them. Add the broth and water into the pot. Add the carrots, cinnamon stick, bay leaf, black pepper, salt, and dill. Bring to a boil. Reduce heat. Simmer, covered, for 30 minutes.

2. Uncover; remove and discard the cinnamon stick and bay leaf. Add the sweet potato. With an immersion blender right in the pot, or in batches in a blender, purée the soup until smooth. Adjust salt and pepper. Add the spinach. Cook for 5 minutes just until spinach is wilted.

*Yield: 6-8 servings*

# cream of sweet potato soup
# with maple-roasted pecans

Meat, Dairy, or Parve

*I dropped off a container at my neighbor Ed David's house and got the following message from him on my answering machine. "Hi, it's Ed, now you're just showing off." Nothing more to say except try this recipe.*

**Maple Roasted Pecans:**

2 tablespoons margarine

1 cup chopped pecans

1 tablespoon pure maple syrup, NOT pancake syrup

**Cream of
Sweet Potato Soup:**

1 tablespoon extra-virgin olive oil

1 stalk celery, chopped

1 leek, white and pale green parts only, chopped

1 large shallot, chopped

1 medium onion, chopped

1½ pounds sweet potatoes, about 3 medium or 2 large, peeled, cut into small chunks

6 cups chicken stock or vegetable stock, divided

½ cup pumpkin purée from a can, NOT pumpkin pie filling

1 teaspoon ground cinnamon

pinch of nutmeg

¼ teaspoon fine sea salt

1 cup light cream or soy milk

1. Prepare the pecans: In a small frying pan over medium-low heat melt the margarine. Add the pecans and maple syrup. Cook, stirring, for 4-5 minutes, until roasted. Transfer to a paper towel. The pecans can be made two days in advance and kept in an airtight container.

2. Prepare the soup: In a large pot, heat the oil over medium-high heat. Sauté the celery, leek, shallot, and onion until soft and shiny, about 4-6 minutes. Add the sweet potatoes; sauté 2 minutes longer.

3. Add 4 cups of stock and bring to a boil.

4. Turn down to a simmer and cook, covered, for 20-25 minutes, until sweet potatoes are soft. Add the pumpkin, cinnamon, nutmeg, and salt.

5. Transfer to a blender or food processor and process until smooth. You can also use an immersion blender right in the pot; purée for a full 3 minutes. Add remaining 2 cups stock and soy milk or light cream. Purée 1 minute and heat through.

6. Ladle the soup into bowls. Serve with a small handful of maple roasted pecans in the center of each bowl.

*Yield: 8-10 servings*

# carrot coconut vichyssoise

*Coconut milk is a thick creamy mixture of coconut meat and hot water. It is parve. It is sold in cans and is different from cream of coconut, which is very sweet and used mostly for drinks. The clear liquid inside a coconut is not coconut milk but called coconut juice. It can be hard to find the coconut milk with a kosher sign. Check on the internet for information on which brands are kosher, do a search under kosher coconut milk, or check the OK or OU website; there are a number of brands available.*

*If you are really desperate and up to the task, you can make your own by cutting the meat of a small coconut into small chunks and puréeing them in a food processor fitted with a metal blade. Pour 2 cups of boiling water over and let sit for ½ hour. Process again until smooth. Pour into a cheesecloth-lined bowl, and squeeze the milk into the bowl. You need to use this within a few days or it will spoil.*

## Carrot Coconut Vichyssoise:

4 cups chicken or vegetable stock

2 medium Idaho or russet potatoes, peeled, diced

16 ounces baby carrots, or 2 cups sliced carrots

1 leek, sliced, white and pale green parts only

1 shallot, diced

dash ground white pepper

⅔ cup coconut milk

½ cup light cream or soy milk

## Balsamic Garnish:

¼ cup balsamic vinegar

1 tablespoon dark molasses

1. Prepare the soup: Place the stock, potatoes, carrots, leek, and shallot into a medium soup pot. Bring to a boil, reduce heat, and simmer for 30 minutes, until vegetables are very tender.

2. Season with white pepper. Simmer for 5 minutes longer. Add the coconut milk. Remove from heat. Transfer to a blender and purée until smooth. You can also use an immersion blender right in the pot; purée for a full 3 minutes. Stir in the light cream or soy milk.

3. Place the soup in the refrigerator and cool for at least 5 hours.

4. Prepare the garnish: Place the balsamic vinegar and molasses into a small pot. Bring to a boil, reduce heat, and simmer on low for 6-8 minutes, until reduced by half. Place in refrigerator; it will thicken as it cools.

5. To serve, ladle the soup into bowls. With the tip of a spoon or a squirt bottle, add a swirl of the balsamic garnish to each bowl.

*Yield: 6-8 servings*

# beef noodle soup

*Chinese-style noodles are made by the same company that makes wonton wrappers and eggroll wrappers. They are usually found in the produce section of the supermarket. If you can't find them, you can use thick spaghetti.*

3 short ribs (1½ pounds)

1 pound hanger or skirt steak, cut into thirds, soaked in water to remove excess salt

freshly ground black pepper

2 tablespoons olive oil

1 medium Spanish onion, cut into ¼-inch dice

3 large celery ribs, sliced in half lengthwise, cut into ¼-inch pieces

2 cloves fresh garlic, minced

1 teaspoon fresh thyme leaves

5 teaspoons beef bouillon powder

6½ cups chicken stock

Chinese-style noodles or spaghetti

water as needed

1. Season the short ribs and hanger steak on both sides with pepper. In a large soup pot, heat the oil over medium-high. Add the ribs and steak, searing until brown on both sides. Remove the meat from the pot.

2. Into the same pot, add the onion and celery. Place over medium heat and sauté for 1 minute. Add the garlic and thyme. Sauté for 2 minutes. Return the meat to the pot.

3. With an immersion blender or whisk, combine the beef bouillon with the chicken stock. Add to the pot. Bring to a boil, then simmer over low heat for 1½ hours.

4. Cut the meat from the short-rib bone and slice. Slice the hanger steak as well. Return the meat to the pot.

5. In a separate pot of boiling water, prepare the noodles according to package directions. Add them to the soup right before serving.

*Yield: 6-8 servings*

# roasted eggplant soup

Meat, Dairy, or Parve

2 medium eggplants, unpeeled, halved lengthwise

olive oil

fine sea salt

freshly ground black pepper

1 medium carrot, chopped

2 ribs celery, chopped

1 Spanish onion, chopped

freshly ground black pepper

2 cloves fresh garlic

2-3 sprigs fresh thyme, leaves picked off, minced, about ½ teaspoon

8-10 fresh mint leaves

4 cups chicken or vegetable stock

3 tablespoons heavy cream, optional, for dairy meals

½ red bell pepper, seeded, cut into tiny dice, for garnish

½ yellow bell pepper, seeded, cut into tiny dice, for garnish

2 chives or 2 sprigs parsley, minced, for garnish

1. Preheat oven to 350°F.

2. Make diagonal score marks over cut side of the eggplant. Generously drizzle with olive oil and season with salt and pepper. Place, cut-side-down, on a baking sheet and roast for 25-35 minutes, until the flesh is tender.

3. Place 1 tablespoon olive oil into a medium soup pot over medium heat. Add the carrot, celery, and onion. Turn the heat to low and slowly cook, uncovered, until tender, about 10-15 minutes. Add the garlic and thyme. Simmer for 2 minutes. Turn off the heat.

4. When the eggplants are roasted, scoop out the flesh and discard the peels. Add the eggplant flesh to the pot. Add the mint leaves and stock. Transfer to a blender or food processor and process until smooth. You can also use an immersion blender right in the pot; purée until smooth. Return to heat and cook until heated through. If making for a dairy meal, add the cream.

5. Prepare the garnish: Mix the red pepper, yellow pepper, and chives or parsley in a small bowl. Place a mound of this garnish in the center of your soup tureen or in a small pile in the center of the soup in each bowl.

*Yield: 6-8 servings*

## Spices:

Spices have a limited shelf life. Whole spices stay fresh for up to 2 years, peppercorns up to 5 years if kept in a cool dark place. Ground spices need to be replaced every 6 months to a year. They don't spoil but become less potent. Crush dried spices in your hand; if there is no aroma or if you taste them and the flavor is not strong, replace your stock.

# wild mushroom velouté

*A velouté is a thickened soup, similar to a bisque. It is quick-cooking and so simple to prepare. In some markets, the wild mushrooms are packaged together. You can just buy 18-20 ounces total of the assorted packages.*

*I love the covered crocks pictured here. I use them often for soups and stews, but my favorite use is for serving individual portions of cholent on Shabbat.*

2 tablespoons olive oil

1 cup (about 4 ounces) sliced shiitake mushroom, stems discarded

2 cups (6-7 ounces) sliced oyster mushrooms

2 cups (6-7 ounces) sliced crimini mushrooms

2 cloves fresh garlic, chopped

1 small onion, cut into small dice

⅛ teaspoon dried thyme

8 tablespoons margarine or butter

½ cup all-purpose flour

7 cups chicken or vegetable broth, warm

⅛ teaspoon fine sea salt

⅛ teaspoon freshly ground black pepper

1. Heat oil in medium pot over medium heat. Add the mushrooms and sauté until tender, about 4 minutes. Add the garlic and onion. Cook for 4-5 minutes. Sprinkle in the thyme. Add the margarine or butter and melt. Slowly sprinkle in the flour. The mixture will form a sticky mixture called a roux. Slowly add the warm stock and simmer, uncovered, for 20 minutes to cook out the floury taste.

2. Season with salt and pepper.

*Yield: 8 servings*

# tomato matzo balls

*What a thrill it was for me as these matzo balls and I proudly made our debut on the Today Show with Katie Couric.*

2 large eggs, plus 1 egg white

2 tablespoons olive oil

3 tablespoons tomato paste

½-¾ cup matzo ball mix (usually 1-1½ bags out of a box)

water or chicken stock, as needed

1. In a medium bowl, whisk the eggs and the oil.

2. Add the tomato paste into the egg mixture. Whisk fully to incorporate.

3. Sprinkle in ½ cup (1 bag) of the matzo ball mix. Stir in with a fork, mixing as little as possible. Don't overwork it.

4. Chill in refrigerator for 20 minutes.

5. Meanwhile, bring a pot of water or chicken stock to a boil.

6. Wet your hands in a bowl of cold water. Using your hand, and manipulating as little as possible, scoop out a Ping-Pong-ball size of the mixture adding more matzo ball mix or matzo meal if the mixture is too thin to shape. Form it into a ball with your fingertips, using no real pressure. Turn the water down to a simmer. Drop the balls into the water. Cover the pot and simmer for 20 minutes.

*Yields: 6 large matzo balls*

# turmeric matzo balls

2 large eggs, plus 1 egg white

2 tablespoons vegetable oil

1 teaspoon turmeric

½-¾ cup matzo ball mix (usually 1-1½ bags out of a box)

water or chicken stock, as needed

1. In a medium bowl, whisk the eggs and the oil.

2. Add the turmeric into the egg mixture. Whisk to incorporate to an even yellow color.

3. Sprinkle in ½ cup (1 bag) of the matzo ball mix. Stir in with a fork, mixing as little as possible. Don't overwork it.

4. Chill in refrigerator for 20 minutes.

5. Meanwhile, bring a pot of water or chicken stock to a boil.

6. Wet your hands in a bowl of cold water. Using your hand, and manipulating as little as possible, scoop out a Ping-Pong-ball size of the mixture adding more matzo ball mix or matzo meal if the mixture is too thin to shape. Form it into a ball with your fingertips, using no real pressure. Turn the water down to a simmer. Drop the balls into the water. Cover the pot and simmer for 20 minutes.

*Yields: 6 large matzo balls*

# spinach matzo balls

*Due to the high water content of fresh spinach, these matzo balls may be a little harder to form than the other two flavors. If this occurs, add some extra matzo ball mix or matzo meal, 1 teaspoon at a time, until the batter can be shaped into balls. You want to use as little extra as possible so that the matzo balls remain light and fluffy.*

2 large eggs, plus 1 egg white

2 tablespoons olive oil

3 ounces fresh baby spinach leaves

1 cup matzo ball mix (usually both bags out of a box)

water or chicken stock, as needed

1. In a medium bowl, whisk the eggs and the oil.

2. In the bowl of a food processor fitted with a metal blade, process the spinach until puréed. Squeeze the liquid out of the spinach.

3. Add the spinach purée into the egg mixture. Whisk to incorporate.

4. Sprinkle in 1 cup (2 bags) of the matzo ball mix. Stir in with a fork, mixing as little as possible. Don't overwork it.

5. Chill in refrigerator for 20 minutes.

6. Meanwhile, bring a pot of water or chicken stock to a boil.

7. Wet your hands in a bowl of cold water. Using your hand, and manipulating as little as possible, scoop out a Ping-Pong-ball size of the mixture. Form it into a ball with your fingertips, using no real pressure. Turn the water down to a simmer. Drop the balls into the water. Cover the pot and simmer for 20 minutes.

*Yields: 6 large matzo balls*

# yellow tomato basil bisque

*This soup tastes great hot or chilled. It is perfect in the summer when yellow tomatoes are abundant and at their best.*

2 shallots, chopped

5 cloves fresh garlic, peeled, whole

1 medium onion, sliced

extra-virgin olive oil

10 yellow tomatoes

2 medium Yukon Gold potatoes, peeled, cut into ½-inch chunks

4 cups chicken or vegetable stock

white pepper

fine sea salt

½ cup light cream, optional, for dairy meals

¼ cup fresh basil leaves, thinly sliced

1. Place the shallots, garlic, and onion into a soup pot. Add olive oil to cover. Slowly cook over a low flame, so that the oil is barely simmering, for 30 minutes.

2. Meanwhile, cut the yellow tomatoes in half. Scoop out and discard the seeds. Place the tomato halves, cut-side-down, on a baking sheet. Broil 6-8 inches from the heat, until blackened and the skin is blistered, about 8-10 minutes.

3. Remove and discard the skins. Set aside.

4. When the onions and garlic have begun to soften, pour off all of the oil. A strainer works well here. (This olive oil is wonderful to keep. It has all of the flavoring of the garlic and onions. Keep it in a non-reactive container in the refrigerator for 2-3 weeks and use it in place of olive oil in any recipe.) Add the potatoes and tomatoes, with any accumulated juices, to the pot. Add the chicken or vegetable stock. Season with white pepper and salt. Bring to a boil. Turn down to a simmer, cover, and cook for 25 minutes, or until the potatoes are soft.

5. Transfer to a blender or food processor and process until smooth. You can also use an immersion blender right in the pot; purée until smooth. Add light cream if you are using it. Sprinkle in the basil. Taste and adjust white pepper and salt as needed. Heat through, about one minute.

*Yield: 6-8 servings*

# ladies' lunch
## stylish lunch format

### Menu

**Popovers with Flavored Butters**
page 248-249

**Smoothie Station**
page 244

**Carrot Coconut Vichyssoise**
page 64

**Mango Tuna Salad**
page 100

**Broccoli Cashew Salad**
page 89

**Salmon Primavera**
page 185

**Berry-Filled Mini Noodle Kugels**
page 241

**Strudel Bites**
page 307

**Caramelized Apple Cheesecake**
page 310

Gather your girlfriends or sisters and get ready for a magical and memorable day! I can think of so many reasons to throw this kind of celebration. A fundraising charity luncheon, a Mother's Day brunch, a bridal shower, a thank-you to your committee luncheon, a friend or sister's special birthday, any time you would enjoy the company of a group of women would fit this party like Cinderella fit the glass slipper. And speaking of slippers, that is exactly what this event is all about: shoes, hats, flowers, and ribbons, all things feminine.

At our Ladies' Lunch, pink and green pastel runners criss-crossed the table and served as placemats. Little craft-store hats were tied around crisp white napkins and set on each plate. Fresh-flower-adorned hats of all colors were set high up on ribbon-wrapped stands so as to not interfere with the constant chatter. Hats were also casually hung from the back of each chair. Fresh pink rose petals were scattered haphazardly around the table, while funky shoes were the perfect stand-in vases. This party really demonstrates how to think beyond the basic flowers-in-a vase for inspiration.

As the women arrived and took in this wonderland, they helped themselves to smoothies. We set out some pre-poured glasses but also set up various fruits and yogurts beside a blender so the ladies could make their own. Quirky rain boots stuffed with flowers were the decor for this station, which was set up in the kitchen near the sink, so the blender could be rinsed out between batches of smoothies. Pretty hat boxes were stacked in the background to complete the space.

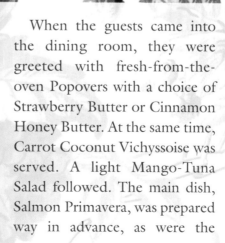

When the guests came into the dining room, they were greeted with fresh-from-the-oven Popovers with a choice of Strawberry Butter or Cinnamon Honey Butter. At the same time, Carrot Coconut Vichyssoise was served. A light Mango-Tuna Salad followed. The main dish, Salmon Primavera, was prepared way in advance, as were the

Broccoli Salad and Mini Kugels that accompanied it. This freed up the hostess to be right where she wanted to be, in the center of the action, enjoying this time with her guests. The meal ended with the dairy decadence of Caramelized Apple Cheesecake and luscious Strudel Bites, which most took home to share with their families.

We took a tip from the children here. Everybody likes party favors, so at each place setting was a pretty box, adorned by a shoe. At the end of the luncheon this little table detail became the vessel for our "bath bar." Out on the patio we set up pretty soaps, lotions, bath salts, nail brushes, and powders, piled high in glass vases. The ladies filled their boxes with the goodies as a parting gift to remember this special day.

# salads

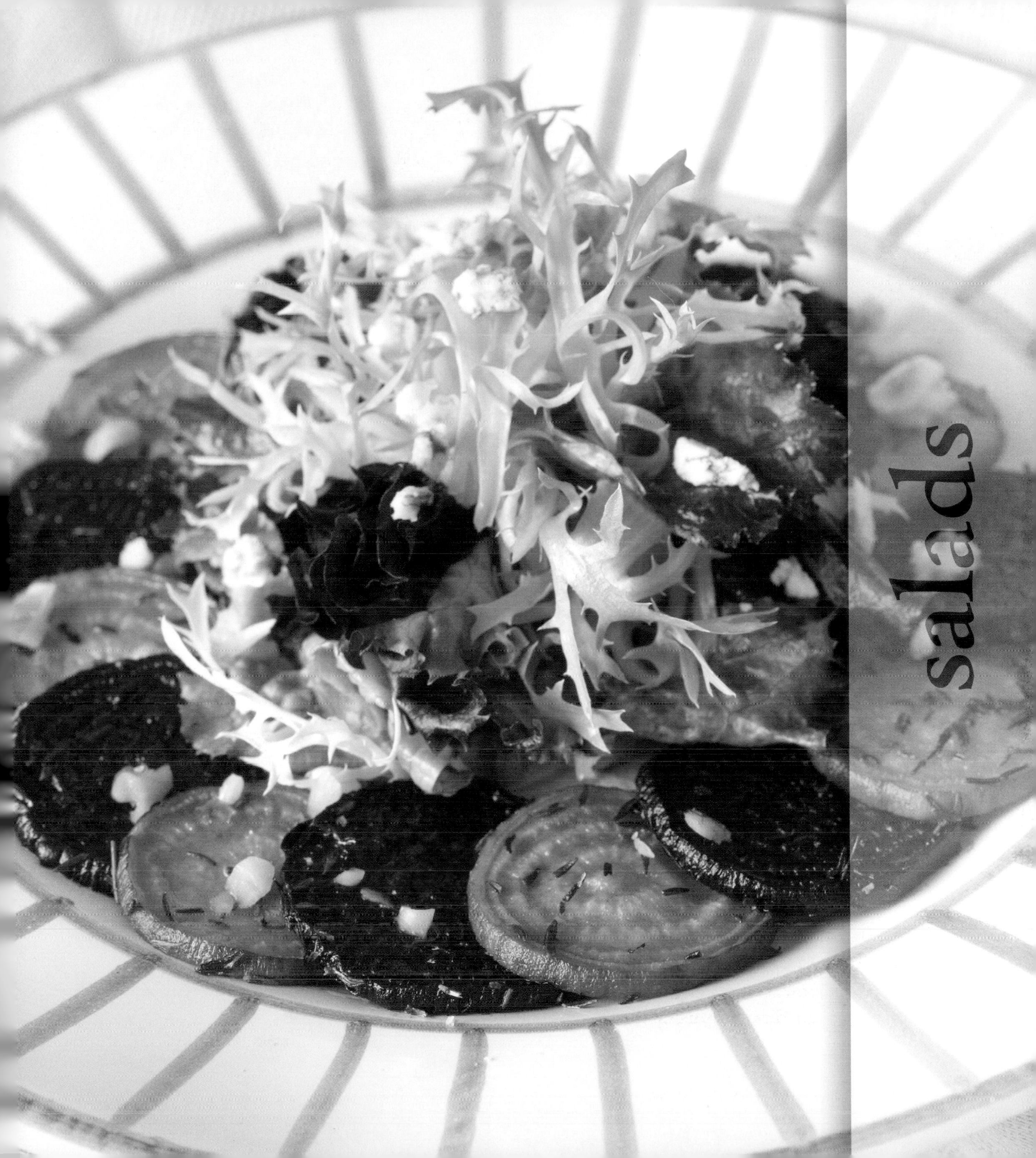

# orange fennel salad with warm tomato vinaigrette

Parve

1 fennel bulb

juice of 1 fresh lemon

1 teaspoon olive oil

1 large tomato, seeded, cut into small dice

½ teaspoon fine sea salt

½ teaspoon freshly ground black pepper

¼ cup orange juice

⅛ cup olive oil

5 ounces mesclun greens with frisée

2 oranges, peeled, segmented, or 2 (11-ounce) cans mandarin oranges, drained

1 medium red onion, halved, thinly sliced

1. Cut the feathery fronds from the fennel bulb (some stores sell the bulb without the fronds) and discard. From the top, where the fronds were, cut paper-thin slices of the fennel on the diagonal and keep in a bowl of water mixed with fresh lemon juice, to keep fennel from turning color. Set aside.

2. Prepare the vinaigrette: Heat a small sauté pan over medium heat. Add the teaspoon of olive oil. Add diced tomato and season with salt and pepper. Sauté for 3 minutes and add the orange juice. Simmer 2 minutes longer to reduce by half. Whisk in the olive oil. Remove from heat. Season with more salt and pepper if needed.

3. In a large bowl toss the mesclun with the oranges and red onion. Drain the fennel and add into the salad. Dress with vinaigrette.

*Yield: 6 servings*

---

**Mounding Salads:**

To shape salad greens into the nice restaurant-style mounds, lightly dress the greens, pack into a plastic pint container, invert onto a plate, lift away container.

# warm sweetbreads salad

*This salad is a real delicacy for the sweetbreads lovers in your life. The dressing is made right in the pan.*

2 pounds sweetbreads

water as needed

2 teaspoons white vinegar

fine sea salt

freshly ground black pepper

unflavored homestyle or fresh bread crumbs

2 tablespoons margarine

6 tablespoons (½ of a medium) red onion, minced

3 cloves fresh garlic, minced

3 scallions, sliced

2 teaspoons fresh ginger, minced

1 pound mesclun lettuce leaves, divided

3 tablespoons seasoned rice wine vinegar

1 tablespoon soy sauce

⅓ cup extra-virgin olive oil, divided

1. Place the sweetbreads into a shallow pan. Cover with water by an inch. Add the vinegar and water. Bring to a boil. Lower heat and simmer, uncovered, for 5-6 minutes. The sweetbreads will plump and feel slightly firmer to the touch. Remove from heat and run under cold water to stop the cooking. Clean the sweetbreads by cutting away any fat and pulling away as much membrane and connective tissue as possible. Cut sweetbreads into pieces.

2. Season the sweetbreads with salt and pepper. Coat with breadcrumbs. Melt the margarine in a pan over medium heat. Add the sweetbreads. Sauté until the breadcrumbs are nice and crispy, about 4-5 minutes.

3. Remove the sweetbreads from the pan and set aside. Add the minced red onion and garlic to the pan. Cook for 1 minute. Add the scallions and the ginger and cook 1 minute. Add the rice wine vinegar and soy sauce; drizzle in half the olive oil. Remove from heat.

4. Add a handful of the greens into the hot pan and toss with the breadcrumbs that you scrape up from the bottom of the pan. The greens will be a little wilted. Season with salt and pepper.

5. In a large bowl, drizzle the remaining fresh greens with the rest of the olive oil. Toss in the wilted greens and mix.

6. Place a mound of salad on each plate and top with the sweetbreads.

*Yield: 8 servings*

# hearts and flowers salad

5 ounces baby arugula leaves

10 fresh chives, sliced into 2-inch pieces

1 carrot, coarsely grated, or ¾ cup pre-bagged shredded carrot

1 jicama, peeled, thinly sliced, or packaged turkey roll

8 edible flowers, any combination; in most markets they come in a package of assorted flowers

⅓ cup olive oil

½ cup Moscato di Asti or Champagne

1 teaspoon fresh lemon juice

⅛ teaspoon freshly ground black pepper

½ teaspoon fine sea salt

1. In a large bowl, combine the arugula, chives, and carrots. Add the petals from 4 of the flowers. Toss.

2. Place the jicama slices or turkey roll slices in a stack. With a medium heart-shaped cookie cutter, cut out stacks of hearts, for a total of 12 hearts. Cut out 4 small hearts with a smaller cookie cutter. Set aside.

3. Prepare the vinaigrette: In a tall container, with an immersion blender, emulsify the olive oil, Moscato or Champagne, lemon juice, pepper, and salt. If doing by hand, whisk vigorously until emulsified.

4. When ready to serve, add 3-4 tablespoons of dressing to the bowl of salad. Arrange 3 of the large jicama or turkey roll hearts on each of the 4 plates. Top with a pile of the dressed salad. Dip the remaining 4 whole flowers into the extra vinaigrette. Arrange a small heart on top of each salad and tuck a flower under each heart.

*Yield: 4 servings*

### Edible Flowers:

Edible flowers can have a sweet or peppery flavor, depending on the type of flower. We used marigolds, carnations, nasturtiums, and dianthus in our salad. You can also use mini roses, snapdragons, pansies, calendulas, violas, yellow daisies, and borage.

# grilled peach salad

2 ripe, firm peaches, pitted, each peach cut into 8 thick wedges

4 sprigs mint, stems discarded, leaves minced

9 large basil leaves, minced

⅓ cup extra-virgin olive oil

1 tablespoon water

¼ cup balsamic vinegar

½ teaspoon honey

fine sea salt

freshly ground black pepper

5 ounces mesclun greens

blue cheese, crumbled (see resource guide, p. 315), optional, for dairy meals

grilled boneless, skinless chicken breasts, cubed, optional, for meat meals

1. Place the peach slices onto a hot oiled barbecue or in 1 tablespoon hot olive oil in a grill pan set over medium heat. To get nice grill marks, do not move the peaches around. Grill for 3 minutes per side until well marked, fragrant, but firm. Remove from heat and set aside.

2. In a small bowl, gently whisk the mint, basil, oil, water, vinegar, and honey. Do not emulsify with an immersion blender because the color will become muddy. Season with salt and pepper.

3. Place the greens into a large bowl. Drizzle with some of the dressing. Place on salad plates. Top with grilled peaches. Drizzle with more dressing to taste.

4. Add the cheese or chicken option if desired.

*Yield: 4 servings*

# stacked jicama and avocado salad with thai vinaigrette

Parve

*You can just as easily toss these great ingredients together in a bowl; in fact, it would look great that way on a buffet table, but the presentation shown here is very artistic.*

½ teaspoon turmeric

½ teaspoon ground cayenne pepper

1½ tablespoons honey

juice of 2 fresh limes

2 tablespoons soy sauce

1 tablespoon roasted or toasted sesame oil

2 tablespoons extra-virgin olive oil

fine sea salt

freshly ground black pepper

1-2 large jicamas, peeled, cut into rectangular french-fry-sized sticks

1 small red onion, minced

1 pint red grape tomatoes, halved

5 ounces baby arugula leaves

2 ripe Haas avocados, peeled, pitted, cut into thin slices

1. In a small bowl, whisk the turmeric, cayenne, honey, lime juice, soy sauce, sesame oil, and olive oil. Season with salt and pepper.

2. Toss the jicama, onion, tomatoes, and arugula in a bowl. Coat with some of the dressing.

3. Lay a few avocado slices on the plate. Arrange 4 jicama sticks in a tic-tac-toe board fashion. Place a fistful of the arugula, with some of the onions and tomatoes, in the center of the jicama. Repeat the pattern of jicama and top with salad. Drizzle remaining dressing on plate.

*Yield: 6 servings*

# blackened steak and asparagus salad

*The spice mixture is a Cajun spice mixture made with basic spices that most people have on hand, but when mixed in the proportions below, it is a fiery delicacy. Mix up some extra and keep on hand to blacken fish or chicken. The dressing is best made a day in advance. In a time pinch, you can easily substitute store-bought Cajun spice mix and bottled Italian dressing for this salad. If you are making the steak a day in advance, don't slice it until you are ready to serve it and make sure you don't overcook it. A perfect medium rare will hold up best in advance preparations.*

**Blackening Spice Mixture:**

2 teaspoons onion powder

2 teaspoons garlic powder

1½ teaspoons cayenne pepper

1 teaspoon white pepper

1 teaspoon freshly ground
black pepper

1 teaspoon paprika

1 teaspoon dried thyme

1 teaspoon dried oregano

1 teaspoon dried basil leaves

1 (1½ pounds) London broil
or ½ filet split

2 tablespoons olive oil, divided

1 pound asparagus

## Dressing:

6 tablespoons olive oil

2 tablespoons white wine
or apple cider vinegar

2 tablespoons fresh parsley,
chopped

1 tablespoon fresh lemon juice

2 cloves fresh garlic, minced

1 teaspoon dried basil

¼ teaspoon crushed red pepper

⅛ teaspoon dried oregano

mesclun mix with radicchio

1. Prepare the blackening spice mixture: In a small bowl or jar, combine the onion powder, garlic powder, cayenne pepper, white pepper, black pepper, paprika, thyme, oregano, and basil. Can be made in advance and stored in a covered container.

2. Generously rub one side of the steak with the blackening spice mixture. If you like your food very hot and spicy, rub the second side with the spice mixture as well.

3. Heat the oil in a large pan over medium heat. Add the steak, spice side down first (if spicing only one side), searing for 10 minutes per side. Remove from pan and allow to rest for 10 minutes. Slice into paper-thin slices. Add 1 tablespoon olive oil to pan. Add the asparagus to the pan and cook until bright green and fork-tender, about 7-8 minutes. Remove from heat.

4. Prepare the dressing: In a small bowl, whisk the olive oil, vinegar, parsley, lemon juice, garlic, basil, red pepper, and oregano.

5. Toss the steak and asparagus with the mesclun and toss with the dressing.

*Yield: 6-8 servings*

# tri-colored pasta salad

16 ounces angel hair pasta, cooked in salted water al denté, according to package directions

2 tablespoons canola oil

3 scallions, sliced

1 red pepper, thinly sliced

1 yellow pepper, thinly sliced

¼ pound snow peas, thinly sliced on the diagonal

½ cup soy sauce

¼ teaspoon ground ginger

¼ cup sugar

1 clove fresh garlic, minced

½ cup extra-virgin olive oil

1 tablespoon roasted or toasted sesame oil

1. Place the prepared noodles into a large bowl. Set aside.

2. Heat the canola oil in a large skillet or wok on medium-high heat. Add the scallions and peppers, Sauté until soft, 4-5 minutes. Add the snow peas and sauté 1 minute longer. Add to the noodles.

3. In a small bowl, whisk the soy sauce, ginger, sugar, garlic, olive oil, and sesame oil. Pour over the vegetables and noodles; toss to combine. Allow flavors to mingle for at least 30 minutes. Toss again. Serve at room temperature.

*Yield: 8-10 servings*

# arugula and pear salad

*This salad works equally well with Granny Smith apples in place of the pears. Think of the apple option for Rosh Hashanah as it also calls for pomegranate molasses, a great Rosh Hashanah ingredient (see resource guide, p. 314).*

¼ cup soy sauce

⅔ cup maple syrup

4-5 ounces pecan halves

2 firm Bosc or Anjou pears

⅔ cup orange juice, divided

¼ cup pomegranate paste, syrup, or molasses, such as Sadaf brand

⅛ cup red wine vinegar

⅔ cup olive oil

1 teaspoon Dijon mustard

pinch of fine sea salt

pinch of freshly ground black pepper

2 heads Belgian endive

5 ounces baby arugula

handful sweetened dried cranberries, such as Craisins

blue cheese, optional, for dairy meals (see resource guide, p. 315)

1. In a medium bowl, combine the soy sauce with the maple syrup. Add the pecans. Toss to coat and set aside to marinate for at least ½ hour.

2. Preheat oven to 350°F.

3. Line a baking sheet with parchment paper.

4. Remove pecans from the marinade, draining off and discarding the liquid. Place in a single layer on the prepared baking sheet.

5. Bake for 15 minutes, tossing the pecans halfway through to prevent them from burning.

6. Remove from oven and, as soon as they are cool enough to touch, but still warm, remove the caramelized pecans to a piece of parchment or wax paper to cool in a single layer so they don't clump. Set aside.

7. Halve the pears lengthwise and remove seeds and core. Keep the peel on one of the halves, and cut this half into 18 very thin slices. Place the slices in a shallow bowl with ⅓ cup orange juice to prevent discoloration.

8. Peel remaining 1½ pears and cut into small dice. Place in another bowl with remaining orange juice.

9. In a small bowl, whisk the pomegranate molasses, vinegar, oil, mustard, salt, and pepper. Set aside.

10. Separate the endive leaves. Stack and thinly slice on the diagonal into julienned thin narrow strips.

11. Toss the endive and arugula greens with the dressing. Remove the diced pears from the orange juice and add the pears into the greens. Toss in some of the caramelized pecans, cranberries, and cheese, if using for a dairy meal.

12. Lay 3 thinly sliced pear slices on each plate. Add a handful of the dressed salad. Garnish with additional caramelized pecans.

*Yield: 6 servings*

# broccoli cashew salad

*An old family favorite that is great at a barbecue or on a buffet.*

1 head broccoli, stems discarded, florets chopped very small

1 cup mayonnaise

½ cup sugar

3 tablespoons red wine vinegar

½ small red onion, finely minced

½ cup raisins

1 package ramen noodles, uncooked, seasoning packet discarded

1 cup raw sunflower seeds, shelled, not roasted or salted

1 cup raw cashews, not roasted or salted

1. Place the broccoli into a large bowl.

2. In a medium bowl, whisk the mayonnaise, sugar, vinegar, and onion.

3. Pour the dressing over the broccoli. Add the raisins, crumbled ramen noodles, sunflower seeds, and cashews. Toss to combine.

*Yield: 8-10 servings*

# watermelon and heirloom tomato salad

¼ ripe watermelon, seeded,
cut into 1-1½ inch chunks

6-7 heirloom tomatoes,
assorted colors, cored,
cut into 1-1½ inch chunks

1-2 tablespoon aged balsamic
vinegar (see box)

½ cup good-quality extra-
virgin olive oil

10 large basil leaves,
cut into thin ribbons

1. Place the watermelon and tomatoes into a large bowl. Toss with the olive oil.

2. Place on plates or platter. Drizzle with aged balsamic. Toss the basil over the salad.

*Yield: 6 servings*

## Heirloom Tomatoes:

Tomatoes have been genetically altered by farmers to be able to make long truck drives to supermarkets without spoiling or bruising. This is what allows beautiful-looking tomatoes to be on the shelves in the dead of winter. However, taste and texture are usually lacking. When summertime arrives, among my favorite things to look for are heirloom tomatoes. Many heirloom seeds have been handed down for generations and are traded by tomato enthusiasts.

The varieties come in gorgeous colors, from purples, to bright yellow, to green stripes. The sizes and shapes are odd and interesting, and most importantly, the taste is unbeatable. Make this salad in the summer and look for heirlooms in organic markets, farm stands, and upscale markets.

## Aged Balsamic Vinegar:

Balsamic vinegar has not been available to the kosher world long enough to be truly aged. Here's a solution to make your own thickened aged balsamic. Pour 4 cups of balsamic (not less, because it will thicken and cook down substantially) into a glass or other non-reactive baking dish. Place in a 200°F oven for 6 hours. The house will smell, so open the windows if you can. The result will be wonderful, syrupy balsamic. It is great on salads, bread, or drizzled into thick creamy soups. Store in a covered container in the refrigerator or in a pantry for up to one month. If kept in refrigerator, bring to room temperature before using.

# layered southwest salad

3 corn tortillas, sliced into long, ½-inch-wide strips

1 tablespoon olive oil, plus extra for brushing tortilla strips

1 pound ground beef

1 small onion, diced into ¼-inch pieces

## Dressing:

½ cup ketchup

1 tablespoon fish-free Worcestershire sauce, (see p. 16)

1 teaspoon red hot sauce, such as Tabasco

½ cup freshly squeezed orange juice; can use store bought but do not use from concentrate

⅔ cup olive oil or canola oil

½ teaspoon spicy brown mustard

1 teaspoon teriyaki sauce

½ head iceberg lettuce, shredded

3 ounces sliced black pearl olives, drained

2 avocados, diced

1. Preheat oven to 350°F.

2. Line a cookie sheet or jelly-roll pan with parchment paper. Lay the strips of tortilla in a single layer on the parchment paper. Lightly brush the strips with olive oil. Bake for 10-15 minutes until crisp and some of the strips begin to curl slightly. Remove from oven and set aside. Can be done 2 days in advance and stored in an airtight container.

3. Meanwhile, place the tablespoon of olive oil into a medium sauté pan. Heat on medium. Add the ground beef. Cook until brown, scraping it and breaking the big pieces with the back of the spatula or spoon as it cooks. When the meat is done, remove it to a bowl with a slotted spoon. Pour off the liquid from the pan. Turn the heat down to medium-low. Add the onion to the same pan and sauté for 5-6 minutes, until soft. Allow the onions to pick up the flavor of the meat by scraping up the browned bits from the pan with a wooden spoon or high-heat spatula. Remove from heat and mix the onions into the meat.

4. Prepare the dressing: In the bowl of a food processor, in a blender, or with an immersion blender, combine the ketchup, Worcestershire sauce, hot sauce, orange juice, oil, mustard, and teriyaki. Pulse to combine and emulsify.

5. In a trifle bowl or other glass salad bowl, carefully arrange a layer of half the shredded lettuce. Top with a layer of olives, reserving a few. Arrange the remaining lettuce. Top with a layer of avocados, reserving a few pieces. Add a layer of the meat. Scatter on reserved olives and avocados. Drizzle with most of the dressing; it will seep down through the layers. Top with tortilla strips scattered on top.

*Yield: 4-6 servings*

# mexican turkey and portobello salad

4 portobello mushrooms

¼ cup balsamic vinegar

¼ cup olive oil

2 cloves fresh garlic, minced

fine sea salt

freshly ground black pepper

½ pound cooked Mexican-style turkey breast, cut into cubes, such as Hod brand

## Dressing:

1 tablespoon balsamic vinegar

1 shallot, sliced

1 clove fresh garlic, chopped

½ cup canola oil

2 tablespoon water

2 teaspoons Dijon mustard


4 ounces mesclun lettuce

5-6 chives, chopped

1. Preheat oven to 375°F.

2. Peel the skin from the head of each portobello. Snap off and discard each stem. Using your hand to support the mushroom, use a spoon to scoop out as much of the gills as possible. Discard the gills. Place the mushrooms into a baking dish. Pour the balsamic, olive oil, and garlic into small bowl. Whisk together. Season with salt and pepper. Pour over the mushrooms.

3. Roast the mushrooms in the oven for 10 minutes, basting halfway through the cooking time. Remove from oven and cool for 5 minutes. Slice the mushrooms and mix with the turkey cubes.

4. Prepare the dressing: Using an immersion blender in a tall container (to reduce splattering) or in the bowl of a food processor fitted with a metal blade, combine the balsamic, shallot, garlic, oil, water, and Dijon mustard. Pulse until emulsified.

5. Dress the lettuce with the dressing. Mix in the turkey and mushrooms. Garnish with chives.

*Yield: 4 servings*

*Mizuna*

*Bibb*

*Green leaf*

*Mix a variety of greens to vary the taste, texture, and nutritional value of your salad.*

*Watercress*

*Arugula*

*Romaine*

*Spinach*

*Red leaf*

*Frisée*

# mizuna, fig, and honey salad

*This is a wonderful salad that combines salty, sticky, and tart in each forkful. Mizuna is a lettuce leaf similar to red oak lettuce, only green and crisper. You can substitute mesclun with a little bit of arugula to get the slight peppery bite. Roasting the figs sweetens them; you can also try white Kadota figs with this recipe. The chestnut honey is the nectar of chestnut blossoms. It is smooth, dark, and robust. It imparts a slightly bitter flavor, which is rich and contrasts well with the sweetness of the honey. You can experiment with various types of honey as well. (See resource guide for moonshinetrading.com, p. 315)*

1 pint Black Mission figs

3 tablespoons extra-virgin olive oil, divided

3 tablespoons chestnut or clover honey, divided

coarse sea salt or kosher salt

freshly ground black pepper

4 cups mizuna lettuce leaves

juice of 1 fresh lemon

1 pint red grape tomatoes, halved

½ cup shredded carrots

1. Preheat oven to 350°F. Halve the figs and place them into a bowl. Drizzle with 1 tablespoon olive oil and 1 tablespoon honey. Season with salt and pepper and toss to coat.

2. Place the figs, cut-side-down, on a baking tray and roast for 8-10 minutes or until figs are slightly wilted. Remove from oven and let cool.

3. Place the mizuna in a bowl and add remaining honey, oil, and the lemon juice. Toss to combine; season with salt and pepper.

4. Place a mound of the lettuce in the center of each plate. Surround with roasted figs. Garnish with tomatoes and shredded carrot.

*Yield: 6-8 servings*

# chicken salad with cherry balsamic vinaigrette

*The dried strawberries are easily found at upscale and organic markets.*

## Candied Walnuts:

2 tablespoons dark brown sugar

liquid from 1 (8-ounce) can sweet dark pitted cherries; reserve cherries

1 teaspoon extra-virgin olive oil

fine sea salt

freshly ground black pepper

4 ounces walnut halves

## Dressing:

2 tablespoons balsamic vinegar

4 tablespoons extra-virgin olive oil

the reserved, drained cherries from above

fine sea salt

freshly ground black pepper

½ teaspoon yellow mustard

## Chicken:

4 boneless, skinless chicken breasts, tenders removed

fine sea salt

freshly ground black pepper

1 tablespoon extra-virgin olive oil

5 ounces mesclun mix

1 cup dried strawberries

1. Preheat oven to 350°F.

2. Cover a jelly-roll pan with parchment paper. Set aside.

3. Prepare the candied walnuts: In a small bowl, whisk the brown sugar, 2 tablespoons cherry juice, and olive oil. Season with salt and pepper. Add the walnuts; toss to coat. Marinate for 30 minutes. Drain the walnuts and spread in a single layer on prepared pan. Bake 8-10 minutes until glazed and golden. Set aside. Can be made in advance and kept in an airtight container for up to 3 days.

4. Prepare the dressing: In a tall container, to prevent splattering, with an immersion blender, emulsify the balsamic, olive oil, cherries, salt, pepper, and mustard. This can also be done in a food processor.

5. Prepare the chicken: Season both sides of each chicken breast with salt and pepper. Place the olive oil into a skillet over medium-high heat. Add the chicken and sear 5-6 minutes per side, until golden brown on both sides. Remove from skillet and cut into dice.

6. Toss most of the dressing with the mesclun leaves. Add the candied walnuts and chicken cubes; sprinkle with the dried strawberries. Drizzle with additional dressing.

*Yield: 4-6 servings*

# chopped salad with honey mustard dressing

*My girlfriend Estee Berman from New York got this salad in an e-mail from her girlfriend i*
*me and I passed it to friends of mine in Israel. Talk about international acclaim! If only I cou*

5 ounces lettuce of choice

handful sweetened dried cranberries, such as Craisins

2 small cucumbers, peeled, cut into ½-inch dice

1 red bell pepper, seeded, cut into ½-inch dice

1 avocado, peeled, pitted, cut into ½-inch dice

1 mango, peeled, pitted, cut into ½-inch dice

12 grape tomatoes, halved

¼ cup mayonnaise

¼ cup honey

¼ cup canola oil

2 tablespoons apple cider vinegar

1 tablespoon spicy brown mustard

1. In a large bowl, toss the lettuce, cranb
   pepper, avocado, mango, and tomatoes
2. In a medium bowl, whisk the mayonna … vinegar,
   and mustard until emulsified.
3. Pour the dressing over the salad as desired and toss; you may have extra dressing.

*Yield: 6 servings*

# duck salad with port dressing

*general kosher butchers don't sell just the duck breast, and you must buy half a duck. Keep the Peking Duck Wontons (p. 43) in mind, as they call for the thigh and leg.*

3 duck breasts, wings removed, boneless, with skin

3 large shallots, sliced

1 cup Port wine

freshly ground black pepper

¼ cup rendered duck fat or olive oil, or more if needed

5 ounces mesclun greens

½ small red onion, cut into narrow strips

cherry-flavored sweetened dried cranberries, such as Craisins

1. With a sharp knife, make score marks across the fat of each duck breast.

2. Heat an empty sauté pan over medium-low. When the pan is hot, add the duck, skin-side-down. Keep the flame at medium-low to give the fat time to render out; pour it off as it does and set aside. It will take some time, about 20 minutes — be patient. When all the fat is out and the skin is crisp, flip the duck and cook on the other side for 3 minutes. Remove duck from pan.

3. Into the same pan, add the shallots and sauté until translucent. Add the Port. Simmer for 6-8 minutes to reduce by half. Season with black pepper. Add ¼ cup of the rendered duck fat or olive oil. Season with salt and pepper. Blend with an immersion blender. If very thick, thin with a little bit of good-quality extra-virgin olive oil. Allow the dressing to cool slightly, for 3-4 minutes, so it doesn't wilt the greens.

4. In a mixing bowl, dress the salad, toss in the onion and a small handful of cranberries. Place a mound of salad on each plate.

5. Slice the duck breast and lay 3 slices over the top of each salad. Sprinkle with a few dried cranberries.

6. Spoon some extra dressing over the duck slices.

*Yield: 4-6 servings*

# mediterranean fatoush salad

*This salad is so simple and refreshing. The spiced pita chips can be made a few days in advance and stored in a ziplock bag. I always make some extra to serve with soup or chummos at another meal.*

Spiced pita chips (see box)

1 (8-10 inch) English cucumber, peeled

3-4 heads Belgian endive, leaves separated

⅛ cup fresh mint leaves, stems discarded

¼ cup flat leaf Italian parsley leaves, stems discarded

1 cup small grape or cherry tomatoes, quartered

1 cup arugula

juice of 1 fresh lemon

4 tablespoons extra-virgin olive oil

1 clove fresh garlic, minced

kosher salt or coarse sea salt

freshly ground black pepper

1. Prepare the spiced pita chips.

2. Slice the cucumbers in half. With a spoon, scoop out and discard the pulp. Chop into ½-inch pieces. Place into a large salad bowl.

3. Thinly slice the endive and place into the bowl. Lay the mint leaves in a pile and tear them, they will bruise if you cut them with a knife. Add to the bowl. Toss in the parsley, tomatoes, and arugula. Mix in the lemon juice, olive oil, and garlic. Season with salt and pepper, tossing to combine. Allow to sit for a few minutes. Divide between individual plates.

4. Stand 2 pita crisps in each salad.

*Yield: 6 servings*

---

## Spiced Pita Chips:

2 (6-inch) pitas, white or whole wheat

olive oil

ground cumin

garlic powder

coarse sea salt

freshly ground black pepper

1. Preheat oven to 350°F.

2. Split the pitas in half to create 2 rounds. Place the pitas, cut-side-up, on a baking sheet. Brush each pita with olive oil. Sprinkle with the cumin, garlic powder, salt, and pepper. Cut into wedges. Bake for 10-12 minutes or until crisp.

# mango-tuna salad with goat cheese, oven-roasted tomatoes, and honeyed walnuts

Dairy

*You could use store-bought sun-dried tomatoes, either drained if they were in oil or reconstituted if they were dry. But try these homemade ones once; you won't go back. Using a low, dry heat adds intense flavor to tomatoes. They laze away as the moisture is slowly drawn out and the sugars caramelize.*

## Dressing:

2 ripe mangoes, peeled, pitted, cut into cubes

¾ cup white wine vinegar or apple cider vinegar

¾ cup orange juice, can use store bought but not from concentrate

1 vanilla bean, split in half lengthwise

1 teaspoon fine sea salt

2 tablespoons extra-virgin olive oil

## Honeyed Walnuts:

1 tablespoon canola oil

1 cup walnut halves

2 tablespoons honey

## Salad:

5 ounces mesclun mix

2 tablespoons olive oil

1 tablespoon balsamic vinegar

6 sun-dried tomatoes, sliced into strips (see box on facing page)

4 ounces goat cheese

½ pound store-bought tuna fish salad, or 1 can tuna prepared to your liking

1. Prepare the dressing: In a small pot, combine the mango, vinegar, orange juice, vanilla bean, and salt. Bring to a boil and then simmer 3 minutes. Carefully remove the vanilla bean. Scrape the seeds back into the pot; discard the pod. Simmer 1 minute longer. Purée with an immersion blender right in the pot or transfer to a food processor and purée. Whisk in the olive oil. Set aside. Can be made 2 days in advance and stored in refrigerator. Bring to room temperature to serve.

2. Prepare the honeyed walnuts: Heat the oil in a small skillet over medium heat. Add the walnuts and honey. Sauté for 3 minutes, making sure they don't burn. Remove from pan and place in a single layer on a piece of parchment or foil. Allow to cool. Keep in an airtight container for up to 1 week.

3. Prepare the salad: Toss the mesclun with the olive oil and balsamic. Arrange on individual plates or serving platter.

4. Lay 3-4 tomato strips on each plate. Toss in the honeyed walnuts.

5. Slice the goat cheese into rounds and place in center of salad. Using a small ice-cream scoop, place scoops of tuna between the goat cheese slices.

6. Drizzle with mango dressing.

*Yield: 6 servings*

## Oven Roasted Tomatoes:

7 medium-large plum tomatoes

⅛ cup extra-virgin olive oil

3-4 cloves fresh garlic

leaves of 2-3 sprigs fresh thyme, or 2 teaspoons dried

fine sea salt

freshly ground black pepper

1. Preheat the oven to 200°F.

2. Cut the tomatoes in half lengthwise. Using a spoon, scrape out the pulp and discard seeds. Place the scooped-out tomatoes into a large bowl. Toss with the oil, garlic, thyme, salt, and pepper.

3. Place the tomatoes, cut-side-down, on a parchment-lined baking sheet. If you have a broiling pan or baking rack, use it so air will circulate. Place the baking sheet in the top third of the oven.

4. Flip the tomatoes after 2 hours or the insides will steam and stew instead of drying out.

5. Roast for a maximum of 6 hours. Remove from oven.

6. When cool, slice into long strips. Can be made up to 1 week in advance and kept in an airtight container in the refrigerator.

# mandarin chicken salad

*This is a winner of a salad. It is a healthy full meal in a bowl. It works well as a main dish, in a picnic basket, or on a buffet.*

4 boneless, skinless chicken breasts

fine sea salt

freshly ground black pepper

1 tablespoon olive oil

4 tablespoons seasoned rice wine vinegar

3 tablespoons roasted or toasted sesame oil

1 tablespoon soy sauce

1 (11-ounce) can mandarin oranges; reserve liquid

1 small red onion, halved, thinly sliced

1 head romaine lettuce

1 cup thin chow mein noodles

black sesame seeds

white sesame seeds

optional: eggroll wrapper cups, see box below

1. Season both sides of each chicken breast with salt and pepper. Place the olive oil into a skillet over medium-high heat. Add the chicken and sear 5-6 minutes per side until golden brown on both sides. Reduce heat if necessary to finish cooking the inside without burning the outside. Remove from skillet and slice on the diagonal. Set aside.

2. In a small bowl, whisk the vinegar, sesame oil, soy sauce, and ½ cup reserved mandarin orange liquid. Season with salt and pepper. Place the onions into a large bowl. Pour half the dressing over the onions and let the onions sit in the dressing for a few minutes. This will mellow their flavor and soften them just a little. Reserve remaining dressing.

3. Break off the leaves of romaine lettuce. Cut off the stem and stack the leaves. Cut on each side of the center rib and discard the rib. Chop the leaves into bite-sized pieces.

4. Add the romaine and mandarin oranges into the bowl of onions and dressing. Add the chow mein noodles.

5. Toss the chicken with the reserved dressing, coating each slice. Toss the dressed chicken slices with the greens. Garnish with black and white sesame seeds.

*Yield: 4-6 salad-sized servings*
*8 eggroll wrapper cup-sized servings*

---

### Eggroll Wrapper Cups:

Preheat oven to 350°F. Invert 8 oven-proof ramekins or custard cups on a cookie sheet. Spray the outside of the cups with nonstick cooking spray. Drape an eggroll wrapper over the outside of each cup. Bake for 10 minutes until golden. Allow to cool for 5 minutes; remove eggroll wrapper from cup. Store in a heavy-duty ziplock bag at room temperature for up to two days.

# thai slaw salad

1½ cups shredded red cabbage

3 cups shredded green cabbage (½ small head)

½ cup grated or shredded carrot (about 1 carrot)

2 scallions, thinly sliced

½ red onion, thinly sliced

½ cup slivered almonds

1 cup sweetened dried cranberries, such as Craisins

½ cup plus 3 tablespoons canola or vegetable oil

1 tablespoon roasted or toasted sesame oil

zest from 1 lime

juice from 2 limes

1 jalapeño pepper, ribs and seeds discarded, minced

¼ teaspoon fine sea salt

freshly ground black pepper

black and white sesame seeds, for garnish

1. In a large bowl, toss the red cabbage, green cabbage, carrot, scallions, red onion, almonds, and cranberries. Toss to combine. Set aside.

2. In a medium bowl, with an immersion blender, combine the canola oil, sesame oil, lime zest, lime juice, jalapeño pepper, salt, and pepper. Blend until emulsified. Pour the dressing over the salad. Mix to combine. Garnish with the sesame seeds. Allow the flavors to mingle for at least ½ hour before serving.

*Yield: 6-8 servings*

# baby bok choy salad

*Cuteness factor aside, baby bok choy are also more tender and milder than regular bok choy. They can be braised whole and are found in many supermarkets and Asian markets year round. If you can't find baby bok choy, you can use regular, use just the bottom 6 inches, discarding the part with the bulk of the leaves. Skip the boiling in water part and cut into paper-thin slices on the diagonal, like cutting a celery stalk.*

*This is where those extra bags of Chinese noodles that come with take-out come in handy. They give the crunch factor to this great salad.*

2 heads baby bok choy,
or 1 head regular bok choy

½ teaspoon roasted or toasted
sesame oil

¼ cup soy sauce

¼ cup water

1-inch fresh ginger, peeled,
cut into 6 thin slices, then into
julienne strips

2 tablespoons rice wine
vinegar

¼ teaspoon chili oil or
crushed red pepper flakes

⅔ cup canola oil

2 tablespoons orange juice

1 teaspoon sugar

5 ounces mesclun greens

packaged Chinese noodles

1. Quarter each head of baby bok choy. Drop into boiling salted water until the core is tender, about 4-5 minutes. Remove and shock in cold water to stop the cooking process.

2. Prepare the dressing: Whisk the sesame oil, soy sauce, and water. Add the ginger, vinegar, chili oil, canola oil, orange juice, and sugar. Whisk until emulsified.

3. Make a criss-cross pattern on each plate with 2 bok choy pieces. Combine the mesclun greens and the Chinese noodles. If you didn't use the baby bok choy, toss the sliced bok choy with the mesclun greens. Toss with prepared dressing to taste; you will have extra dressing.

## Optional garnish:

Cut 1 inch of peeled ginger into threadlike julienne strips. Dry on paper towels. Heat 1 inch of vegetable or corn oil. Fry the ginger for 10 seconds until it frizzles. Sprinkle over the top of each salad.

*Yield: 4-6 servings*

# roasted beet salad

*Not one person in my family likes beets. Not one person left over a drop of this salad when I served it and it was requested the very next night! The roasted beets become almost like beet chips. They are incredible. The procedure can be done with taro root or other root vegetables as well. One of the unique aspects to this recipe is not needing to peel the beets.*

*Cutting the beets on newspaper keeps the red from dying your kitchen pink; gloves keep it off your hands. If you can't find golden beets, just double the amount of red beets.*

2 medium/large red beets, scrubbed but not peeled

2 medium/large golden beets, scrubbed but not peeled

olive oil

kosher salt

dried thyme

## Dressing:

1 tablespoon honey

1 tablespoon Dijon mustard

3 tablespoons orange juice

3 tablespoons olive oil

1 tablespoon balsamic or apple cider vinegar

fine sea salt

freshly ground black pepper

2 ounce frisée lettuce

3 ounces red leaf lettuce

½ cup chopped walnuts

3 ounces blue or gorgonzola cheese, optional, for dairy meals (see resource guide, p. 315)

1. Preheat oven to 450°F. Line 2 baking sheets with parchment paper. Slice off the top and bottom of each beet. Slice into rounds as thin as possible, ¼-inch thick or less. Drizzle each beet slice with olive oil, brushing it to evenly coat. Sprinkle with coarse salt and thyme. Place on prepared baking sheet. Roast 18-22 minutes, until the beets are soft and slightly shrunken. The smaller or thinner beets will need to come out of the oven so they don't burn. Set aside. Keep the colors separate as they will bleed otherwise.

2. Prepare the dressing. Using an immersion blender or with a whisk, combine the honey, mustard, orange juice, olive oil, and vinegar. Blend or whisk until emulsified. Season with salt and pepper.

3. Place the frisée and red leaf lettuce leaves into a bowl and lightly dress, tossing to combine, reserving 6 teaspoons of the dressing.

4. Arrange the roasted beet slices, in alternating colors, in a single layer on each plate. Drizzle a scant teaspoon of the dressing over the beets. Place a tall mound of the greens in the center of each plate, allowing the beets to peek out. Sprinkle walnuts evenly over each plate. If using cheese, crumble over each mound of lettuce.

*Yield: 4-6 servings*

oh baby!

# oh baby!
## dessert buffet format

### Menu

❧

Blueberry Lemon
Crème Brûlée Tart
page 297

∼

Chocolate Peanut Butter Diamonds
page 273

∼

Fudge Covered Brownie Cheesecake
page 281

∼

Chocolate-Dipped Almond Horns
page 268

∼

Cupcakes
page 304

∼

Plum Crumble Cake
page 267

∼

Peanut Brittle
page 280

∼

Fresh Fruit Lollipops
page 279

∼

Chocolate Layer Cake with
Creamy Coconut Glaze
page 298

∼

Peach and Berry Crisp
page 303

∼

Fruit Spritzers

To welcome a new baby or celebrate a 1st birthday, what could be more fun than a dessert buffet? It is a practical, inexpensive offering made up entirely of sweets, presented in a beautiful buffet format with a touch of indulgence. Children love helping with the setup of this charming display.

Begin by breaking out your stuffed animals and baby accouterments. A teddy bear in a diaper holds the silverware. Diaper pins are a darling touch to the napkins. Baby bottles are filled with Majolica spray roses, baby's breath, blue delphinium, and daisies. There are so many ways to be creative here. Party stores are filled with small baby-themed charms, like those pacifier elastics in which we wrapped our cupcakes.

The table was covered with an inexpensive teddy bear fabric and overlayed with a pastel sheer. It was gathered in the front and secured by pins which are masked by a teddy bear.

Varying the heights of your desserts gives great visual appeal. The guests felt like kids in a candy store as they used silver scoops to scoop candy from 4-foot tall martini glasses. Parchment paper cones of Peanut Brittle displayed in an ice-cream cone holder (which held them upright) added eye-appeal.

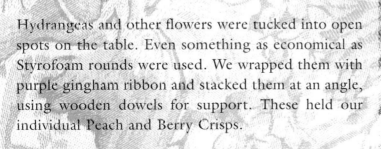

Hydrangeas and other flowers were tucked into open spots on the table. Even something as economical as Styrofoam rounds were used. We wrapped them with purple gingham ribbon and stacked them at an angle, using wooden dowels for support. These held our individual Peach and Berry Crisps.

With this menu, which is all done in advance, we included something for everyone; from the peanut butter lovers, to the chocoholics, to the cheesecake fiends. We didn't even forget our diet-conscious friends. Our Fresh Fruit Lollipops are a simply delightful way to allow everyone to partake. Lay them flat on a platter or set them up in a lollipop stand, as we show here.

The beverage of choice at this party, Fruit Spritzers, are a beautiful, healthful, non-alcoholic drink that will appeal to the whole family. We froze berries in fun shaped ice-cubes trays as a festive touch.

As a parting gift to the children in our crowd, we made a name tag for every child attending the party and tied it around the neck of a small baby bottle. At the end of the party, the kids filled their baby bottles with the extra candy, a party favor for the road.

# marinated spring chicken breast

*This recipe is great on the grill. It is perfect for summer. If you can't find the Pereg brand dry spice soup blend, you can make your own. Mix ¼ teaspoon each of cumin, ground tumeric, coriander, black pepper, cardemon, and 1 whole clove in a food processor. Process to form spice blend.*

4 teaspoons olive oil

¼ teaspoon garlic powder

¼ teaspoon paprika

juice of 1 fresh lemon

2 teaspoons Pereg brand
soup mixture spice blend

1 onion, sliced

4 boneless, skinless chicken
breasts

2 tablespoons olive oil

1 head iceburg lettuce

2 tomatoes, cut into 8 wedges

extra-virgin olive oil

store-bought techina sauce

1. In a large bowl, make a paste of the 4 teaspoons olive oil, garlic powder, paprika, lemon juice, and the soup spice or homemade spice blend. Mix in the onion. Add the chicken breasts and toss to coat. Marinate at least 6 hours or overnight. (If you have less time, slice the chicken horizontally and in half.)

2. Remove the chicken, reserving the onions. Sear the chicken on an oiled preheated grill or in an oiled preheated frying pan, 5-6 minutes per side until done. Try not to move the chicken too much while cooking so you can achieve pretty grill marks on it.

3. Heat the 2 tablespoons olive oil in a medium sauté pan over medium heat. Add the onions and cook for 5-6 minutes, until slightly wilted.

4. Shred the lettuce and make an oval heap on each plate or serving platter. Lay 4 tomato wedges around the lettuce on each plate. Drizzle with olive oil. Season with salt and pepper.

5. Slice chicken on the diagonal. Lay the chicken slices over the lettuce. Drizzle onions over the plate.

6. Drizzle plate with techina sauce.

*Yield: 4 servings*

# ratatouille chicken stew

olive oil

1 chicken, cut into eighths, or 10 chicken thighs

1 small Asian eggplant, cut into ½-inch cubes, or 1 small Italian eggplant, peeled, cut into ½-inch cubes

2 carrots, cut into small chunks

1 onion, cut into small chunks

1 celery stalk, cut into small chunks

1 bay leaf

2 teaspoons dried thyme

1 teaspoon whole black peppercorns

2 shallots, thinly sliced

3 cloves fresh garlic, sliced

⅓ cup sliced black olives, optional

1 (13.5-ounce) can artichokes, drained

½ cup red wine

1 (28-ounce) can crushed tomatoes

2 roasted red peppers (jarred) sliced

fresh basil leaves

1. Preheat oven to 400°F.

2. Place 1 tablespoon olive oil into a very large Dutch oven or very large ovenproof sauté pan, or prepare in two batches in medium pans. When oil is hot, add the chicken pieces, skin-side-down. Sear the skin until nice and evenly golden. Flip the pieces to get color on the bottom side as well. The chicken will render out some of the fat. Remove the chicken pieces from the pan and set aside; do not drain off the oil.

3. Into the same frying pan, add the eggplant. Add olive oil as needed. Sauté for 3-4 minutes. Add the carrots, onion, celery, bay leaf, thyme, and peppercorns. Sauté for 6-8 minutes, until onions soften. Add the shallots and garlic; sauté until soft, 4-6 minutes. Add the olives, if using, and the artichokes. Add the red wine. Shake the pan and then let the wine cook down to 2 teaspoons.

4. Add the crushed tomatoes and the roasted red peppers. Simmer for 5-10 minutes.

5. Bring to a low boil, and cook until the vegetables are soft, about 10 minutes

6. Place chicken, skin-side-up, on top of the vegetables; do not submerge or skin will become rubbery.

7. Put into the oven, uncovered, for 50 minutes. Spoon some of the juices and vegetables over the chicken and bake for another 2 minutes. Garnish with fresh chopped basil.

*Yield: 4-6 servings*

# roasted garlic chicken
# stuffed with dried fruits and nuts

Meat

*You can prepare this dish with chicken parts as well. Lay the orange slices and sprigs of rosemary in your baking pan. Place the stuffed chicken pieces on top. Bake, uncovered, for one hour.*

1 head garlic

extra-virgin olive oil

fine sea salt

freshly ground black pepper

10-12 dried apricots

5 dried Mission figs

½ cup shelled, raw pistachio nuts, (unsalted, not roasted)

1 whole (3-5 pound) chicken or pullet, washed, patted dry

½ orange, unpeeled, sliced

2 sprigs fresh rosemary

kitchen twine

3 tablespoons margarine, melted

1. Preheat oven to 375°F.

2. Holding the head of garlic on its side, cut the top 1-2 inches off the top of the bulb to expose the cloves. Place the head in the center of a square of foil, on a small baking pan. Drizzle with olive oil and season with salt and pepper. Close the foil packet. Roast for 45 minutes-1 hour.

3. Meanwhile, in a food processor fitted with a metal blade, chop the apricots, dried figs, and pistachios into very small pieces.

4. With your fingers, loosen the skin of the chicken at the breasts, thighs, and drumsticks.

5. Massage the fruit mixture under the skin, getting it into the cavities where the skin was loosened.

6. Stuff the orange slices and the rosemary into the cavity of the chicken. Tie the legs closed with kitchen twine. Place the chicken on a rack in a roasting pan; try not to let too much of the fruit and nuts drip out into the pan, as they will burn.

7. When the garlic is soft and caramelized, remove it from the oven and squeeze the roasted garlic out of the skin. Rub it all over the outside of the chicken.

8. Drizzle the margarine over the top of the chicken, letting it run down the sides.

9. Bake, uncovered, for 1½ hours, basting 2-3 times with the pan juices.

*Yield: 4 servings*

# mushroom stuffed chicken

Meat

3 tablespoons olive oil, divided

1 large shallot, finely minced

6 ounces fresh button or crimini mushrooms, sliced

fine sea salt

freshly ground black pepper

8 fresh sage leaves, chiffonade

½ cup white wine, such as Sauvignon Blanc, divided

4 chicken breasts, bone-in, with skin

4 chicken thighs, bone-in, with skin

¼ cup chicken stock

2 sage leaves, chiffonade, for garnish

1. Preheat oven to 375°F.

2. In a large frying pan, heat 2 tablespoons of olive oil. Add the shallots and mushrooms. Cook until soft and shiny, 4-6 minutes. Season with salt and pepper. Add 8 sage leaves and ¼ cup of wine. Cook for 6-8 minutes, until all the liquid has evaporated. Set aside until cool enough to handle.

3. Using your fingers, loosen the skin on each piece of chicken. Stuff under the skin of each thigh and breast with the mushroom-sage mixture.

4. Salt and pepper both sides of each piece of chicken.

5. In the same pan, heat 1 tablespoon olive oil. Sear chicken, skin-side-down, until golden. Flip and brown on other side. Remove to a baking pan and bake for 15 minutes, skin-side-up, uncovered.

6. Drain all but 1 tablespoon of fat from the frying pan. Add ¼ cup white wine and stock. Pour the sauce over the chicken and bake another 15 minutes, basting once or twice during the last 5 minutes.

7. Immediately before serving; garnish with a sprinkle of sage leaf chiffonade.

*Yield: 6-8 servings*

---

### Chiffonade:

To create a chiffonade, stack the leaves and cut them into narrow ribbons. These elegant strips can be used to garnish any number of dishes and are an attractive addiiton to salads.

# chicken with beer and tomatoes

⅔ cup all-purpose flour

2 teaspoons salt

1 teaspoon freshly ground
black pepper

1 teaspoon paprika

2 chickens cut into eighths

½ cup vegetable oil

8 cloves fresh garlic, sliced

1 large onion, chopped

1 (35-ounce) can Italian
peeled tomatoes, drained,
coarsely chopped

1 (16-ounce) can or bottle
full-flavored beer

1 (6-ounce) can tomato paste

1 teaspoon dried thyme

1 teaspoon dried marjoram
or oregano leaves

1 teaspoon freshly ground
black pepper

1. Preheat oven to 350°F.

2. Place the flour, salt, pepper, and paprika into a heavy-duty ziplock bag. Shake to mix. Add the chicken pieces, three at a time, shaking to coat. Remove chicken from bag and shake off excess flour.

3. Place the oil into a large frying pan over medium heat. Add the chicken. Cook, turning, until chicken is browned on all sides, about 10 minutes. Transfer the chicken to a baking pan. Do this in batches, if necessary, until all chicken is browned.

4. To the same pan, add the garlic and onion. Sauté until soft, about 4-6 minutes.

5. Sprinkle the garlic and onion over the chicken.

6. In a bowl, mix the tomatoes, beer, and tomato paste. Pour over the chicken. In a small cup or bowl, combine the thyme, marjoram, and pepper. Sprinkle over the top.

7. Bake, uncovered, for 1 hour 30 minutes.

*Yield: 8 servings*

# cornish hens with pistachio paste

*The pistachio paste is fine at room temperature, which makes this dish great for Shabbos lunch.*

4 (1 pound) baby Cornish hens, butterflied, backbone removed, pressed flat with your palm

2 cups shelled raw unsalted pistachio nuts, finely chopped, divided

fine sea salt

freshly ground black pepper

3-4 tablespoons olive oil

6 shallots, sliced

2 tablespoons fresh thyme or 2 teaspoons dried

12 ounces chicken stock, plus a little extra, if needed

4 basil or other brightly colored flat leaves for garnish

1. Preheat oven to 350°F.

2. Stuff ¼ cup chopped pistachio nuts under the skin of each of the hens. Massage the nuts under the skin to help spread them out evenly. Salt and pepper both sides of each hen.

3. Heat the olive oil in 2 large sauté pans (or plan to sear in batches). Sear the hens, skin-side-down, until golden brown. Remove hens from the pan and place in roasting pans in a single layer. Set aside. Add the shallots to the pan with the hen drippings. Sauté 6-7 minutes. Sprinkle in the thyme. Deglaze the pan with the chicken stock, using a wooden spoon to unstick any nuts from the pan.

4. Meanwhile, place the hens, uncovered, in the oven. Roast for 30 minutes, or until done.

5. Prepare the pistachio paste: In a deep container, or in the bowl of a food processor, place ½ cup chopped pistachio nuts. Add the shallots and pan drippings. Using an immersion blender or food processor, blend into a paste. Thin with a little stock if needed.

6. Dollop 1-2 tablespoons of the pistachio paste onto a basil or other flat leaf; place at the side of the hen. Sprinkle all with the remaining chopped pistachios.

*Yield: 4 servings*

# chicken tagine

¼ teaspoon garlic powder

⅛ teaspoon cayenne pepper

¼ teaspoon ground cumin

¼ teaspoon ground coriander

¼ teaspoon curry powder

¼ teaspoon cinnamon

¼ teaspoon ground allspice

3 tablespoons olive oil

4 chicken drumsticks, bone-in, with skin

4 chicken thighs, bone-in, with skin

4 chicken breasts, bone-in, with skin

1 head fennel

fine sea salt

freshly ground black pepper

2 large Spanish onions, cut into 1-inch chunks

1 carrot, peeled, cut into 1-inch chunks

3 parsnips, peeled, cut into 1-inch chunks

2-3 cups chicken broth

Moroccan Couscous, optional (see box)

1. Preheat oven to 350°F.

2. In a small bowl, mix the garlic powder, cayenne, cumin, coriander, curry, cinnamon, and allspice. Set aside.

3. If the fennel has long fronds, cut them off and remove for garnish. Slice the fennel into 1-inch bias-cut strips.

4. Season the chicken pieces on both sides with salt and black pepper.

5. Heat olive oil in a large frying pan over medium-high heat. Add the chicken pieces, skin-side-down, in batches. Sear until skin is nice and brown, try not to shake the pan too much.

6. Remove chicken to a baking dish or oven-to-table casserole dish. Sprinkle half the spice mixture on the chicken, rubbing it into the pieces.

7. Add the fennel, onions, carrot, and parsnips to the pan. It should still have olive oil in it, plus some fat rendered out of the chicken pieces. If necessary, add a drop of olive oil. Sauté and scrape up all the browned bits from the bottom of the pan. Add the remaining spice mixture. Cook for 3 minutes, until nice and shiny.

8. Surround the chicken with the vegetables. Add chicken broth to come halfway up on the chicken.

9. Bake, covered, for 1 hour.

10. Serve with Moroccan Couscous, if desired.

*Yield: 6-8 servings*

---

**Moroccan Couscous:**

Prepare a 10-ounce box of couscous as per directions on box. Soak a cup of golden raisins in rum (or orange juice) while the chicken cooks. When ready to serve, toss the couscous with the drained raisins, 1 cup of chopped green pitted olives, and ½ cup chopped almonds.

122   ···   KOSHER BY DESIGN ENTERTAINS

# coq au vin

*It is best to marinate the chicken in the wine the night before. It will really soak up the flavor of the wine and the color will be magnificent.*

4 chicken drumsticks, bone-in, with skin

4 chicken thighs, bone-in, with skin

4 chicken breasts, bone-in, with skin

fine sea salt

freshly ground black pepper

1 bottle good-quality Cabernet Sauvignon

3 tablespoons olive oil, divided

2 cups wild mushroom caps (oysters, shiitake, crimini), stems discarded

1 medium carrot, peeled, cut into chunks

1 large onion, cut into chunks

1 cup chicken stock

4 tablespoons cornstarch

4 tablespoons water

1. Season the chicken pieces on both sides with salt and pepper. Place into a large container in a single layer. Add enough wine to cover the chicken and place, uncovered, in the refrigerator overnight.

2. The next day, remove the chicken pieces from the container, reserving the wine marinade.

3. Preheat oven to 325°F.

4. Place 2 tablespoons of oil into a large frying pan over medium-high heat. Add the chicken pieces, skin side down, in batches. Sear the chicken on both sides until nice and brown. The sugars from the wine will help caramelize the skin quickly.

5. As the chicken pieces are done, remove them to a baking dish, skin-side-up. To the same pan, add the mushrooms and remaining tablespoon of olive oil. Sauté for 2 minutes. Add the carrot and onion. Season with salt and pepper. Sauté for 2 minutes, until nice and shiny. Add 1 cup of the wine marinade and 1 cup of stock to deglaze the pan.

6. Pour the mushroom mixture and remaining wine marinade over the chicken. Loosely cover and bake for 1 hour.

7. When the chicken is done, strain the juices into a medium pot. In a small bowl, whisk the cornstarch with the water. Bring the juices to a boil. Reduce heat to low. Whisk in the cornstarch slurry and return to a boil. The mixture will thicken. Stir. Simmer for 5 minutes. Pour the sauce back over the chicken.

*Yield: 6-8 servings*

# glazed chicken breasts with strawberry salsa

## Glazed Chicken Breasts:

4 boneless skinless, chicken breasts, tenders removed

fine sea salt

freshly ground black pepper

2 tablespoons olive oil

1 shallot, minced

½ cup chicken stock

1 teaspoon cornstarch

3 tablespoons strawberry jelly

1½ tablespoons balsamic vinegar

## Strawberry Salsa:

2 cups fresh strawberries, chopped

2 tablespoons red onion, chopped

1½ tablespoons balsamic vinegar

¼ teaspoon freshly ground black pepper

1 tablespoon chopped fresh mint

juice of 1 fresh lime

1. Season the chicken with salt and pepper on both sides.

2. Heat the oil in a medium skillet or grill pan over medium heat. Add the chicken and sear on both sides, 4-5 minutes per side, until browned. You can also grill the chicken on a barbecue grill. Remove the chicken to a plate.

3. To the same pan, add the shallots and sauté on low heat until soft, about 4 minutes. (If you grilled the chicken on a barbecue, heat 2 tablespoons olive oil in a pan, sauté the shallots in it, and continue.)

4. In a small bowl, dissolve the cornstarch in the chicken stock. Add it to the pan. Add the jelly and balsamic vinegar. Cook until thickened, about 1-2 minutes. Return the chicken to the pan and coat both sides with the glaze. Remove from heat.

5. Prepare the salsa: Place the chopped strawberries into a small bowl. Toss with the red onion, balsamic vinegar, pepper, mint, and lime juice. Allow flavors to blend for 10 minutes.

6. Serve chicken with the salsa, warm or at room temperature.

*Yield: 4 servings*

# chicken with rum

1 chicken, cut into eighths

fine sea salt

freshly ground black pepper

all-purpose flour

2 tablespoons olive oil

1 large onion, thinly sliced

2 red bell peppers, seeded, very thinly sliced

6 cloves fresh garlic, thinly sliced

juice and zest of 1 lime, green part only, not the white pith

4-5 tablespoons rum

8 tablespoons crushed pineapple and 3 tablespoons of the juice

2 tablespoons water

1. Preheat oven to 400°F.

2. Season the chicken pieces with salt and pepper. Lightly dust each piece with flour, shaking off any excess.

3. Heat the olive oil in a skillet over medium heat. Add the chicken, skin-side-down. Let the skin get golden and crisp; try not to move the pieces around. Turn pieces over and brown. Remove the chicken to a baking dish.

4. To the same skillet, add the onion and peppers and sauté for 3 minutes. Add the sliced garlic, lime zest, and lime juice. Turn heat down to low and cook for 10 minutes.

5. Add the rum; cook for 3 minutes. Add the crushed pineapple and 3 tablespoons of the pineapple juice. Add 2 tablespoons water. Bring to a boil.

6. Pour the pineapple mixture over the chicken pieces. Roast, uncovered, for 45 minutes.

*Yield: 4 servings*

# zinfandel chicken

1½ cups red Zinfandel wine, or other dry red wine

½ cup olive oil

3 tablespoons soy sauce

1 tablespoon fish-free Worcestershire sauce (see p. 16)

2 tablespoons Dijon mustard

⅛ teaspoon freshly ground black pepper

3 scallions, sliced

1 chicken, cut into eighths

1. In a bowl combine the wine, oil, soy sauce, Worcestershire sauce, mustard, pepper, and scallions.

2. Place the chicken pieces in a heavy-duty ziplock bag. Pour the marinade over the chicken. Seal the bag, squeezing out as much air as possible so that the marinade is forced up around the chicken. Refrigerate for at least 4 hours or overnight.

3. Preheat oven to 350°F.

4. Remove the chicken from the marinade and spread in a single layer on a baking sheet. Bake, uncovered, for 1 hour 15 minutes, until the chicken is cooked through. Turn the oven to broil and broil for 2 minutes so that the skin of the chicken becomes nice and crisp.

*Yield: 4 servings*

# walnut-crusted turkey cutlets with cranberry sauce

¾ cup walnut pieces

½ cup all-purpose flour

1 egg, beaten

4 boneless, skinless, turkey cutlets, pounded to ¼-inch thickness

fine sea salt

freshly ground black pepper

2 tablespoons margarine

1 tablespoon canola oil

1 cup jellied cranberry sauce, from a small can

¼ cup red currant jelly

1 tablespoon red wine, such as Cabernet Sauvignon or Port

1 tablespoon Dijon mustard

1. Place the walnuts and flour into the bowl of a food processor. Making sure not to process too finely, chop the walnuts. You want a little texture from the nuts. You can also finely chop the nuts by hand and mix with flour. Pour the walnut mixture into a dish or pie plate.

2. Place the beaten egg into a dish or pie plate.

3. Season both sides of the turkey cutlets with salt and pepper. Dip them into the egg and then into the walnut mixture to form an even coating.

4. Place the margarine and oil into a large skillet. Melt over medium heat, Add the turkey and cook until golden brown and cooked through, about 4-5 minutes per side. Transfer to a plate or serving platter.

5. Place the cranberry sauce, currant jelly, wine, and mustard into a small saucepan set over medium-low heat. Whisk until smooth. Cook for 3 minutes. Remove from heat. Serve with the turkey cutlets.

*Yield: 4 servings*

# lemon chicken scalloppine with lemon aïoli

*This subtle, light-flavored dish is great hot out of the pan or even at room temperature the next day.*

6 boneless, skinless chicken breasts, tenders removed

½ cup all-purpose flour

2 teaspoons fine sea salt

1 teaspoon freshly ground black pepper

3 eggs, lightly beaten

1 cup homestyle or panko breadcrumbs

1 teaspoon dried oregano

⅛ cup pine nuts, coarsely chopped

⅛ cup raw, shelled sunflower seeds, not roasted or salted, coarsely chopped

1 lemon

3 tablespoons olive oil

## Lemon Aïoli:

zest of 1 lemon

juice of 1 fresh lemon

2 cloves fresh garlic, minced

¼ teaspoon fine sea salt

1 teaspoon sugar

⅔ cup mayonnaise

1 tablespoon olive oil

1. Place the chicken breasts between two pieces of waxed or parchment paper. Using a meat mallet or bottom of a heavy frying pan, pound the chicken cutlets until they are ¼-inch thick.

2. Set three shallow bowls or pans in front of you. Place the flour, salt, and pepper in one. Stir with a fork. Place the beaten eggs in the second bowl or pan. Place the breadcrumbs, oregano, pine nuts, and sunflower seeds in the third bowl, stirring to combine. Add the zest from the lemon, reserving the lemon.

3. Starting at the first bowl, dredge the chicken in flour on both sides, shaking off excess.

4. Coat in the eggs, allowing extra to drip off. Coat in breadcrumb mixture, pressing the coating into the chicken.

5. In a large skillet over medium heat, heat the oil. When the oil is hot, add the chicken. Squeeze the lemon over the pan, so that the juice squirts onto the chicken breasts. Cook 5-6 minutes per side, until golden and cooked through.

6. Prepare the aïoli: In a small bowl, mix the lemon zest, juice, garlic, salt, and sugar. Whisk in the mayonnaise and olive oil.

7. Serve the chicken with aïoli sauce on the side.

*Yield: 6 servings*

# pastrami-stuffed turkey roast with pineapple glaze

*When ArtScroll ran their recipe contest, a friend of Miriam L. Wallach of Woodmere submitted some recipes on her behalf, with the note that Miriam is one of the best and most creative cooks in her community. She bakes and distributes challahs every Shabbat for fun and relaxation. Enough said.*

*Just a cooking note: Turkey breast dries out very easily, so keep a close eye on the cooking time. If you are using a smaller roast, decrease the cooking time. If you have leftovers, don't reheat, just bring to room temperature.*

1 (4-5) pound boneless turkey roast, with skin, tied

¼ pound sliced pastrami

fine sea salt

freshly ground black pepper

garlic powder

onion powder

paprika

parsley flakes

2 tablespoons olive oil

kitchen twine

1 (20-ounce) can pineapple chunks

1. Preheat oven to 350°F.

2. Untie the turkey breast. If in a plastic sleeve, discard the sleeve or it will burn when you sear the turkey. Slide your fingers under the skin to loosen it and make a pocket. Slide the pastrami slices into this pocket.

3. Retie the turkey with kitchen twine. Liberally season both sides of the breast with the salt, pepper, garlic powder, onion powder, paprika, and parsley.

4. Heat the olive oil in a large skillet. When the oil shimmers, add the turkey, skin-side-down. Allow to sear until the skin is golden brown, 4-5 minutes. Turn and sear the other sides for 4-5 minutes each.

5. Transfer the turkey to a shallow baking dish that snugly holds it.

6. While the pan is still hot, add the pineapple chunks with their juices. Turn the heat to medium-low. Scrape up the browned bits. Simmer until the sauce becomes syrupy and the pineapple turns an amber color, about 5-8 minutes. Pour this glaze over the turkey.

7. Bake 1½-1¾ hours. The turkey will continue to cook when removed from the oven.

8. Allow the turkey to rest for 15 minutes before slicing and serving.

9. Garnish with the pineapple sauce.

*Yield: 8-10 servings*

# citrus-and-garlic crusted duck breasts

4 boneless duck breasts, with skin

zest of 1 lemon

zest of 1 orange

6 cloves roasted garlic (see box), or ½ teaspoon garlic powder mixed into a paste with ¼ teaspoon water

3 sprigs flat leaf parsley, leaves finely chopped, stems discarded

1. Preheat oven to 350°F.

2. Trim excess fat from the duck breasts. Score the fat, making deep diamond cut marks through the layers of fat, but be sure not to cut into the duck meat. Heat an empty frying pan over medium heat. Place the duck, fat-side-down, into the hot pan. Allow the fat to render out, pouring it off as it releases. It will take about 15 minutes for all the fat to render out and for the skin to get browned and crisp. Turn over and cook for 4 minutes on the other side.

3. Using a sharp knife, finely chop the lemon zest, orange zest, roasted garlic, and parsley. Keep going over it with the knife, chopping until it forms a paste.

4. Gently spread the citrus paste over the skin side of each duck breast to form a crust.

5. Place in preheated oven for 10 minutes.

6. Allow the duck to rest for a few minutes. Slice on the diagonal into ¼-inch slices. Serve over a bed of greens or a grain such as rice or couscous.

*Yield: 4 servings*

## Roasted Garlic:

Roasted garlic is a fabulous building-block recipe. Once you know how to make it, you can use it in hundreds of dishes. Place whole, peeled cloves of garlic into a small pot. Add olive oil to cover. Bring to a boil over medium-low heat. Boil for 5 minutes; the garlic may turn brown. Remove from heat. Allow to stand in the oil for 20 minutes. The garlic will be soft and caramelized. The oil can be stored in an airtight non-metal container in the refrigerator for 3 weeks and used anywhere olive oil is called for; the garlic flavor infuses into the oil, adding a wonderful taste.

# chicken osso buco with orange-lemon gremolata

## Chicken Osso Buco:

4 tablespoons all-purpose flour

4 chicken drumsticks
bone-in, with skin

4 chicken thighs,
bone-in, with skin

4 chicken breasts,
bone-in, with skin

2 tablespoons olive oil

1 medium onion, minced

2 cloves fresh garlic, minced

¾ cup dry white wine

½ cup pearl barley

1 can (14.5 ounces)
whole tomatoes,
chopped, with their juices

¾ cup chicken broth

zest and juice of 1 orange

1¼ teaspoon fine sea salt

½ teaspoon dried sage

½ teaspoon dried rosemary

## Orange-Lemon Gremolata:

boiling water, as needed

2 cloves fresh garlic

¼ cup chopped parsley

zest of ½ orange

zest of ½ lemon

1. Preheat oven to 350°F.

2. Place the flour into a large ziplock bag. Add the chicken pieces a few at a time, shaking to coat.

3. Heat the oil in a Dutch oven or large ovenproof pot on medium heat. Add the chicken and brown on both sides, about 6 minutes per side. Transfer chicken to a plate. Lower the heat and add the onions and garlic to the pot; cook for 5-7 minutes, until onions are soft. Raise the heat back to medium. Add the wine. Cook until slightly reduced, scraping up the browned bits from the pan. Add the barley, tomatoes and their juices, broth, zest and juice of the orange, salt, sage, and rosemary. Bring to a boil.

4. Add the chicken, cover, and transfer to the oven. Bake 1½ hours.

5. While chicken is cooking, prepare the gremolata: In a small pan of boiling water, place 2 cloves garlic. Boil for 2 minutes. Drain and finely chop. Place into a small bowl. Mix with the parsley, orange zest, and lemon zest.

6. Sprinkle over the chicken right before serving.

*Yield: 6-8 servings*

# caribbean jerk chicken

*My friend Aline Grossman is always experimenting with new recipes and flavors in her kitchen. While in a spicy phase, she shared this winner with me, although she warned that for her kids she prepares it with bell peppers, as the hot peppers are too spicy for them. Jerk seasoning is the hot, spicy, and sweet flavor of the islands. Make sure you get the rub under the skin and into every part of the chicken. Give the chicken enough time to absorb the flavors.*

3 cloves fresh garlic

2 bunches scallions, roots trimmed, halved

1 medium red onion, quartered

1 habanero or other hot pepper, with seeds, any color, stem removed

3 tablespoons fresh thyme leaves

1 tablespoon ground allspice

8 whole cloves

1 tablespoon molasses

1 tablespoon apple cider vinegar

1 teaspoon fine sea salt

1 chicken, cut into eighths

½ cup beer

½ cup ketchup

1. Into the bowl of a food processor fitted with a metal blade, place the garlic, scallions, onion, hot pepper, thyme, allspice, cloves, molasses, vinegar, and salt. Pulse until a wet paste forms.

2. Rub this jerk seasoning over and under the skin of the chicken. Refrigerate, uncovered, in a glass non-reactive baking dish for 4 hours or overnight.

3. Preheat an outdoor barbecue or grill. This can also be done indoors in a grill pan. Lightly oil the grill or pan. Place the chicken on the grill, skin-side-down, and cook for 20 minutes. Turn over and cook for 20 minutes longer.

4. In a small bowl, mix the beer and ketchup. Cook the chicken for an additional 10 minutes, basting the chicken with the beer mixture often.

*Yield: 4 servings*

# terra chip chummos chicken

*Every so often, when we are really desperado at dinner time, my husband and I play our own version of The Iron Chef. We give each other 6 minutes and the ability to use up to 5 ingredients that we have in the fridge or pantry, and the winner is the one who creates a better dinner. Here is my favorite entry. It is fun, colorful, and unique.*

*Terra chips are a more exotic version of a potato chip. They are made from root vegetables, such as sweet potato, taro, ruby taro, and parsnip, and are sold in supermarkets in the chip/snack aisle.*

6 tablespoons extra-virgin olive oil

3 cloves fresh garlic, minced

12 tablespoons store-bought chummos, plain or roasted red pepper

6 boneless, skinless chicken breasts, pounded flat to an even thickness

1 (7.5-ounce) bag Terra Chips, original flavor

1. Preheat oven to 375°F.

2. Place the oil into a small pot. Add the minced garlic. Bring to a simmer over low heat and cook for 3 minutes, stirring occasionally. Remove from heat; the garlic will continue to cook.

3. Spread 1 tablespoon of the chummos on both sides of each cutlet.

4. In a large ziplock bag, crush the Terra Chips. Don't overcrush, you want some texture and to be able to see the different colors of the chips. Coat each side of the chicken with a handful of the crushed chips, pressing them to adhere. Place on a broiler pan. Drizzle 1 tablespoon of the garlic oil over each breast. Bake for 20 minutes.

*Yield: 6 servings*

# slow-roasted rotisserie chicken

*Once a month I mix up a huge batch of this seasoning mixture and keep it in a jar with my spices. This cuts my preparation time to under a minute each time I make this dish, and it is often! It is my kids' most-requested chicken dish. I make mine on a small rotisserie but have gotten equally great results using this low and slow oven-cooking method.*

½ teaspoon fine sea salt

½ teaspoon garlic salt

¼ teaspoon black pepper

1 teaspoon dark brown sugar

¼ teaspoon cayenne pepper

½ teaspoon paprika

¼ teaspoon onion powder

1 teaspoon barbecue seasoning; check ingredient list for hickory or mesquite flavoring

1 (3-5 pound) whole chicken

1. Preheat oven to 300°F.

2. In a small bowl, mix the salt, garlic salt, pepper, brown sugar, cayenne, paprika, onion powder, and barbecue seasoning.

3. Rub the spice mix all over the skin of the chicken. If time permits, place the chicken into the refrigerator, uncovered, for 2-3 hours or up to overnight; this will help the skin crisp.

4. Place the chicken on a rack in a baking dish. Roast for 2 hours at this low temperature. During the last hour of cooking time, baste every ½ hour with the pan juices.

*Yield: 4 servings*

# whole roasted autumn chicken

*The recipe can be prepped a day ahead and left overnight in the refrigerator, uncovered, this will give the chicken a crisper skin when roasted. The honey oozes around the vegetables and the result is outstanding.*

leaves of 1 stem fresh rosemary, stem discarded

leaves of 2 stems fresh thyme, stems discarded

8 cloves fresh garlic, chopped

¼ cup chopped hazelnuts or roasted peeled chopped chestnuts

1 whole chicken, about 3 pounds, washed, patted dry

2 Yukon Gold potatoes, unpeeled

1 white turnip, peeled

2 large carrots, peeled, or 8 baby carrots

1 medium red onion

3-4 tablespoons extra-virgin olive oil, plus more for drizzling

fine sea salt

freshly ground black pepper

½ cup wildflower honey

1. Preheat oven to 375°F.

2. Either by hand with a sharp knife, or in the bowl of a food processor fitted with a metal blade, finely chop the rosemary, thyme, garlic, and nuts.

3. Slide your fingers under the chicke breast and thighs and loosen the skin. Gently place the garlic mixture under the loosened skin.

4. Cut the potatoes, turnip, carrots, and red onion into uniform ¼-inch pieces. Place into a bowl and toss with olive oil, salt, and pepper.

5. Place the vegetables into a medium roasting pan. Place the chicken on the vegetables. Drizzle the honey over the chicken, letting it run down the sides.

6. Drizzle the chicken with olive oil. Season with salt and pepper.

7. Place, uncovered, into the oven for 1½ hours. Stir the vegetables after an hour to prevent burning. The internal temperature should be 175°F and the top will look brown and gorgeous. If you would like, carefully turn the chicken over (make sure not to prick the skin or the juices will run out), turn the oven to broil, and broil for 2 minutes, until the skin on the underside looks nice and golden.

8. Carefully turn the chicken back over and let it rest for 10 minutes before cutting.

*Yield: 4 servings*

# pineapple chicken piccata

1 medium fresh, ripe pineapple

4 tablespoons margarine, divided

6 boneless, skinless chicken breasts

fine sea salt

freshly ground black pepper

2 tablespoons Dijon mustard

flour

2 cups assorted sliced mushrooms, white, baby bella, shiitake caps, etc.

1 scallion, thinly sliced

**Lemon Sauce:**

4 ounces orange juice

4 ounces pineapple juice

juice of 1 fresh lemon

2 teaspoons cornstarch

1 teaspoon chicken bouillon powder

4 tablespoons fresh parsley, chopped

1 whole tomato, seeded, chopped

2 tablespoons capers, drained

1. Cut off crown and end of the pineapple and discard. Slice pineapple lengthwise down the middle. Slice each half lengthwise into 4 long wedges. Cut out the core from each wedge. Cut the pineapple wedges out of their shells. Slice each wedge into ½-inch-thick triangles.

2. In a large skillet, melt 2 tablespoons margarine over medium heat. Sauté the pineapple triangles until lightly golden, 5-6 minutes. Remove from pan.

3. Pound the chicken breasts to an even thickness between 2 sheets of parchment or waxed paper. Sprinkle with salt and pepper. Using a spatula or pastry brush, spread one side of each breast with mustard.

4. Place the flour into a pie plate or shallow tin. Working with one chicken breast at time, coat with flour and shake to remove excess.

5. Add the remaining 2 tablespoons margarine to the skillet and melt. Add the chicken, mustard-side-down, and sauté until brown, about 5 minutes, without moving the cutlets. Flip the chicken over and add the mushrooms and scallion to the pan. Cook for 10 minutes.

6. Prepare the lemon sauce: In a small skillet, mix the orange juice, pineapple juice, and lemon juice. Add the cornstarch and bouillon and stir until dissolved. Turn the heat to medium and cook, stirring, until thickened. Pour over the chicken. Add the parsley, tomato, and capers. Add the pineapple to the pan. Heat through. Serve warm.

*Yield: 6 servings*

# orange chicken over whipped carrots

*This dish is a collaboration of one of my favorite chicken dishes and my friend Beth Eidman's favorite side dish. They go great together, but feel free to use them separately.*

## Orange Chicken:

2 large oranges

2 tablespoons honey

1½ tablespoons soy sauce

1 tablespoon roasted or toasted sesame oil

¼ teaspoon ground ginger

⅛ teaspoon crushed red pepper flakes

2 cloves fresh garlic, minced

1 chicken, cut into eighths

fine sea salt

freshly ground black pepper

1 tablespoon cornstarch, dissolved in ¼ cup cold water

## Whipped Carrots:

2 pounds carrots, peeled, sliced into ½-inch rounds

3 tablespoons sugar

zest and juice of 1 small orange

6 tablespoons margarine, sliced into pieces

pinch of ground ginger

fine sea salt

1. Grate the orange zest from the into a medium bowl. Juice the oranges into the same bowl.

2. Add the honey, soy sauce, sesame oil, ginger, red pepper flakes, and garlic. Whisk together.

3. Season the chicken pieces on both sides with salt and pepper. Place into a ziplock bag or glass baking dish. Pour the orange marinade over the chicken and marinate 6 hours or overnight.

4. Preheat oven to 375°F.

5. Remove chicken from marinade; pour marinade into a small pan.

6. Place the chicken into a baking dish. Bake, uncovered, for 1 hour.

7. Pour the dissolved cornstarch into the marinade. Bring to a simmer over low heat and cook for 5-6 minutes until thickened. Baste the chicken several times with this sauce while it bakes.

8. Meanwhile, prepare the carrots: Place the carrots and sugar into a large pot. Cover with water and season with salt. Bring to a boil and cook for 25-30 minutes, until carrots are soft. Drain the carrots, reserving 1 cup of the cooking water. Return the carrots to the pot. Heat until any remaining moisture is gone. Add the orange juice, zest, margarine, ginger, and salt to taste. With an immersion blender right in the pot, or in a blender, purée the carrots until whipped and smooth. Thin with the reserved cooking water if they are too dry. The carrots can be made in advance and reheated.

9. Serve the chicken over a mound of the carrots.

*Yield: 4 servings*

# farfalle chicken

*Finally, a one-skillet dish that your kids may even request! This is best served fresh. If you have leftovers, you may need to add a little chicken broth to the sauce, as it thickens when rewarmed. A loaf of garlic bread and a lightly dressed green salad are all you need to complete this meal.*

8 ounces farfalle or bow tie pasta

3 tablespoons olive oil

3 cloves fresh garlic, minced

3-4 boneless, skinless chicken breasts, cut into bite-sized pieces

1 teaspoon dried oregano

½ teaspoon crushed red pepper flakes

1 teaspoon garlic salt

¾ cup chicken broth

¼ cup oil packed sun-dried tomatoes, cut into thin strips

¼ cup dry white wine

2 Roma tomatoes, seeded, chopped

½ cup frozen green peas, (from a 10-ounce box) unthawed

½ cup soy milk

1. Cook the pasta al denté, according to package directions and drain.

2. Meanwhile, heat the oil in a large pan over medium heat. Add the garlic, cook for 30 seconds; do not brown it. Add the chicken, oregano, red pepper flakes, and garlic salt. Cook for 4 minutes. Add the broth, sun-dried tomatoes, and wine. Bring to a boil. Add the fresh tomatoes and peas. Reduce heat to low and simmer for 5-6 minutes, uncovered. Make sure chicken is no longer pink.

3. Stir in the soymilk. Simmer 2 minutes more. Watch the entire time to make sure the sauce does not cook out. Add the cooked pasta and toss to combine all. Heat through.

*Yield: 6-8 servings*

---

### Ovenproofing Your Skillet:

To ovenproof a skillet with a plastic or wooden handle, wrap the handle with a few layers of heavy-duty aluminum foil. The foil will still get very hot, but it will keep the handle from getting ruined.

# homestyle roasted chicken

*One of the simplest yet most satisfying dishes is a perfectly roasted chicken. The best pan to make this dish in is an ovenproof skillet. It will allow the chicken to roast on most of the exposed surfaces, and when you remove the chicken it is a snap to make the sauce from the pan juices. If you are using a disposable tin, you will need to transfer the pan juices to a small pot to make the sauce.*

1 whole chicken

5-6 sprigs fresh thyme or lemon thyme

½ lemon

16 cloves fresh garlic, divided

coarsely ground black pepper

coarse sea salt or kosher salt

4 tablespoons margarine, melted

4 Idaho potatoes, peeled, cut into small chunks

2 tablespoons red wine

1 tablespoon water

1. Preheat oven to 375°F.

2. Stuff the thyme sprigs, lemon and 8 garlic cloves into the cavity of the chicken. Sprinkle in a little salt and pepper. If you have kitchen twine, tie up the legs for a nicer presentation.

3. Place the chicken into a baking pan or ovenproof skillet.

4. Rub salt and pepper over the chicken breast. Spoon or ladle half the melted margarine onto the breast side of the chicken, allowing it to run down the sides of the chicken.

5. Surround the chicken with the potatoes and the remaining garlic cloves. Sprinkle the potatoes with salt and pepper. Brush the potatoes with a little of the melted margarine.

6. Place the pan into the oven. Roast, uncovered, for 35 minutes. Remove from oven. Ladle remaining margarine over the top of the chicken breast and baste the chicken with the pan juices.

7. Return the chicken to the oven for 45 minutes more. If the chicken does not look pretty, turn your oven to broil and broil until the skin looks nice and golden, about 2-3 minutes.

8. Remove chicken and most of the garlic from the pan. Add the wine and 1 tablespoon water to the pan. Place it over medium heat and bring to a simmer, scraping up the browned bits and smashing the roasted garlic cloves with the back of your spoon.

9. Serve the chicken with the pan juices.

*Yield: 4 servings*

# chicken curry

*I am not normally a curry fan, so when Chef Alex Petard excitedly told me that he can't wait to give me his recipe for a great curry, I was less than excited. As he was going on about the great chef he worked with in England, who was himself Indian, who taught him this recipe, all I could seem to focus on was how I hated the smell of the raw curry spice, and how my family would never go for this recipe, and how could I get out of eating this meal with my manners intact. An hour later, as I feasted on my second helping of Chicken Curry, I admitted I was won over. The flavors in this recipe are not overwhelming, the color is gorgeous, and, like many stews, it cooks a whole meal in one pot. Give this one a try, you may become a curry convert — I did.*

3 tablespoons margarine

1 large onion, halved, sliced

2 teaspoons Indian curry

2 teaspoons ground cumin

3 cloves fresh garlic, minced

2 teaspoons fresh minced ginger

2 Idaho potatoes, peeled, cut into 1-inch cubes

10 baby carrots, sliced, or 2 carrots, peeled, sliced

8 pieces chicken, bone-in, with skin, preferably drumsticks and thighs

1 teaspoon chicken bouillon powder

water as needed

fine sea salt

freshly ground black pepper

1. Select a large frying pan with a cover and 2-3-inch-high sides. Melt the margarine over medium heat. Add the onion slices. Cook until they are shiny and begin to soften; do not brown them or get color on them. Stir often. Add the curry and continue to cook, mixing the onions with the curry. You are trying to get all of the liquid from the onion to evaporate while you release the flavor of the curry and concentrate it into the onions. Add the cumin.

2. Add the garlic and ginger and cook for another 2-3 minutes.

3. Add the potatoes and carrots to the pan. Cook for 5 minutes.

4. Add the chicken and stir to coat with the spices.

5. Add the bouillon and water to just cover the chicken.

6. Cover the pot and simmer for 1 hour. Add salt and pepper to taste.

*Yield: 4-6 servings*

dinner for two

# dinner for two
## small plated meal format

## Menu

❧

**Peking Duck Wontons**
page 43

~

**Cream of Sweet Potato Soup
with Maple Roasted Pecans**
page 63

~

**Hearts and Flowers Salad**
page 83

~

**Roasted Garlic Chicken Stuffed
with Dried Fruit and Nuts**
page 116

~

**Oven-Roasted Asparagus**
page 219

~

**Assorted Truffles**
pages 285 and 312

 An intimate dinner for two. This party is perfect for the unexpected celebration — a promotion, a birthday, an anniversary. The sharing of any good news is a great reason to serve a fancy supper and make a fuss over someone you care about.

When you have a house full of company, the last place you want to be is in your kitchen, but when you have only one guest, the kitchen is a great place to be together. You want to spend time together, so this menu is built around some foods which have been prepared in advance and others that you can cook while working side by side. All of the food comes out to the table at once and you sample each dish as you savor your moments together.

Don't forget to make some musical selections in advance. Plan for some upbeat music for your preparation time in the kitchen and something more subdued as background music for your dinner conversation.

We had our soup, wonton filling, and Roasted Garlic Chicken completely prepared the night before and left them in the refrigerator. An hour before dinner, we popped the chicken into the oven to cook. A half-hour before dinner, while the Cream of Sweet Potato Soup warmed, we assembled and cooked the Peking Duck Wontons and roasted the asparagus. We whipped up the salad dressing and assembled the Hearts and Flowers Salad.

This dinner can be set out on a small table in the kitchen or dining room, or for a nice change, use your cocktail table. Toss some comfortable cushions on the floor for this easy, casual, yet elegant, menu.

MENU
DUCK WONTONS
SWEET POTATO SOU
RTS & FLOWER SA
GARLIC CHICK
ASTED ASPARAG
TRUFFLES

Move the table out in front of a fireplace if you have one. The glow of the fire provides flattering illumination. If you don't have a fireplace, long tapered candles set in crystal or sterling candlesticks will do the trick.

As a cute touch, we used a white paint marker to write out the menu on a wine bottle. We served a bottle of red and a bottle of white at this meal. We selected Kinneret Red Ella Valley Cabernet and Weinstock Contour, but there are many good bottles of kosher wines at varied prices to choose from.

Break out old photo albums and use this time to reminisce over the past and look toward the future.

No four-star meal would be complete without a special dessert. The assorted truffles were just the thing. We set ours out in a tea light holder, but they could be served in champagne glasses, small bowls, or small boxes. They were all prepared days before, and were the perfect little ending to this memorable meal.

meat

# beef carbonnade

*Thanks for this recipe go to Edward Magel and Susan Holland of Susan Holland & Company Event Design.*

2 pounds beef cubes, trimmed of fat

fine sea salt

freshly ground black pepper

6 tablespoons all-purpose flour, divided

3 tablespoons olive oil

2 sweet yellow onions, such as Vidalia, cut into ½-inch dice

2 large cloves fresh garlic, coarsely chopped

6 ounces cremini or baby bella mushrooms

2 large bay leaves

2 tablespoons light brown sugar

¼ teaspoon ground allspice

⅛ teaspoon ground cloves

⅛ teaspoon ground nutmeg

1 teaspoon coarse salt

¼ teaspoon freshly ground black pepper

12 ounces good-quality dark beer

water as needed

## Garnish:

1 crusty French baguette

3-4 tablespoons whole grain mustard

1 tablespoon fresh parsley, chopped

1. Preheat oven to 325°F.

2. Place the beef cubes into a large bowl or ziplock bag. Season with salt and pepper. Add 4 tablespoons flour and toss until the cubes are evenly dusted. Shake off excess flour.

3. Heat the olive oil in a large skillet over medium-high heat. When well-heated, add the beef; brown on all sides. You may need to do this in batches, depending on the size of your pan. Remove the beef to a casserole dish or a pretty oven-to-table ceramic dish.

4. Lower the heat and add the onions. Sauté for 5-6 minutes, stirring often, until onions begin to soften. Add the garlic and sauté 2-3 minutes longer. Add remaining 2 tablespoons flour to the pan. Stir to combine, cooking for 1 minute until flour is no longer visibly white. Add the onions to the meat in the casserole dish. Add in the whole mushrooms.

5. In a small bowl, toss the bay leaves, brown sugar, allspice, cloves, nutmeg, coarse salt, and black pepper. Sprinkle over the top of the meat. Pour the beer over the meat. If more liquid is needed to come halfway up on the meat, add water. Cover with a lid or heavy-duty aluminum foil. Bake for 2½ hours.

6. Remove from oven.

7. Prepare the garnish: Slice the baguette evenly into 10 (½-inch) slices. Spread mustard on one side of each slice. Remove the lid or foil from the casserole and place the bread, mustard-side-down, on top of the carbonnade. Return to oven, uncovered, for 30 minutes, or until bread is toasted.

8. Garnish with fresh parsley.

*Yield: 10 servings*

# veal paprikash over caraway noodles

8 ounces fettuccine noodles
or medium egg noodles

2 tablespoons margarine,
melted

¾ teaspoon caraway seeds,
divided

4 tablespoons canola oil

2 large onions, thinly sliced

3 cloves fresh garlic, minced

fine sea salt

freshly ground black pepper

2½ pounds veal cutlets,
pounded thin

all-purpose flour

1 (14.5-ounce) can diced
tomatoes, with their juice

2 tablespoons Hungarian
sweet paprika

¼- ½ teaspoon cayenne pepper

1 teaspoon dried oregano

½ cup non-dairy sour cream,
such as Tofutti brand Sour
Supreme

1. Cook noodles al denté, according to package directions. Drain. Add margarine and ½ teaspoon caraway seeds to the noodles. Set aside.

2. Heat the oil in a large skillet over medium heat. Add the onions and sauté until soft, about 10 minutes, stirring occasionally. Add the garlic and sauté 5 minutes longer. Transfer onions and garlic to a small bowl, leaving behind the oil in the pan.

3. Sprinkle the veal on both sides with salt and pepper. Dredge in the flour, shaking off excess. Add the veal in a single layer to the pan and sauté until brown, about 3-4 minutes; flip over and brown the other side. If necessary, do this in batches, removing first batch to platter as it is done and adding 1 additional tablespoon oil to the pan to brown the second batch. Remove to platter.

4. Return the onions and garlic to the pan. Add the tomatoes and their juice, paprika, cayenne to taste, and oregano. Simmer for 5 minutes, stirring up the browned bits from the bottom of the pan.

5. Mix the remaining caraway seeds and parve sour cream into the pan and heat though. Pour over the veal.

6. Serve the veal alongside the noodles.

*Yield: 8-10 servings*

# moroccan short ribs

2-3 large racks beef ribs, not cut into spare ribs or flanken; leave fat on meat side, (can be trimmed later but you need it or the ribs will be dry) trim fat from bone side; allow 2 bones per person

3-4 tablespoons olive oil, divided

coarse sea salt or kosher salt

freshly ground black pepper

2 carrots, unpeeled, halved

1 parsnip, unpeeled, halved

1 stalk celery, halved

3 cloves fresh garlic

1 onion, quartered; leave end root attached so it stays together

¾-ounce fresh thyme or 1 teaspoon dried thyme

1 bottle Syrah or other red wine

water as needed

## Spice Rub:

1 tablespoon ground fennel

2 teaspoons ground cinnamon

1 tablespoon ground coriander

1 tablespoon dried oregano

2 teaspoons dried mustard powder

1 teaspoon ground cumin

½ teaspoon crushed red pepper flakes

¾ teaspoon ground cardamom

½ cup dark brown sugar

1. In a large soup pot over medium heat, heat 3 tablespoons olive oil.

2. Season both sides of ribs with salt and black pepper.

3. Sear meat on both sides until nicely browned; about 6-7 minutes per side.

4. When the meat is seared on both sides, add the carrots, parsnip, celery, garlic, onion, and thyme. Add the wine. Add water to cover completely.

5. Reduce heat to medium-low and cover the pot. Slowly braise the ribs for 1½ – 2 hours. Remove ribs from the pot. Cool. The recipe can be done in advance up to this point. When ready to serve, cut into individual portions.

6. You can continue cooking the braising liquid, reducing it down to use in gravy for this or another dish. You can also freeze it and use as beef stock.

7. If chilled, bring meat to room temperature.

8. Prepare the spice rub: In a bowl, combine the fennel, cinnamon, coriander, oregano, mustard, cumin, red pepper, cardamom, and brown sugar. Rub into the meat.

9. Heat a large skillet until very hot. Add a drizzle of olive oil. Sear the meat for just a few minutes; it is already cooked.

10. To serve, stack 2 ribs for individual serving, or pile all ribs onto a platter.

*Yield: 6 servings*

# pasta bolognaise

2-3 tablespoons olive oil

2 onions, finely chopped

8 cloves fresh garlic, minced

1 pound ground beef

1 cup Merlot or Cabernet Sauvignon

1 (28-ounce) can crushed tomatoes

1½ teaspoons dried oregano

½ cup soy milk

¼ teaspoon fine sea salt

¼ teaspoon freshly ground black pepper

1 pound pasta of your choice, cooked al denté, according to package directions

1. Heat olive oil in a large pot over medium heat. Add the onions and garlic. Sauté until nice and soft, being careful not to brown them, about 4-6 minutes. Add the meat, breaking up the chunks. Sauté until brown and liquid is cooked out, about 8 minutes.

2. Add the wine. Cook until liquid is reduced to ½ cup, about 15-20 minutes.

3. Add the crushed tomatoes and oregano. Simmer for 10 minutes. Blend in the soy milk. Season with salt and pepper.

4. Serve over prepared pasta.

*Yields: 10-12 servings*

### Freshly Ground Black Pepper:

10 grinds of a pepper mill yields about ¼ teaspoon freshly ground black pepper.

Every so often, peppercorn residue builds up, making it tough to turn the mill. To clean a pepper mill, never expose it to water. It will rust the mechanisms. Instead, grind 1 tablespoon raw rice through the mill. It will dislodge any stuck peppercorns. Dust pepper residue from the bottom, using a pastry brush.

# barbecue beef

*There are some restaurant managers who choose not to feed their staff, but in venues where there is a nice caring environment, someone is delegated the task of preparing the "family meal." This is the typically modest grub that feeds the staff after the big rush of lunch and before dinner service begins. When I gave a few classes at the now defunct Shallots Restaurant in Manhattan, the staff was well taken care of. My friend Jean Chin was often on "family meal" duty. This is one of my favorites that she "threw together" in 10 minutes flat, just using whatever was at arm's length. I call it from family style to fabulous.*

1 tablespoon olive oil

2 pounds large boneless beef cubes, or boneless lamb cubes

¼ cup steak sauce, such as A-1

¼ cup apple cider vinegar

¼ cup molasses

½ teaspoon ground cumin

1 teaspoon garlic powder

½ teaspoon freshly ground black pepper

1 teaspoon fine sea salt

1 teaspoon barbecue spice

¼ teaspoon chili powder

1. Heat the olive oil in a large skillet over medium heat. Add the beef or lamb cubes; sear on all sides, about 4 minutes per side. Try not to move the meat around; it will release when it is properly seared.

2. Add the steak sauce, vinegar, and molasses. Stir with a wooden spoon or silicon spatula until combined. Season with cumin, garlic powder, pepper, salt, barbecue spice, and chili powder. Cook for 5-6 minutes, until meat is cooked through.

3. Serve over mashed potatoes, rice, egg noodles, or couscous.

*Yield: 6-8 servings*

## Skillets:

When shopping for skillets, look for the heaviest stainless steel you can find, at least 18 gauge. A solid stainless steel or copper core pan will retain heat well, resulting in evenly cooked foods.

I find a 14 inch frying pan indispensable, as it allows me to cook larger amounts of food in single batches.

# balsamic braised brisket
# with shallots and potatoes

1 (3-pound) beef brisket

fine sea salt

freshly ground black pepper

10 cloves fresh garlic, divided

3 tablespoons margarine, divided

2 tablespoons olive oil

3 Yukon Gold potatoes, peeled, cut into chunks

6 whole shallots, peeled

¼ cup balsamic vinegar

¼ cup red wine

1 (14½-ounce) can crushed tomatoes

water as needed

1. Preheat oven to 400° F.

2. Season the brisket on both sides with salt and pepper. Using the tip of a sharp knife, make 10 sliver cuts all along the brisket. Cut 5 of the garlic cloves in half. Place a piece of garlic into each slit. Place 2 tablespoons margarine and oil into a large skillet or pot set over medium heat. When the margarine is melted and hot, add the meat; you should hear it sear on contact. Let it cook for 8 minutes; don't move it around. After 8 minutes, lift the meat up, add remaining tablespoon of margarine to the pan, and turn the meat over. Sear on the second side for 8 minutes. Remove the brisket to a baking pan. Surround the brisket with the potatoes, shallots, and remaining whole garlic cloves.

3. Add balsamic vinegar and wine to the skillet or pan. Add the tomatoes. Turn the heat down to medium and cook for 5 minutes, stirring to combine. While the mixture cooks down, scrape up the browned bits from the pan; a wooden spoon works well here. Pour balsamic mixture over the brisket and vegetables. Add water to just cover the brisket.

4. Place in the oven and bake for 2-2½ hours, covered. Allow to cool before slicing.

*Yield: 6-8 servings*

---

**Searing Meat:**

Searing meat means exposing it to high heat to brown the surface. This seals in the flavor. It forms a crust that enables the meat to retain its juices.

# braised rib roast with melted tomatoes

*This recipe is elegant enough to be the centerpiece of a formal dinner, but simple enough to follow using single rib steaks. If making with rib steaks, cut the eye away from the bone and discard the bone. Reduce the oven cooking time to 20 minutes. After cooking, slice the steak into strips and serve.*

1 (5-6) pound standing
 beef rib roast

fine sea salt

freshly ground black pepper

4 tablespoons margarine

2 onions, coarsely chopped

4 cloves fresh garlic, coarsely
chopped

2 beefsteak tomatoes,
cut into large chunks

6 sprigs thyme; remove
leaves, discard stems

water as needed

1. Preheat oven to 450°F.

2. Season the rib roast with salt and pepper. Melt the margarine in a large ovenproof pot or Dutch oven. Add the roast to the hot margarine, turning to sear evenly on all sides, about 3-4 minutes per side. Try not to manipulate the meat while it is searing. The meat will release itself when it is properly seared.

3. Add the onions, garlic, and tomatoes to the pot. Add the thyme leaves. Sauté 3-4 minutes. Add water to come up halfway on the roast.

4. Place the pot, uncovered, into the oven for 1 hour and 30 minutes, until thermometer inserted in center reads between 150° and 160°F. Remove roast from the oven and let stand for 10 minutes.

5. Scrve with the tomatoes and onions from the pot.

*Yield: 6 servings*

# juniper berry and peppercorn-crusted skirt steak with spiced onions

*Juniper berries are a dry, whole spice found in the spice section of the supermarket. The easiest way to crush them is with a spice mill or small food processor. Don't grind them too finely; you want some coarseness and texture to remain. An alternate way is to place them in a heavy-duty ziplock bag and smash them with a rolling pin. Use the weight of your body to press down on the rolling pin as it rolls over the whole spices.*

½ tablespoon whole juniper berries

1 tablespoon whole black peppercorns

4 skirt steaks or hanger steaks (20-24 ounces total), soaked overnight in water to remove saltiness; pat dry

1 tablespoon olive oil

1 small red onion, halved, thinly sliced

1 small Spanish onion, halved, thinly sliced

1 teaspoon favorite dry barbecue spice

¼ cup apple cider vinegar

¼ cup beef stock; can be made from beef consommé powder dissolved in water

1. Coarsely crush together the juniper berries and peppercorns (see note above).

2. Pat the spice mixture into the steaks on one side, pressing the cracked spices into the meat to form a light crust.

3. Heat the olive oil in a large skillet over medium-high heat until it shimmers. Add the steaks, crust-side-down. Sear for 3 minutes. Flip the steaks and sear on the other side for 3 minutes for medium. This can also be done on a hot grill. Remove to a platter and set aside.

4. Add the onions to the pan, scraping up the browned bits. If meat was grilled on an outdoor grill, heat 1 tablespoon olive oil in a small pan or pot. Add the onions and continue from here. Cook until translucent, 5-6 minutes. Add the barbecue spice and stir. Add the vinegar and beef stock. Cook for 3-4 minutes. Turn the heat down to a simmer and cook the onions for about 12-14 minutes longer, until they are soft and shiny. Serve the onions with the steaks.

*Yield: 4 servings*

# asian style silver tip roast beef

*Don't be shy with the cumin, it mellows as it cooks and it adds a wonderful flavor.*

1 (5-6 pound) silver tip roast beef

8 cloves fresh garlic, sliced

fine sea salt

freshly ground black pepper

5 carrots, peeled, cut into 1-inch chunks

2 medium onions, cut into ½-inch dice

1-inch fresh ginger, peeled, minced

ground cumin

white pepper

paprika

1 cup water

1 teaspoon lemon juice

1 teaspoon soy sauce

sliced scallions, garnish

1. Preheat oven to 350°F.

2. With the tip of a sharp knife, cut slits all over the roast. Place a slice of garlic into each slit. Sprinkle with salt and pepper.

3. Place the roast into a heavy baking dish or Dutch oven. Surround the roast with the carrots and onions. Sprinkle the top of the meat with the ginger and a generous sprinkling of cumin. Sprinkle the carrots and onions with white pepper and paprika.

4. Place the roast into the hot oven and cook, covered, for 1 hour and 45 minutes – 2 hours, until center is medium rare. Remove meat from pan and allow it to sit for 10 minutes. Meanwhile, add 1 cup of water to the pan of vegetables. Add a sprinkle of salt and pepper. Return the pan to the oven. Raise the temperature to 400°F. Allow the water to come to a boil. Remove from oven. Add lemon juice and soy sauce. Scrape up the brown bits from the bottom of the pan.

5. Slice the roast into thin slices. Place overlapping slices on a large platter. Sprinkle with the carrots and onions and juices from pan. Garnish with scallions.

6. Serve hot or at room temperature.

*Yield: 8-10 servings*

# lamb stew with toasted barley

1 (750 ml.) bottle Merlot or Port wine

1 tablespoon olive oil

3 pounds boneless lamb cubes or one (3-pound) lamb shoulder, untied, trimmed of fat, cut into cubes

fine sea salt

freshly ground black pepper

3 carrots, cut into ½-inch dice

1 leek, halved lengthwise, thinly sliced

2 stalks celery, thinly sliced

water as needed

1 tablespoon margarine

½ pound pearl barley, uncooked

1 tablespoon beef bouillon powder

2 tablespoons cornstarch

1. Preheat oven to 350°F.

2. Pour the bottle of wine into a pot. Bring to a boil over medium heat. Cook for 15-20 minutes until reduced by three-quarters.

3. Meanwhile, heat the oil in a large skillet. Season the lamb with salt and pepper. Place the lamb into the pan in a single layer. Sear the lamb on all sides, 4-6 minutes. You may need to do this in batches. Add more oil as necessary. Remove to a baking dish or casserole dish as the lamb is seared.

4. Once all the lamb is seared, add the carrots, leek, and celery to the skillet. Add 1½ cups water to deglaze the pan, scraping up the browned bits with a wooden spoon. When all the water has evaporated, after about ten minutes on medium/high heat, pour the vegetables over the lamb in the baking dish. Toss. Add the reduced wine and water to cover. Bake, covered, for one hour. Uncover and bake for an additional hour.

5. Prepare the barley: Place the margarine into a pot and melt over medium heat. Add the barley, tossing to coat with margarine. Lower the heat to medium low and toast the barley, 6-7 minutes; toss it every so often. It will darken and release a nutty aroma.

6. In a container or bowl, combine 3 cups water and the beef bouillon. Add to pot and simmer until the barley is tender and liquid has evaporated, about 15-20 minutes. Remove to a platter or if making in advance, to a casserole dish.

7. When the lamb is done, pour the liquid through a strainer into a pot, reserving 3 cups of this liquid. Discard any remaining liquid. Spoon the lamb over the barley.

8. Over medium-high heat, bring the strained liquid to a boil and reduce by half, about 20 minutes.

9. In a small bowl mix the cornstarch with ¾ cup cold water. Stir until dissolved. Add it into the liquid, bring to a boil and cook until the liquid thickens. Ladle over the lamb and barley.

*Yield: 6-8 servings*

# kalamata and mustard-crusted roast beef

*The technique here is roasting the beef until almost done before adding the spice crusting. This will enable the meat to cook perfectly, uncovered, without worrying about burning the crust.*

4-5 pound silver tip roast or standing rib roast

8 cloves fresh garlic, quartered lengthwise

3 tablespoons olive oil

1 tablespoon nonpareil capers, drained

½ cup fresh rosemary leaves

15 Kalamata or Niçoise olives (⅓ cup), pitted

¾ cup whole grain mustard

1 teaspoon dried thyme

2 tablespoons homestyle unflavored breadcrumbs or panko (see resource guide, page 317)

1. Preheat oven to 375°F.

2. With the tip of a sharp knife, cut slits all over the surface of the meat. Place a garlic sliver into each slit.

3. Heat the olive oil in a large skillet over medium-high heat. Add the roast and sear on all sides until it is nice and brown, about 4 minutes per side.

4. Remove the meat to a roasting pan and place into the oven, uncovered, for 1½ hours.

5. Meanwhile, prepare the crust: In the bowl of a food processor fitted with a metal blade, or by hand with a sharp knife, finely mince the capers, rosemary, and olives. Mix in the mustard, thyme, and breadcrumbs.

6. Remove the meat from the oven and lower the oven to 300°F.

7. Cut off the strings if your roast was tied.

8. Using the palm of your hand or a spatula, pat on the mustard crust. It will form a nice thick layer over the top and sides of the roast beef.

9. Return to the oven for 15 minutes.

10. Remove from oven and allow the meat to rest for 15 minutes before slicing.

*Yield: 8-10 servings*

# potato-stuffed rib steaks

## Marinade:

3 tablespoons fish-free Worcestershire sauce (see p.16)

2 medium shallots, finely chopped

2 teaspoons fresh thyme leaves

2 fresh chives, thinly sliced

2 tablespoons soy sauce

1 tablespoon balsamic vinegar

⅓ cup olive oil or canola oil

½ teaspoon freshly ground black pepper

½ teaspoon ground white pepper

## Stuffing:

1 Idaho potato, peeled, cut into ½-inch cubes

water as needed

1 tablespoon canola oil

3 ounces sliced button mushrooms

2 cloves fresh garlic, thinly sliced

4 (1½-inch thick) rib steaks

1 cup chicken stock

1. Prepare the marinade: Combine the Worcestershire sauce, shallots, thyme, chives, soy sauce, vinegar, oil, black pepper, and white pepper. Using an immersion blender or a whisk, combine until emulsified. Pour into a heavy-duty ziplock bag or a non-reactive baking dish. Add the steaks. Cover or seal bag. Marinate in the refrigerator at least 30 minutes or up to 2 hours. Halfway through the marinating time, turn the bag over or turn the steaks to make sure both sides are marinated.

2. Meanwhile, prepare the stuffing: Place the potato cubes into a pot with water to cover. Bring to a boil. Reduce heat slightly and boil for 20-30 minutes until potato cubes are soft.

3. Meanwhile, in a medium skillet over medium, heat the oil. Add the mushrooms and sauté 5-6 minutes until wilted. Add the garlic and sauté 3 minutes longer.

4. When potatoes are soft, drain, and mash with a fork. Add to the pan of mushrooms. Mix to combine. Set aside.

5. Remove the steaks from the marinade. Pour the marinade into a small pot. Set aside.

6. Cut a deep pocket into the side of each steak, making sure not to cut all the way through. Spoon ¼ of the stuffing into the pocket of each steak. Secure with toothpicks or skewers.

7. Grill, broil, or pan sear the steaks, 6-8 minutes per side.

8. Add the chicken stock to the pot of marinade. Bring to a boil over medium high. Boil for a full 5 minutes. Serve the steak with the hot marinade.

*Yield: 4 servings*

# steak with eggplant in roasted garlic sauce

*The hot cut of meat in restaurants this year was the Flatiron steak. It is known to some butchers as top blade steak or chicken steak. It is flavorful, tender, and inexpensive. If you can't find it, fillet split or London broil stand in fine in this recipe.*

## Steak with Eggplant:

4 Asian or Japanese eggplants (the long, thin bright purple eggplants)

6 (4-6 ounce portions) Flatiron steaks, or 2 pounds fillet split (this will be 2 large pieces)

juice of 2 medium lemons

4 cloves fresh garlic, thinly sliced

⅔ cup olive oil

½ cup soy sauce

½ teaspoon ground cayenne pepper

## Roasted Garlic Sauce:

10 cloves fresh garlic

good-quality extra-virgin olive oil

1 cup chicken stock

2 teaspoons cornstarch dissolved in 3 teaspoons water

1. Trim the ends from each eggplant and discard. Slice each eggplant in half lengthwise. Cut each half on the diagonal into 4 equal pieces.

2. If using the fillet split or London broil, cut each steak on the diagonal, against the grain, into 3 equal pieces. Place the steak and eggplant into a large bowl. Add the lemon juice, sliced garlic, olive oil, soy sauce, and cayenne pepper. Toss together to combine and coat the meat and eggplant. Allow to sit at room temperature for 20 minutes.

3. Meanwhile, prepare the garlic sauce: Place the 10 whole cloves of garlic into a small pot. Add enough olive oil to cover the garlic. Over medium heat, bring to a boil. Reduce heat and allow to simmer for 5 minutes. Remove from heat and allow the garlic to sit in the oil for a few minutes off the flame. Set aside.

4. If you have a nonstick grill pan or George Forman-type grill, there is no need to oil it. If not, or if you are using a barbecue, grease with a little olive oil. Heat the pan or grill. Place the meat and the eggplant, cut-side-down, on the grill or grill pan. Sear the meat for 7 minutes per side, for medium. The eggplant will take only 5 minutes per side. Remove from pan or grill and keep warm. To achieve pretty grill marks on the eggplant, don't shake the pan around.

5. Place the grilled eggplant chunks in a sunburst pattern around the platter. Slice the steaks into very thin slices, against the grain and on the diagonal. Arrange them in the center of the platter.

6. Finish the garlic sauce: Place the 10 cloves of roasted garlic and 1 tablespoon of the oil it cooked in into a small pot. (Reserve the remaining garlic oil in a plastic container in the refrigerator for up to 3 weeks; it is wonderfully flavored and can be used for dressings, sauces, or to sear chicken or meat in). Add the chicken stock and dissolved cornstarch. Bring to a boil. Season with salt and pepper. Blend with an immersion blender or transfer to a food processor and blend. Drizzle over the steak and eggplant.

*Yield: 6 servings*

# shepherd's pie

*What to do with leftover mashed potatoes, leftover chopped meat, leftover vegetables? How about the ultimate comfort food? It's right out of my childhood: Shepherd's Pie. If you don't have leftover mashed potatoes, just peel some Yukon Gold, Russet, or Idaho potatoes, cut into chunks, and boil. When soft, mash with some salt, pepper, and non-dairy creamer or soymilk. Don't mash in a food processor, as they will become gluey, but the job can be done in a Kitchen Aid with a whisk attachment.*

*If the occasion calls for a more formal presentation, divide the filling among individual ramekins before piping with potatoes and baking. To make the potatoes easier to pipe, add a little more soymilk.*

3 tablespoons margarine

1½ onions, cut into
¼-inch dice

16 baby carrots, sliced,
or 2 regular carrots, cut
into ¼-inch slices

2 stalks celery, sliced into
¼-inch pieces

4 cloves fresh garlic, chopped

¼ teaspoon sea salt

¼ teaspoon freshly ground
black pepper

1 sprig fresh thyme

1 bay leaf

1 (28-ounce) can whole
peeled tomatoes

2 pounds ground beef
(can use 1 lb. ground turkey
and 1 lb. ground beef)

1 teaspoon sugar

1 teaspoon beef- or chicken-
flavored bouillon powder

leftover mashed potatoes,
or fresh mashed potatoes
from 2 large Idaho potatoes,
cooked and mashed with 1
tablespoon margarine, salt,
and 1 tablespoon soymilk

1. Preheat oven to 425°F.

2. In a large frying pan, over medium heat, melt the margarine. Add the onion, carrots, and celery. Sauté 3-4 minutes. Add the garlic. Add the salt and pepper. Add the leaves from the sprig of thyme and the bay leaf.

3. Lift the tomatoes out of their liquid and drain well. Chop and add to the pan. Add in the ground beef and sauté until brown, about 12-15 minutes. Remove and discard the bay leaf.

4. Add the sugar and bouillon powder.

5. Place the meat mixture into a medium ovenproof casserole dish. Cover with mashed potatoes. For a decorative touch, you can pipe the mashed potatoes through a large star tip of a pastry bag.

6. Place in oven and bake for 20-30 minutes, until potatoes are just starting to brown.

*Yield: 6-8 servings*

# braised roasted veal provençal

3-4 pound boneless veal shoulder

8 cloves fresh garlic, coarsely chopped, divided

fresh sage leaves

15 Kalamata olives, pits removed, divided

2 teaspoon fresh or dried rosemary leaves, chopped, divided

freshly ground black pepper

¼ cup plus 1 tablespoon olive oil, divided

2 red bell peppers, seeded, cut into chunks

2 large beefsteak tomatoes, stems removed, cut into chunks

1 large onion, chopped

fine sea salt

1 cup white wine

1. Preheat oven to 450°F.

2. Using the tip of a sharp knife, cut random slits all along the top and sides of the veal.

3. Using 6 of the garlic cloves, place a garlic chunk and a sage leaf into each slit.

4. In the bowl of a food processor fitted with a metal blade, or with an immersion blender in a bowl, finely chop 5 pitted olives and 2 cloves of garlic. Mix in 1 teaspoon rosemary and ½ teaspoon black pepper. Drizzle in 1 tablespoon of olive oil; blend to form a paste.

5. Rub this olive paste all over the veal.

6. Heat the ¼ cup olive oil in an ovenproof pot or Dutch oven just big enough to hold the roast. Add the veal and sear on all sides.

7. Surround the veal with the red peppers. Add the 10 remaining olives, tomatoes, and onion. Mince 1 sage leaf; sprinkle it over the top of the roast. Season with salt and pepper. Sprinkle on the other teaspoon of chopped rosemary. Cook for 5 minutes over medium heat. Add the wine to the pot. Cook for 5 minutes. Bring to a boil.

8. Transfer the pot to the oven and roast, uncovered, for 1 hour, basting occasionally with pan juices. Cut into the meat; it may need up to an additional 15 minutes.

9. Let the roast rest for 15 minutes, then slice.

*Yield: 8 servings*

# mexican brisket

*This simple one-dish meal is a great spin on an old standby cut of meat. You can control the spiciness with the heat level of your salsa. Go for a mild salsa if you don't love hot foods — but if you do, go for a medium or even a spicy hot bottled salsa for some great kick and heat.*

3 tablespoons olive oil

3-4 pound beef brisket

freshly ground black pepper

5 Yukon Gold potatoes, peeled, cut into large chunks

1 onion, sliced

2 cups baby carrots, sliced into thirds on an angle

6 cloves fresh garlic, chopped

1 (12-ounce) can beer

24 ounces store-bought salsa

¼ cup cilantro leaves, chopped

¼ cup fresh flat leaf parsley leaves, chopped

1. Place the oil into a large pot over medium heat. Season both sides of the brisket with pepper. Once the oil is hot, add the meat to the pot and sear on both sides, about 3-5 minutes, or until nicely browned and no longer sticking to the pot.

2. Add the potatoes, onion, carrots, and garlic. Pour the beer and salsa over the meat and vegetables. Top with cilantro and parsley.

3. Bring to a boil, and then simmer, covered, on a low flame for 3 hours. It is easiest to slice this meat when it is cold, and then return it to the pot to reheat.

*Yield: 6-8 servings*

## Getting Organized:

Getting organized a day or two before a party will take the last-minute rush out of your preparation. Pressing the linens, pre-setting the table and the like will create a more relaxed atmopshere. Here we set out our serving pieces with the utensils in advance. A small post-it note or placecard indicates which platter is assigned which dish. If the party is a buffet, set the placecards in front of each food for easy identification by your guests.

# hazelnut-and-honey-crusted veal chop

1½ cups shelled hazelnuts

1 clove garlic, sliced

1 shallot, sliced

4 tablespoons buckwheat honey or other dark honey

2 tablespoons chopped fresh chives, plus extra for garnish

6 (1½-inch thick) veal chops

fine sea salt

ground white pepper

1. Preheat oven to broil.

2. In the bowl of a food processor fitted with a metal blade, process the nuts, garlic, and shallot until finely minced. Add in the honey and pulse to form a paste. Stir in the chopped chives. Set aside.

3. Season the veal chops on both sides with salt and pepper.

4. Place the veal chops on a baking tray 6 inches from the heat and broil 5 minutes per side.

5. Spread a layer of the honey paste over the top of each veal chop. Place crust-side-up on the baking tray.

6. Return the tray, uncovered, to the oven on the rack farthest from the heat. Broil for 10 minutes longer, checking to make sure the honey crust is not burning.

7. Garnish with chopped chives.

*Yield: 6 servings*

---

### Chilling Champagne:

To quickly chill a bottle of champagne, place it in a bucket of ice water; the cold water envelops the bottle to cool it better than ice alone. Let sit for 10 minutes.

# pomegranate-glazed london broil
# with caramelized onions

1 tablespoon olive oil

4 onions, sliced into rings

¼ cup dark brown sugar

¼ cup and 1 tablespoon pomegranate molasses, divided (see resource guide, page 314)

¼ cup chicken broth

½ teaspoon freshly ground black pepper, plus more for sprinkling

⅓ cup bottled barbecue sauce

1 tablespoon yellow mustard

2 pounds London broil or fillet split

fine sea salt

1. Heat the oil in a large pan over medium heat. Add the onions and brown sugar. Cook, uncovered, for about 20-30 minutes, until caramelized and sticky.

2. Add the ¼ cup pomegranate molasses, chicken broth, and pepper to the pan. Cook for 2-3 minutes, until thick. Keep warm.

3. In a small bowl, mix the barbecue sauce, mustard and 1 tablespoon pomegranate molasses. Set aside.

4. Sprinkle both sides of the meat with salt and pepper.

5. On an outdoor oiled grill, or in the oven set to broil, with the meat 6-8 inches from broiler, cook the meat 8 minutes per side. Baste the meat with the prepared sauce. Finish cooking, 2-4 minutes per side.

6. Remove the meat to a cutting board and let it rest for 10 minutes. Slice the meat into strips and drizzle with the onions.

*Yield: 6 servings*

# veal roast with pearl onions

1 cup olive oil

6 tablespoons white wine vinegar or apple cider vinegar

6 tablespoons white wine

½ cup capers, drained

½ cup fresh parsley, finely chopped

3 pounds boneless veal roast, tied

2 pints (12 ounces) white pearl onions

½ cup beer

1. In a small bowl, combine the oil, vinegar, wine, capers, and parsley. Pour it into a large ziplock bag or container. Add the veal roast.

2. Bring a medium pot of water to a boil. Slice off the root end of each onion and discard. Cut a small x into the root end of each onion. Drop the onions into the boiling water. Remove them after 3 minutes. Let cool until easy to handle. The skins will pop right off. Remove and discard the onion skins. Add the onions to the veal. Marinate 6 hours or overnight in the refrigerator, turning the bag every so often.

3. Preheat oven to 350°F.

4. Place the veal into a roasting pan just large enough to hold it. Pour the onions and contents of the bag over the top of the roast. Drizzle the beer over the veal.

5. Roast in the oven, uncovered, for 2 hours, basting with the pan juices a few times during the roasting process.

6. Allow the roast to rest for fifteen minutes before slicing.

*Yield: 8-10 servings*

# sesame beef and broccoli over ramen noodles

¼ cup low-sodium soy sauce

3 tablespoons rice vinegar

2 tablespoons hoisin sauce

2 tablespoons dark brown sugar

1 tablespoon chopped fresh ginger, or ¼ teaspoon ground ginger

3 teaspoons roasted or toasted sesame oil, divided

2 teaspoons cornstarch

¼ teaspoon crushed red pepper flakes

2 pounds pepper steak, sliced into long, thin strips

4 cups water

2 (3-ounce) packages beef- or Oriental-flavored ramen noodles; reserve 1 spice packet, discard the other

4 scallions, sliced

1 tablespoon canola oil

3 cloves fresh garlic, minced

12 ounces broccoli florets, cut into small pieces

sesame seeds

1. In a ziplock bag or non-reactive bowl, combine the soy sauce, vinegar, hoisin sauce, brown sugar, ginger, 2 teaspoons sesame oil, cornstarch, and pepper flakes. Add the meat and marinate for 30 minutes in the refrigerator.

2. Place 4 cups water into a medium pot. Bring to a boil and add the 2 packages ramen noodles with one of the spice packets. Add the scallions and remaining teaspoon sesame oil. Remove from heat, let stand, covered. Set aside.

3. In a large skillet or wok, heat the canola oil over medium heat. Remove the meat from the marinade, reserving marinade, and add the meat to the skillet. Cook for 3 minutes. Add in the minced garlic. Add the broccoli and sauté for 6-8 minutes. Add the marinade to the pan and stir until thickened. Toss to combine.

4. Serve over the ramen noodles. You can drain them or serve them in the broth.

5. Sprinkle with sesame seeds.

*Yield: 6 servings*

# fillet split with mushroom-wine reduction sauce

Meat

*Even you real beginners can dive right into the gourmet world with this one. A quick meal that is so simple, yet so elegant. The wine reduction sauce is that thick syrupy wine sauce that is right off the plate of an expensive steak house dinner. This dish can be made with London broil as well as hanger steak. It goes perfectly with the Mushroom Barley Risotto (see page 215) and a side of fresh steamed vegetables.*

1 tablespoon olive oil

4 ounces shiitake mushroom caps, sliced

1 shallot, sliced

3¼ cups Cabernet Sauvignon, divided

¼ cup red currant jelly

2 pounds fillet split or London broil

fine sea salt

freshly ground black pepper

2 tablespoons total fresh herbs (any combination of basil, oregano, parsley, thyme), finely chopped

1 teaspoon extra-virgin olive oil

1. Place the tablespoon of olive oil into a small saucepan over medium heat. Add the mushrooms and shallot and sauté for 3-4 minutes. Add 3 cups of wine and the currant jelly; bring to a boil. Reduce heat to medium-low and cook until reduced to a syrupy consistency, about 15-20 minutes. Set aside until ready to serve.

2. Meanwhile, rinse the fillet with cold water. Pat dry with paper towels. Sprinkle with salt, pepper, and herbs. Place into a plastic ziplock bag or a non-reactive dish with a lid. Add remaining ¼ cup of wine. Allow to marinate 15 minutes or up to 8 hours in the refrigerator. Place reduction in refrigerator as well.

3. When ready to cook, bring the meat to room temperature and reheat reduction if chilled. Discard any remaining marinade. Preheat broiler. Broil 6 inches from heat for 10 minutes per side. Allow to sit for 10 minutes.

4. Slice the fillet on the diagonal into ¼-inch slices. Drizzle with wine reduction, scattering the mushrooms over the meat.

*Yield: 8 servings*

### Knives:

Short of schechting (slaughtering) your own cattle or rolling your own sushi, 90% of kitchen work can be accomplished with a set of 3 good-quality stainless steel knives. You need a large (7-10 inch) chef's knife for the majority of your kitchen work, a 3-5 inch paring knife for small jobs, and a serrated knife. The key is to keep them sharp.

A chef's knife is a large multipurpose knife ideal for mincing, chopping, and slicing. Shown here is Global's 7½-inch vegetable knife which I use in place of a chef's knife.

A paring knife is shorter and lighter than a chef's knife and is ideal for cutting and peeling fruits and vegetables.

A serrated knife gently and neatly slices breads and cakes.

# family outing
## picnic format

Menu

Barbecue Buffalo Wings
page 16

Garlic Knots with Olive Tapenade
page 31

Coconut Chicken Strips
with Two Dipping Sauces
page 34

Sesame Beef and Broccoli over
Ramen Noodles
page 172

Zucchini Carrot Bread
page 223

Multi-Grain Chick Pea Pilaf
page 214

Stacked Jicama Avocado Salad
with Thai Vinaigrette
page 85

Cookie Crunch Brownies
page 286

Summer is over, but the weather is calling us outdoors one last time. For a few weeks in autumn, the sun is shining and the breeze is delicious. There is no more perfect time than this for a picnic.

Served with effortless simplicity in your favorite setting, a picnic is unbeatable as a backdrop for an unforgettable celebration. There are so many wonderful locations to hold a picnic. We chose a quiet spot in a wooded area near our backyard, but you could have a picnic at a park, on a beach, an apartment house rooftop, out on a boat, near a playground — really anywhere peaceful and picturesque.

The key to a successful picnic is in the planning. Keep lists for a few days leading up to the picnic. Remember things like: a tablecloth or blanket to sit on; plates, cups, cutlery; serving utensils; bottle opener and/or wine opener — and remember to pack a large garbage bag for cleanup. Fill resealable bags with ice and place them

around the items in your cooler. This will keep the food cold and provide ice for drinks once the party has started.

To make transporting all of our supplies easier, we used a large wicker chest. We filled it with quilts, pillows, silverware, napkins, and serving trays. When we arrived at the perfect spot, we just threw open the chest and had our party set up within minutes. The top of the chest was then a great spot on which to set up our food.

Our patchwork quilt was perfectly suited to the feel of the season. Pillows were strewn around for our guests to laze and recline on.

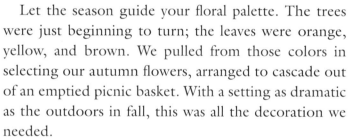

Let the season guide your floral palette. The trees were just beginning to turn; the leaves were orange, yellow, and brown. We pulled from those colors in selecting our autumn flowers, arranged to cascade out of an emptied picnic basket. With a setting as dramatic as the outdoors in fall, this was all the decoration we needed.

We served an array of family-friendly foods set in interesting serving pieces. Barbecue Buffalo Wings were heaped into galvanized pails; wicker trays of Zucchini Carrot Bread, Sesame Beef and Broccoli, Multi-Grain Pilaf, and Stacked Jicama Avocado Salad filled the buffet. The guests were given compartmentalized wicker trays lined with squares of parchment paper to fill with thier favorite foods.

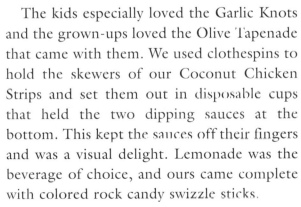

The kids especially loved the Garlic Knots and the grown-ups loved the Olive Tapenade that came with them. We used clothespins to hold the skewers of our Coconut Chicken Strips and set them out in disposable cups that held the two dipping sauces at the bottom. This kept the sauces off their fingers and was a visual delight. Lemonade was the beverage of choice, and ours came complete with colored rock candy swizzle sticks.

The Cookie Crunch Brownies were a huge hit. Cutting them with round cookie cutters gave them a new look. We packed additional brownies into round wicker boxes tied with ribbon to give our guests at the end of the picnic, as a gift for the road.

Washcloths, perfumed with lemon and thyme, were very welcome after eating with our hands. The morning of the picnic we took washcloths and wet them. We folded them and placed them into individual ziplock sandwich bags. Before sealing, we added a slice of lemon and a sprig of thyme to each bag. Our guests loved this lavish touch.

Our picnic came complete with giggling children. To entertain them while the grown-ups lazed away, we brought along a fun activity and a small table. The kids made candy sand art from edible colored sugar, which kept them busy and happy for almost an hour. We also packed a ball, a jump rope, and a frisbee, which were easy to carry and added to their fun.

On a practical note, any protein left out of refrigeration for two hours should be thrown out and not taken home as leftovers. The ice in your cooler is sufficient to keep food cold after it has been chilled, but it won't be able to keep it re-chilled the rest of the day.

Just as the crickets start to call and the air takes on a chill, pack all your things into the trunk and gather your family. Turn around and take one last look — you will want to return to this scene again and again.

# snapper in parchment

4 (6-ounce) red snapper fillets

fine sea salt

freshly ground black pepper

1 lemon

4 teaspoons soy sauce

parchment paper

3 tablespoons olive oil

2 leeks, white and pale green parts only, cleaned, sliced into julienne matchsticks

2 medium zucchini, peeled, sliced into julienne matchsticks

1 red bell pepper, seeded, cut into julienne matchsticks

1 carrot, peeled, sliced into julienne matchsticks (can use 1 cup pre-bagged)

2 shallots, halved, thinly sliced

4 tablespoons white wine

4 tablespoons water

1. Preheat oven to 375°F.

2. Score the skin side of each snapper fillet and place into a tray. Season generously with salt and pepper. Drizzle with lemon juice and soy sauce. Set aside.

3. Cut 4 (18-inch) rectangles of parchment paper. Fold in half and cut half a heart shape. Make a crease mark down the center of each heart. Set aside. Cover one large or two medium baking trays with another piece of parchment paper. Set aside.

4. Heat the olive oil in a large skillet over medium heat. Add the leeks, zucchini, red pepper, carrot, and shallots. Sauté for 5-7 minutes, until slightly wilted. Season with salt and pepper.

5. Place ¼ of the vegetables onto the center of one side of each parchment heart. Place a snapper fillet over the vegetables, flesh-side-down. Add 1 tablespoon wine and 1 tablespoon water to each packet. Fold the other side of parchment heart over the fish. Pleat the edges to secure the packet and keep it closed.

6. Place the packets onto the prepared baking tray. Bake for 20 minutes. The packets will puff. To serve in the parchment, carefully remove each packet to a plate. Cut an "X" into the top of each packet to let steam escape. Serve immediately.

*Yield: 4 servings*

# tuna tataki teriyaki with radish salad

Parve

*You can make this on Friday to serve for Shabbos, just don't slice the tuna or dress the radish until ready to serve. Make sure you are using the freshest Ahi tuna you can find. To make the radish in advance soak as directed. Dry shreds and place on paper towels in a covered bowl.*

½ cup teriyaki sauce, divided

1 tablespoon Dijon mustard

1 teaspoon minced garlic

½ cup and 2 teaspoons corn oil, divided

1 daikon root

water as needed

4 (3-ounce) fillets Ahi tuna, cut into squares

3-4 tablespoons teriyaki sauce

3-4 tablespoons sesame seeds

1 scallion, thinly sliced

1. Prepare the dressing: In a small bowl or jar, whisk the teriyaki, mustard, garlic, and ½ cup corn oil. Set aside.

2. Using the coarse grating disc of a food processor or by hand, thinly shred the daikon into long, thin, spaghetti-like strands. Let the daikon soak in water for 1 hour. Remove and dry.

3. Rub each square of tuna with teriyaki sauce. Sprinkle sesame seeds on all surfaces.

4. Heat 2 teaspoons corn oil in a skillet over medium heat. Add the tuna. Sear for 10 seconds on each of the 6 sides. You may need tongs to hold it in place for the top sides.

5. Place the daikon into a bowl and mix with some of the dressing.

6. Using your palm, make a mound of the dressed daikon in the center of the plate. Slice the tuna into thin strips. Lean the strips around the mound of daikon. Drizzle the sauce around the outside of the plate. Scatter scallion slices around platter.

*Yield: 4-6 servings*

How to Tell When Fish Is Done:

Fish is done when the flesh is firm. Poke the tip of a knife between two flakes; the shiny flesh should be opaque.

# salmon primavera

*This simple preparation yields such a wow factor in taste and presentation. I love serving it at room temperature. If you start out with good-quality fresh fish, it will taste like a good poached salmon.*

2½ -3 pounds wild Pacific or Sockeye salmon fillet

fine sea salt

freshly ground black pepper

Dijon mustard or thick honey mustard, such as Honeycup brand

1 small zucchini, unpeeled, thinly sliced

1 small yellow squash, unpeeled, thinly sliced

2 Roma or plum tomatoes, thinly sliced

¼ cup unflavored breadcrumbs or panko (see resource guide, page 317)

2 tablespoons chopped fresh dill

2 tablespoons olive oil

1. Preheat oven to 375° F.

2. Season the salmon fillet with salt and pepper. Brush an even, thick coating of the mustard all over the salmon.

3. Place the salmon on a parchment- or foil-lined baking sheet. Place the fish horizontally in front of you. Starting at the left end of the fillet, lay a column of overlapping slices of the zucchini. On the next row, lay a column of overlapping slices of the squash; they should overlap the zucchini a bit as well. On the next row, lay a column of overlapping slices of tomatoes; they should slightly overlap onto the squash. Begin again with the zucchini, followed by the squash and the tomato. Continue in this fashion until the whole fillet is covered.

4. In a small bowl, mix the breadcrumbs, dill, and olive oil. Sprinkle over the top of the vegetables.

5. Bake for 30-35 minutes. Remove one of the vegetables in the thickest part of the fillet and test to make sure the fish is done, and then cover it back up with the vegetable.

6. Serve hot or at room temperature. Can be refrigerated overnight and brought to room temperature the next day.

*Yield: 8-10 servings*

# tuna with pico de gallo sauce

*Pico de Gallo is a Mexican relish similar to a salsa. Make some extra and serve with steak, hamburgers, burritos, or eggs. You can even just serve it with tortilla chips for a great snack at a party or barbecue.*

### Pico de Gallo:

4 plum tomatoes, seeds discarded, cut into ½-inch dice

¼ cup cilantro leaves, finely chopped

1 lime

1 small red onion, minced

1 clove garlic, minced

1 tablespoon minced, seeded, jalapeño chili pepper (optional)

fine sea salt

freshly ground black pepper

### Tuna:

4 (6-ounce) tuna fillets

olive oil

1 teaspoon ground cumin

fine sea salt

freshly ground black pepper

1. Prepare the Pico de Gallo: In a medium bowl, toss the tomatoes, cilantro, juice of ½ the lime, onion, garlic, and chili pepper if using. Season with salt and pepper. Let the mixture sit at room temperature for at least 15 minutes.

2. Rub the tuna on all sides with olive oil, salt, pepper, and ground cumin.

3. Heat 1 tablespoon olive oil in a medium skillet set over medium heat. When the oil is hot, add the fish, searing 2 minutes per side for medium-rare, 3 minutes per side for medium to well done.

4. Drain the liquid from the Pico de Gallo.

5. Serve the tuna with a spoonful of the Pico de Gallo. Finish each plate with a small squeeze of the remaining lime half.

*Yield: 4 servings*

---

### Removing Parsley Leaves:

To shave the leaves from parsley or cilantro stems, scrape the stems with a sharp blade. This will easily remove the leaves. Store the parsley and cilantro whole, tightly wrapped, in slightly damp paper towels in the refrigerator. Shave the leaves right before using.

# pesce arrabbiata

Parve

4 teaspoons olive oil, plus more for searing the fish

12 cloves fresh garlic, minced

2 teaspoons ground fennel

2 (28-ounce) cans crushed tomatoes

¼ teaspoon crushed red pepper flakes

2 tablespoons capers, chopped into tiny pieces

6-8 tablespoons sliced black olives

2 tablespoons Merlot or Cabernet Sauvignon

zest of ½ small orange

8-ounces capellini or angel hair pasta

good quality extra-virgin olive oil

6 (6-ounce) white flesh fish fillets, such as flounder, Mahi Mahi, halibut, or cod

1. Heat 4 teaspoons olive oil in a large pot over medium heat. Add the garlic and fennel. Sauté for 2 minutes. Add the tomatoes and crushed red pepper. Cook until reduced by half, about 20 minutes.

2. Add the capers and olives and cook for 5 minutes. Add the wine and cook for 5 minutes more. Add the orange zest. Allow the sauce to simmer as you prepare the fish.

3. Cook the capellini pasta according to package directions.

4. Place 2-3 tablespoons olive oil into a medium skillet over medium heat. When the oil is hot, add the fish fillets. Sear for 5 minutes per side until cooked through; thicker fillets will need more time.

5. Serve the fish on a bed of capellini with the arrabbiata sauce spooned over. Finish with a drizzle of olive oil for sheen.

*Yield: 6 servings*

# cod, potatoes, and sun-dried tomatoes

⅓ cup extra-virgin olive oil

2 pounds Yukon Gold potatoes, unpeeled, cut into ¾-inch dice

fine sea salt

freshly ground black pepper

1 teaspoon dried oregano, divided

1 cup homemade oven-roasted tomatoes (see page 101) or storebought sun-dried tomatoes

2 cups vegetable stock

½ cup Wondra or all-purpose flour

2 pounds cod, boneless and skinless

3 tablespoons olive oil

1 tablespoon canola oil

1 cup dry white wine, such as Chardonnay

1 cup black Niçoise or Kalamata olives, pitted, chopped (see box)

1. Heat the oil in a large sauté pan over medium heat. Add the potatoes and sauté. Season with salt and pepper. Add ½ teaspoon of the oregano. When the potatoes begin to brown, add the tomatoes and stock. Simmer until the potatoes are tender, about 10 minutes. Set aside.

2. Place the flour into a plate. Coat the cod in the flour, shaking off the excess. Season both sides with salt and pepper. In a separate large pan, heat the olive oil and canola oil over medium heat. Add cod to the pan. Cook until golden brown, flipping fish once, about 5 minutes per side.

3. Remove the potatoes and tomatoes to individual plates or serving platter. Place the cod on top of this mixture.

4. Add the wine and remaining ½ teaspoon of oregano to the pan in which you cooked the fish. Scrape up the browned bits with a wooden spoon. Turn the heat to medium-high and simmer for 3 minutes. Pour over the fish. Sprinkle with chopped olives.

*Yield: 6 servings*

---

Pitting Olives:

The easiest way to pit olives is to smack them against a hard surface with the palm of your hand. The pit will pop right out.

# sesame salmon with bok choy

*The dressing in this recipe is Chef Alex Petard's "Secret Sauce." The dressing can be made in advance and stored in the refrigerator. It can also be made in larger quantities and used for other recipes. It makes a great salad dressing or dipping sauce for fish or meat.*

½ cup soy sauce

½ cup sugar

3 teaspoons fresh ginger, minced, divided

4 cloves fresh garlic, minced, divided

1 teaspoon Jack Daniels or other whiskey

4 (6-ounce) salmon fillets, skin removed

fine sea salt

½ teaspoon crushed red pepper flakes, divided

2 teaspoons sesame seeds, divided

2 tablespoons margarine

4 stalks bok choy, chopped

4 thyme sprigs, for garnish

1. Prepare the dressing: In a small pot, mix the soy sauce and sugar. Bring to a boil. Add 1 teaspoon ginger, 1 teaspoon garlic, and whiskey. Reduce heat and simmer for 30 minute. Strain through a fine mesh strainer or chinois. Set aside.

2. Preheat oven to 375°F.

3. Season one side of the salmon with salt, ¼ teaspoon red pepper flakes, and ½ teaspoon sesame seeds.

4. In an ovenproof skillet, over medium/high heat, melt 2 tablespoons margarine.

5. Place the salmon, seasoned-side-down, into the margarine. While that side is searing, season the top side with salt, ¼ teaspoon crushed red pepper flakes, and ½ teaspoon sesame seeds.

6. Place the skillet into the hot oven to finish cooking, about 8-10 minutes.

7. Remove the pan from the oven. Remove the salmon and set aside. Without cleaning it out, place the skillet back onto medium heat. Add the bok choy and 1 teaspoon sesame seeds. Add remaining garlic and remaining ginger. Toss to combine and cook for 1 minute. Add 2 teaspoons of the prepared dressing and stir.

8. Place one-quarter of the bok choy on each plate. Top with a salmon fillet. Drizzle some of the sauce around the rim of the plate. Stick a sprig of thyme into the salmon.

*Yield: 4 servings*

# flounder over smashed chick peas

3½ tablespoons olive oil, divided, plus more for searing fish

1 clove garlic, minced

1 (15.5-ounce) can chick peas (garbanzo beans), rinsed and drained, smashed with the back of a fork

fine sea salt

freshly ground black pepper

1 sprig fresh rosemary, leaves finely chopped, about 1 teaspoon

⅓ cup water

1 jarred roasted red pepper half, cut into ¼-inch dice

Wondra or all-purpose flour

4 (6-ounce) fillets of flounder, snapper, sole, or trout

1. In a medium pan, heat 1 tablespoon olive oil over medium heat. Add the garlic and smashed chick peas. Season with salt and pepper. Cook for 2 minutes.

2. Add 2 tablespoons olive oil to the pan. Sprinkle in the rosemary. Add the water. Sauté for 3 minutes, stirring the mixture. Add the red pepper and ½ teaspoon black pepper. Add remaining ½ tablespoon olive oil. Cook for two minutes longer, and stir until creamy.

3. Remove the chick pea mixture and place ¼ of it into the center of each of 4 plates.

4. Heat 2-3 tablespoons olive oil in the pan. Dust each fish fillet with Wondra or all-purpose flour, shaking off the excess. Sear for 3 minutes on each side, until cooked through.

5. Lay each fillet over a mound of the smashed chick peas.

*Yield: 4 servings*

# halibut with zucchini confit

1 medium lemon

4 (6-ounce) halibut fillets, skin removed

olive oil

fine sea salt

freshly ground black pepper

1 small zucchini, unpeeled, cut into ¼-inch dice

1 tablespoon water

1 teaspoon fresh thyme

1. Preheat oven to 400°F.

2. Using a microplane, zest the lemon, being sure to get only the yellow part, not the bitter white pith. Set aside, reserving the lemon as well.

3. Brush the halibut with olive oil. Season both sides with salt and pepper.

4. Heat a heavy ovenproof skillet over medium heat until hot. Add the fish and sear for 1 minute per side until golden on each side. Place the skillet into the hot oven and roast until just cooked through, about 4-5 minutes.

5. Carefully remove the fish from the pan; the pan handle will be hot. Add 1 teaspoon olive oil to the pan. Add the zucchini. Cook over medium heat; don't brown it. Season with salt and pepper and add water.

6. Add the reserved lemon zest, juice of the lemon, and thyme. Sauté 30 seconds. Top the halibut fillets with the zucchini confit.

*Yield: 4 servings*

# dover sole meunière

*Meunière is a simple style of cooking whereby a food is lightly dusted with flour and sautéed simply in butter. If Dover Sole is unavailable you can use lemon sole which is really a flounder.*

7 tablespoons clarified butter, divided (see box below) or 4 tablespoons clarified butter and 3 tablespoons butter, divided

4 (6-8 ounces) fillets of Dover sole

fine sea salt

freshly ground black pepper

all-purpose flour, for dredging

2 tablespoons fresh onion, minced

1 tablespoon capers

1½ medium lemons, divided

2 cups frozen shoestring french fries (from a bag), thawed for 15 minutes

1 clove garlic, minced

6 chives, finely chopped

Garnish:

½ lemon, cut into paper-thin slices

2 chives, finely chopped

1. Place 4 tablespoons of clarified butter into a skillet that is large enough so that the fish can lie flat and in a single layer while cooking; use two pans if necessary. Set over medium heat.

2. Season the fish with salt and pepper. Place the flour into a paper or ziplock bag. Add the fillets and shake to coat. Shake off the excess flour.

3. Place the fish into the hot butter. Cook, turning once until cooked through, about 4 minutes per side; you are looking to form a crust, so don't move it around too much. During the last 2 minutes, add minced onion, capers, and juice of 1 lemon. Remove fish to a platter. Keep warm and reserve pan sauce.

4. Cut the thawed french fries into small cubes. Place 3 tablespoons butter (can be clarified) into another medium pan over medium heat. Add the cubed potatoes with minced garlic, salt, and pepper. Cook until golden brown, about 3-4 minutes. Add chopped chives to the potatoes.

5. Place a mound of potatoes on a platter or on each plate. Lay the fish over, and garnish with paper-thin slices of the lemon half. Sprinkle with chopped chives. Spoon any pan sauce around plate or platter.

*Yield: 4 servings*

## Clarified Butter:

Clarified butter is golden melted butter that has had the milk solids removed. This allows it to reach higher temperatures without burning and turning brown. To make clarified butter, place 1 stick of butter into a saucepan. Melt over low heat until completely liquified. Remove from heat. It will separate into 3 layers, a foamy surface, golden yellow butterfat, and milk solids on the bottom. Skim the foamy part off the top and discard it. Slowly pour the golden butterfat into another container, leaving the milk solids behind. You will end up with 6-8 tablespoons butter that can be kept covered in the refrigerator for up to 1 month.

# pecan-crusted grouper
# over amaretto whipped potatoes

*For a non-alcoholic version, use maple syrup in place of the amaretto liquor.*

5 Yukon Gold potatoes, peeled, cut into equal-sized chunks

fine sea salt

water as needed

5 (6-ounce) grouper or salmon fillets

Dijon mustard

¾ cup finely chopped pecans

4 tablespoons (½ stick) butter

⅛ cup heavy cream, warmed in microwave for 20 seconds

3 tablespoons Amaretto liquor or maple syrup

1. Preheat oven to 375°F.

2. Place the potatoes into a large pot. Add water to cover and a large pinch of salt. Bring to a boil. Simmer for 15 minutes or until potatoes are easily pierced with a fork.

3. Meanwhile, prepare the fish: Lightly brush each fish fillet with the Dijon mustard. Press the pecans into the fish, making sure to cover all surfaces of the fish except the skin side. Place, skin-side-down, on a baking tray and bake for 15-20 minutes, until done.

4. Drain the potatoes, reserving ½ cup of the cooking liquid in case the potatoes turn out dry. Transfer to a large mixing bowl. Add butter, cream, and Amaretto. Mash the potatoes with a potato masher or ricer. When well-mashed, whip for 1-2 minutes with an electric mixer set at a medium speed. Add reserved cooking liquid if needed. Season with salt.

5. Serve the fish over a dollop of the whipped potatoes.

*Yield: 5 servings*

194 ॐ KOSHER BY DESIGN ENTERTAINS

# poached salmon with roasted red pepper sauce

1 onion, cut into 1-inch dice

1 stalk celery, cut into 1-inch chunks

1 carrot, peeled, cut into 1-inch chunks

1 cup white wine

2 cups water

4 (6-ounce) salmon fillets, preferable Sockeye or wild Pacific salmon

### Roasted Red Pepper Sauce:

2 roasted red bell peppers (see box)

1 tablespoon extra-virgin olive oil

fine sea salt

freshly ground black pepper

½ bunch (about 40) chives, minced on the diagonal

additional chives, thinly chopped, for garnish

1. Place the onion, celery, carrot, wine, and water into a fish poacher or a straight-sided sauté pan. Bring to a boil over medium heat. Turn heat down and simmer for 5 minutes. Add the salmon fillets. Spoon some of the liquid over the fish. Cook, covered, for 10 minutes or until salmon is firm and cooked through; may need longer if fillets are thick in the middle. Using a slotted spatula, remove the fillets from the pan or poacher. Discard the vegetables and broth. Place the salmon in refrigerator for 6 hours or overnight.

2. Prepare the red pepper sauce: Place the roasted red peppers into the bowl of a food processor or into a tall container. With a food processor or an immersion blender, purée the peppers with the olive oil until creamy and smooth. Add the chives. Season with salt and pepper. Can be made 3-4 days in advance.

3. Place a spoonful of the pepper sauce in the center of each plate. Top with salmon fillet. Drizzle a little sauce on top of each fillet in a zigzag fashion. Scatter chopped chives around the plate.

*Yield: 4 servings*

### Roasting Red Bell Peppers:

Preheat the broiler with racks 5 inches from the heat. Cut your peppers in half and remove the seeds. Place the peppers, skin-side-up, on a foil-lined baking sheet. Broil about 5 minutes or until peppers look blistered and blackened. Place peppers into a paper bag. Seal and let stand 10 minutes to loosen skin. Remove skin. It is okay if some of the black pieces remain; they enhance the flavor.

# beer-battered fish with tartar sauce

*My friend Naomi Nachman sent me this recipe to use with flounder. Authentic British fish and chips traditionally uses cod, but I have tried this recipe with everything from Mahi Mahi to salmon. It is just a great tempura-like batter. When I have extra batter I even coat some zucchini and sweet potatoes and deep-fry them as well. Be careful with your oil temperature; 360°–375°F is perfect and a thermometer is a must or else the fish may brown too quickly on the outside while remaining raw on the inside.*

*Open the beer and allow it to come to room temperature or to sit at room temperature for at least 30 minutes.*

*If you want to add the "chips" to this recipe, peel three potatoes and cut into ½-inch strips. Drop into the hot oil and fry. Remove to paper towels to cool and then fry the potatoes again until brown and crisp.*

1½ cups flour, divided

1 teaspoon fine sea salt

¼ teaspoon freshly ground black pepper

4 large eggs

1 (12-ounce) bottle of beer, room temperature

canola or peanut oil for frying

1½ pounds sole, cod, haddock, or other lean, firm, white-fleshed fish fillets, pin bones removed, cut into 2- by 2-inch chunks

Tartar Sauce:

4 tablespoons mayonnaise

2 tablespoons sweet relish

2 teaspoons Dijon mustard

2 teaspoons white wine or apple cider vinegar

1. Sift 1 cup flour into a bowl. Add salt and pepper. Whisk in the eggs. Slowly add the beer, whisking after each addition. Allow the batter to sit at room temperature for 30 minutes.

2. Meanwhile, preheat oven to 250°F.

3. Heat 3 inches of oil in a large pot, skillet, or deep fryer to 360°–375°F.

4. Dredge the fish in the remaining ½ cup flour, shaking off excess. Coat the fish in the batter. Continue until all the pieces are coated.

5. Add the fish to the oil, a few pieces at a time, and fry until golden brown, 3-4 minutes, depending on the thickness of the fish. Using a slotted spoon, transfer to paper towels to drain briefly, then place into warm oven until all the fish is fried.

6. Prepare the tartar sauce: In a small bowl, mix the mayonnaise, relish, mustard, and vinegar. Stir to combine.

7. Serve fish with tartar sauce.

*Yield: 6 servings*

# Jake

Salmon Mousse with Horseradish Aioli

Winter White Soup

Seared Duck Salad

Kalamata and Mustard Crusted Roast Beef

Broccolini with Mustard Vinaigrette

Oranges Stuffed with Cranberry-Cherry Relish

Jewel Toned Orzo

Glazed Cinnamon Chocolate Ribbon Cake

anniversary party

# anniversary party
## formal dinner format

### Menu

Salmon Mousse
with Horseradish Aïoli
page 14

Winter White Soup
page 56

Seared Duck Salad
with Port Dressing
page 98

Kalamata and Mustard-Crusted
Roast Beef
page 161

Broccolini with Mustard Vinaigrette
page 211

Oranges Stuffed
with Cranberry-Cherry Relish
page 206

Jewel-Toned Orzo
page 210

Glazed Cinnamon
Chocolate Ribbon Cake
page 295

It is hard to imagine a more worthy event for formal entertaining than a celebration of a 50th wedding anniversary. A lifetime together deserves no less. You can turn a formal meal into a meaningful family event by adding creative surprises and unique personal accents.

Our beautiful toile tablecloth was a great backdrop for our gorgeous place settings. Simple silver, crystal, and plain linen napkins were all that were needed to create the proper ambiance. My grandmother's jewelry box was the source of inspiration for the various broaches that adorned each toile napkin band.

Gabriella

Salmon Mousse with Horseradish Aioli

Jewel Toned Orzo

Glazed Cinnamon Chocolate Ribbon Cake

Guests love the welcome that personalized place cards deliver. We loved the way the beautiful calligraphy dressed up each place setting. This place card was also a menu, to let the guests know of the feast that awaited them. The point is that the smallest of details conveys the warmth and caring that put this party together.

In keeping with the formality of this meal, the menu selected was more refined than that of a casual dinner. Each course was pre-plated, beginning with the Salmon Mousse and followed by the Seared Duck Salad and Winter White Soup with its gorgeous pesto garnish. Both the mousse and soup were prepared the day before. At a pre-plated dinner, it is important to make sure that most of your dishes can be made in advance so that you are only away from the table for a short amount of time, just long enough to plate and serve. The simple, yet impressive roast beef, with its three colorful side dishes, made the guests feel like royalty.

As demonstrated here with our yellow roses, we designed our centerpiece around a single type of flower. Use one striking enough to stand alone for a sophisticated look.

To personalize this party, we added some very cute touches. We had heart-shaped confetti made of the anniversary couple's wedding picture and sprinkled it onto the dessert table. Our tablecloth of old family wedding photos, spanning three generations, is sure to become a family heirloom. It wasn't hard to create this unique tablecloth. We photocopied the photos onto iron-on transfer paper, which can be bought at office-supply stores. Then we ironed them on to a simple white silk cloth. Don't worry if the edges don't iron on cleanly, that adds to the antique feel.

During dinner, we played a CD that we compiled of songs that included their wedding song, some Hebrew *chupah* music, and other meaningful songs. As a parting gift, we used the couple's wedding photo as the cover for a CD case of this music and gave one to each guest.

Toasting our special couple with Nicolas Fueillat Champagne was the final touch to an evening that was 50 years in the making.

# side dishes

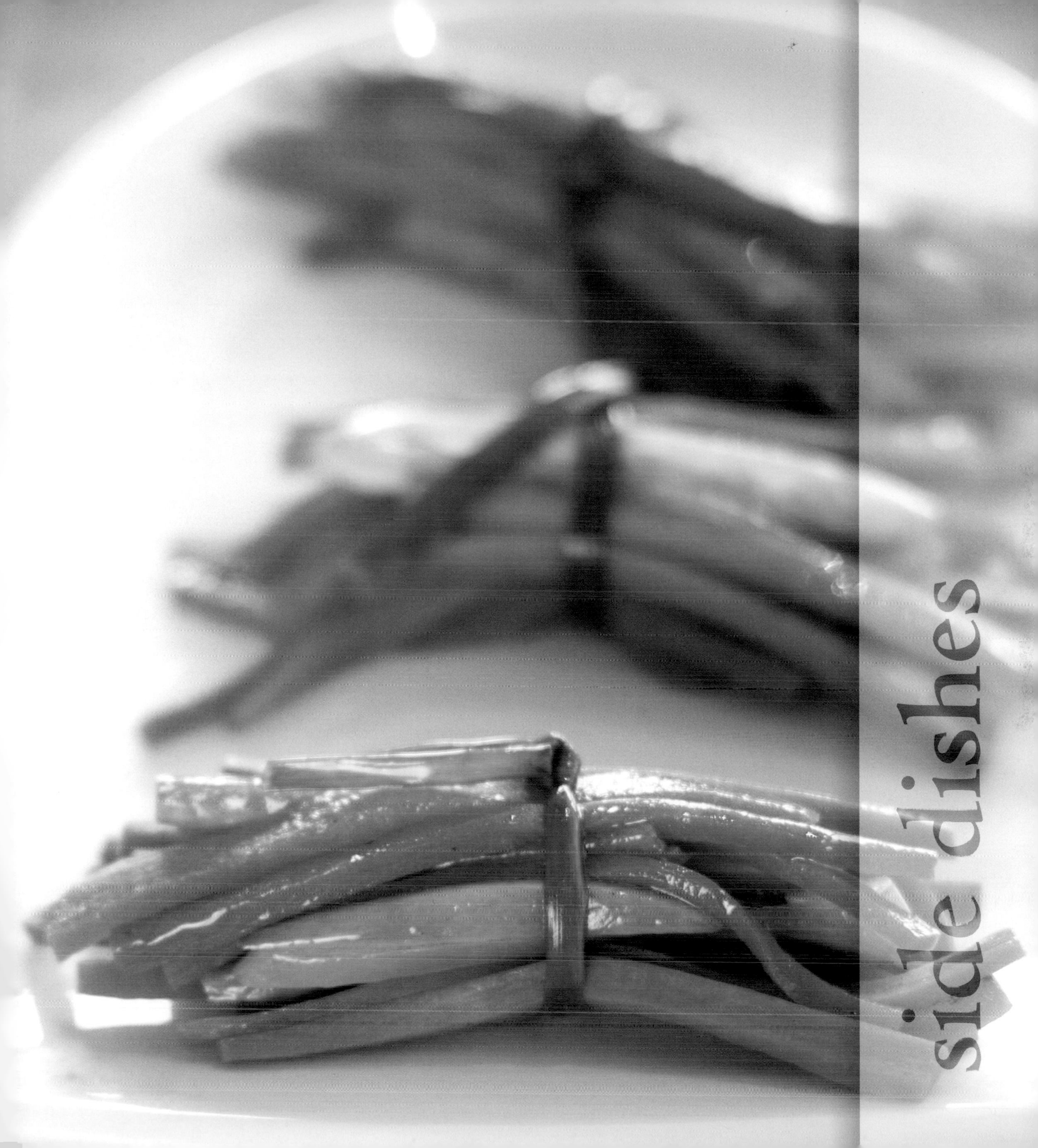

# tomato basil lentils and rice

Meat or Parve

3½ cups chicken or vegetable stock

¼ cup tomato sauce, from a small can

2 teaspoons olive oil

¼ teaspoon fine sea salt

⅓ cup dried lentils

1 cup long-grain white rice, uncooked

1 teaspoon dried basil

2 tablespoons sun-dried or oven-roasted tomatoes (see page 101), minced

1. Place the chicken or vegetable stock, tomato sauce, olive oil, and salt into a medium pot with a tight lid. Bring to a boil. Add the lentils and cover. Turn the heat down and cook over low heat for 20 minutes.

2. Add the rice, basil, and sun-dried tomatoes. Cover and simmer on low for 20 minutes. Do not open the lid during cooking, as the steam helps the rice cook. Remove from the heat and let stand covered for 5 minutes. Fluff with a fork.

*Yield: 4-6 servings*

# sweet noodle kugel roulade

Parve

*This kugel has a lovely and unusual rolled presentation. Don't skip the parchment paper, it makes rolling up the kugel much easier. The pan to use is a jelly-roll pan. A jelly-roll pan is a cookie sheet that has sides (see p. 273).*

margarine or non-stick cooking spray

8 ounces fine noodles

½ cup sugar

4 large eggs

¼ cup crushed pineapple, drained

¼ cup raisins

¼ cup canola oil

ground cinnamon

1. Preheat oven to 350°F.

2. Cover an 11- by 17-inch jelly-roll pan with parchment paper. Lightly grease the parchment with margarine or non-stick cooking spray. Set aside.

3. Cook the noodles according to the package directions; do not overcook. Drain.

4. Place the noodles into a large bowl and with a whisk, mix in the sugar, eggs, pineapple, raisins, and oil. Whisk until all combined.

5. Pour the noodle mixture onto the prepared sheet and spread it into an even layer. Bake for 15-18 minutes, until the kugel is set.

6. Remove from oven. Allow to cool for a few minutes. Starting from one of the shorter ends, and using the parchment paper to assist, roll the kugel into a tight spiral. Sprinkle the top and sides with cinnamon.

*Yield: 8-10 servings*

# moroccan sweet potato stew

*This was another recipe that was given to me by the crew on the Windstar cruise when I traveled with Chosen Voyage. It is from their Sail Light menu and is a nice, hearty, healthy side dish or can even be made with the vegetable broth as a vegetarian main dish.*

1 large onion, cut into
½-inch dice

3 cloves fresh garlic, minced

¼ cup water or more as
needed

1½ teaspoons turmeric

1 teaspoon ground cinnamon

¾ teaspoon curry powder

¾ teaspoon ground cumin

¼ teaspoon ground nutmeg

¼ teaspoon crushed red
pepper flakes

¾ teaspoon fine sea salt

¾ teaspoon freshly ground
black pepper

3-4 sweet potatoes
(3½ pounds), peeled,
cut into 1-inch cubes

1 large red bell pepper,
seeded, cut into 1-inch pieces

1 eggplant, peeled,
cut into 1-inch cubes

¾ cup chicken broth or
vegetable broth

2 cups canned chick peas,
(garbanzo beans), rinsed
and drained

1 (28-ounce) can diced
tomatoes, undrained

fresh cilantro leaves,
chopped, for garnish

1. Place the onions and garlic into a large pot with ¼ cup water. Cook, covered, over low heat until tender, about 10-12 minutes, adding more water as necessary to prevent scorching.

2. Stir in the turmeric, cinnamon, curry, cumin, nutmeg, red pepper flakes, salt, and pepper. Cook for 3 minutes. Stir in the sweet potatoes, bell pepper, eggplant, and broth. Raise the heat to medium and bring to a boil. Reduce heat to low and simmer, covered, for 5 minutes.

3. Add chick peas and tomatoes, and simmer, covered, until sweet potatoes are tender, about 45-60 minutes, stirring occasionally. Garnish with fresh cilantro before serving.

*Yield: 10-12 servings*

# oranges stuffed with cranberry-cherry relish

*When my brother got married, not only did I get Jessica, a sister-in-law whom I adore, but the bonus was that she brought along some great family recipes. This is one of them.*

2 cups firmly packed dark brown sugar

1½ cups golden raisins

1 orange, unpeeled, quartered, seeded, cut into ¼-inch dice

1 lemon, unpeeled, quartered, seeded, cut into ¼-inch dice

1 cup canned pitted sweet dark cherries, drained

½ cup white vinegar

1 cinnamon stick

½ teaspoon ground cinnamon

½ teaspoon ground nutmeg

½ teaspoon ground cloves

1½ cups fresh cranberries

½ cup chopped walnuts

small navel oranges, optional, for garnish

cinnamon sticks, optional, for garnish

1. In a large pot, combine the brown sugar, raisins, orange, lemon, cherries, vinegar, cinnamon stick, ground cinnamon, nutmeg, and cloves. Bring to a boil over medium heat, stirring frequently. Reduce heat and simmer for 10 minutes. Add the cranberries and simmer until they begin to pop, about 15 minutes longer. Remove cinnamon stick. Cover and refrigerate until cold. Can be made in advance. When ready to serve, mix in the walnuts.

2. You can serve the relish in a pretty bowl, or halve and hollow out small navel oranges. Stuff each with a mound of relish and stick a cinnamon stick in each.

*Yield: 10-12 servings*

# hasselback potatoes

*My friend Jill Raff was the stylist on Kosher by Design. She shared this recipe concept with me. It is an old family favorite technique for dressing up a plain baked potato.*

*Here is a neat trick for cutting the potatoes so that you cut even slices but don't cut through to the bottom. Place the potato into a wooden spoon. The sides of the spoon will keep you from cutting through. For bigger potatoes, such as Idaho potatoes, place a chopstick or wooden spoon along each of the two long sides. With one hand holding the potato and chopsticks or spoons in place, slice the potato widthwise. The knife should touch the chopsticks or spoon handles at every slice, leaving the slices attached at the bottom of the potato. This will serve as a guide to keep your slices even and keep from slicing through as well.*

8 small Idaho baking potatoes or Yukon Gold potatoes, unpeeled

8 cloves fresh garlic, sliced into thin slivers

fine sea salt

freshly ground black pepper

olive oil

1. Preheat oven to 450°F.

2. Using a sharp or electric knife starting at one end and going to the other end, cut slits into each potato, ⅛ of an inch apart, being careful not to cut all the way to the bottom of the potato (see methods above). Place the potatoes onto a baking sheet.

3. Place a garlic sliver into each slit. Sprinkle each potato with salt and pepper. Drizzle with olive oil.

4. Bake 1 hour; baste with the pan oil and then continue to bake for another 30 minutes, until potatoes are soft.

*Yield: 8 servings*

# herbed roasted corn on the cob

*These are fabulous served in the summertime. I like to keep the cooking indoors in my oven, as the husks burn when exposed to the flames of a grill for a long period of time. If you prefer to use the grill, just soak the corn in their husks for 20 minutes in a pot or sink of water, then prepare as directed in the recipe and cook on the grill.*

8 ears fresh corn

8 tablespoons butter or margarine, softened for 15 minutes at room temperature

2 tablespoons fresh chives, chopped

2 tablespoons fresh parsley leaves, chopped

1 tablespoon fresh thyme leaves, chopped

2 teaspoons fresh dill, chopped

¼ teaspoon cayenne pepper

fine sea salt

freshly ground black pepper

kitchen twine

1. Preheat oven to 375°F.

2. In a small bowl, mix the butter or margarine with the chives, parsley, thyme, dill, salt, and cayenne. Stir until the herbs are evenly distributed.

3. Trim the stems and discard tough outer husks from corncobs. Peel back remaining husks, being careful not to detach them from the corn. Remove and discard the corn silks.

4. Spread 1 tablespoon of the butter mixture evenly over each ear of corn. Sprinkle each ear with salt and black pepper.

5. Pull the husks back up to enclose the corn. Tie kitchen twine around each ear to secure the husks.

6. Place on a baking sheet and roast, turning once, until corn is fragrant and tender, about 25-28 minutes.

7. When ready to serve, remove string, pull back the husks and tie them with the string.

*Yield: 8 servings*

208    KOSHER BY DESIGN ENTERTAINS

# jewel-toned orzo

2 tablespoons margarine

2 large onions, cut into
¼-inch dice

1 green bell pepper, seeded,
cut into ¼-inch dice

1 yellow bell pepper, seeded,
cut into ¼-inch dice

8 ounces fresh sliced
mushrooms

½ cup sweetened dried
cranberries, such as Craisins

¼ teaspoon fine sea salt

¼ teaspoon ground white
pepper

1 tablespoon canola oil

1 (16-ounce) box orzo

boiling water as needed

1½ teaspoons chicken bouillon
powder (can be parve)

1. In a large pan, over medium heat, melt the margarine. Add the onions, peppers, mushrooms, and cranberries. Sauté until softened, about 6-8 minutes, making sure not to let the vegetables brown or burn. Season with salt and white pepper. Set aside.

2. Meanwhile, in a medium pot, heat the oil. Add the orzo and toast until golden, stirring often. It will be all different shades of brown and have a nutty aroma. Add boiling water to cover by a few inches; add the bouillon powder. Cook until the orzo is al denté, about 8-9 minutes. If the water boils out and the orzo is still too hard, add more hot water ½ cup at a time, stirring to make sure the orzo is not sticking to the bottom of the pot, until orzo is done and water has evaporated.

3. Combine the vegetables with the orzo. Serve hot or at room temperature.

*Yield: 8-10 servings*

# broccolini with mustard vinaigrette

*Broccolini is a cross between broccoli and Chinese broccoli, which is a leafy variety with thick stems. Broccolini has thinner stems and is sometimes called Aspiration.*

*This dressing is also great over asparagus or green beans or a mix of both. The dressing can be made up to a week in advance and kept in the refrigerator.*

1 shallot

2 teaspoons Chinese mustard
or ¼ teaspoon dry mustard
powder

2 tablespoons Dijon mustard

8 sprigs fresh thyme, stems
discarded

¼ cup red-wine vinegar

½ cup olive oil

water as needed

fine sea salt

1 pound broccolini

1. Place the shallot, Chinese mustard, Dijon mustard, thyme leaves, and vinegar into a blender or food processor. Pulse to blend. Drizzle in the olive oil and pulse to emulsify.

2. Bring a pot of salted water to a boil. Drop the broccolini into the water and cook for 4-6 minutes, until it turns a bright green and can be pierced with a fork; do not overcook. Remove from pot and shock in cold water to prevent further cooking. Drain and pat dry with paper towels.

3. Drizzle with some of the dressing. Serve at room temperature.

*Yield: 6 servings*

# two-tone potatoes with pesto sauce

Parve

1 cup fresh basil leaves

2 large shallots

4 cloves fresh garlic

2 tablespoons pine nuts

⅓ cup olive oil, plus more for drizzling

1½ pounds small red new potatoes, unpeeled

1½ pounds small white round potatoes, unpeeled

fine sea salt

freshly ground black pepper

1. Preheat oven to 400°F.

2. In the bowl of a food processor fitted with a metal blade, process the basil, shallots, garlic, and pine nuts until finely chopped. Drizzle in the olive oil. Pulse to combine into a smooth paste.

3. Place the potatoes into a large baking dish. Drizzle with olive oil. Season generously with salt and pepper. Roast, uncovered, for 40 minutes.

4. Pour the pesto over the potatoes; toss to coat. Continue roasting until potatoes are fork-tender and golden brown, about 25-30 minutes longer.

*Yield: 8 servings*

# apple kugel

Parve

*Although it works fine in a disposable tin, this dish is worthy of a beautiful ceramic baking dish. I bake it in a rectangular oven-to-table ceramic dish; my girlfriend Shari Alter, who gave me the recipe, uses a very large round fluted one. Just make sure that whatever you bake it in is big enough to hold all the apple slices.*

½ cup sugar

1 cup all-purpose flour

3 large eggs

¾ cup vegetable or canola oil

1 teaspoon baking powder

2 heaping tablespoons vanilla sugar, or 2 packets vanilla sugar

9 Granny Smith apples, peeled, halved, cored, thinly sliced

1 (12-ounce) jar apricot preserves

ground cinnamon

1. Preheat oven to 350°F.

2. Grease an 8½- by 11-inch baking dish. Set aside.

3. In a mixing bowl, combine the sugar, flour, eggs, oil, baking powder, and vanilla sugar. Whisk to combine.

4. Place apples into the prepared pan. Using a spatula, spread an even layer of the apricot preserves over the apples.

5. Spread the batter over the jelly; it will seep into the apples a bit.

6. Sprinkle the top with cinnamon.

7. Bake, uncovered, for 1 hour.

*Yield: 8-10 servings*

# multi-grain chick pea pilaf

*Growing up, Friday nights in my house meant opening a can of "arbis," a.k.a. chick peas, with my Dad. Together we would dry them and pepper them. My siblings and I would toss them in the air and try to catch them in our mouths.*

*As a grownup, besides the memory of chick peas, what appeals to me about this side dish is that the grains pack a powerhouse of nutrients. They need no cooking, just a rinsing. This salad is great at room temperature, which makes it perfect picnic food or a Shabbat lunch side dish.*

½ cup bulgur, also known as tabbouleh, or cracked wheat

½ cup kasha, also known as buckwheat groats, medium granulation

1 cup chicken or vegetable broth

8 red grape or cherry tomatoes, halved

6 small scallions, thinly sliced on the diagonal, white and pale green parts only

½ cup fresh flat-leaf parsley, chopped

juice and zest from 1 small or ½ large lemon

¼ cup extra-virgin olive oil

½ teaspoon fine sea salt

¼- ½ teaspoon freshly ground black pepper

½ teaspoon crushed red pepper flakes

1 (15-ounce) can chick peas, (garbanzo beans), rinsed and drained

1. Place the bulgur and kasha into a medium bowl.

2. In a small saucepan, heat the broth to boiling. Pour the boiling broth into the bowl of grains and cover. Set aside for 30 minutes.

3. In a large bowl, combine the tomatoes, scallions, parsley, lemon juice, lemon zest, olive oil, salt, ¼ teaspoon pepper, red pepper flakes, and chick peas. Toss to mix. Stir in the bulgur and kasha.

4. Taste and add more black pepper to taste. Serve at room temperature.

*Yield: 4-6 servings*

# mushroom barley risotto

Meat or Parve

*I love risotto, the creamy arborio rice that you gently cook over a period of 45 minutes, slowly adding in stock as the grains absorb it cup by cup. However, I don't always have the time for that kind of recipe. This is one of those "cheat" recipes. All the creaminess of risotto without all the work and constant attention. The substitution of barley in place of rice is a nice textural and taste change. Although it's not technically a risotto, the end result of this dish tastes like one.*

*The result will be much better if you use homemade chicken or vegetable stock. If you have none on hand, sometimes the butcher or local deli will sell you stock, and the sodium content is much lower than in canned stock or broth, which is very salty.*

*Like most risotto, this recipe is best served fresh; when re-heated, it loses some of its creaminess.*

2 tablespoons margarine

3 medium onions, finely chopped

1 tablespoon sugar

9 ounces sliced mushrooms (can be button, baby bella, etc.)

8 ounces shiitake mushroom caps, chopped

2 cups pearl barley, uncooked

¼ teaspoon freshly ground black pepper

⅛ teaspoon dried thyme

6 cups chicken broth or vegetable stock

fine sea salt

freshly ground black pepper

1. Preheat oven to 350°F.

2. In a large Dutch oven or ovenproof pot, melt the margarine. Add the onions and sugar. Cover and cook for 20 minutes, until golden brown. Stir frequently to make sure the onions are not burning. Add the mushrooms and cook, uncovered, 10 minutes longer, stirring every few minutes. Add the barley. Cook 2 minutes so that it toasts, which enhances its nutty flavor and keeps it from becoming mushy. Stir in pepper and thyme. Remove from heat.

3. In a medium saucepan, bring the broth to a boil. Pour over the mushroom-barley mixture. Cover and bake for 1 hour. Season with salt and pepper as needed.

*Yield: 8-10 servings*

## Cutting Onions:

When you cut an onion it releases a sulfuric compound. This compound reacts with the saline in your eyes to create mild sulfuric acid. Your eyes produce tears to rinse the acid away. One trick to reduce tears is to slow down the release of the compound by refrigerating onions for an hour before cutting them. Using a sharp knife helps too. My best trick came from an unlikely source, my friend Marisa's husband, who enters the kitchen only to check on dinnertime: wear protective goggles. It works!

# wasabi mashed potatoes

*There are many fun garnishes for mashed potatoes. Use a mandolin and cut paper-thin slices of Idaho potato, place onto parchment on a baking sheet. Brush with oil, sprinkle with sesame seeds, and top with another baking sheet. Bake in a 350°F oven for 8 minutes. Uncover and bake an additional 7-8 minutes. You can also use a spiral vegetable slicer to make continuous curly ribbon-like slices out of vegetables such as turnips, parsnips, sweet potatoes, or carrots. Just deep fry for 2-3 minutes. You can also slice ginger into julienne threads and fry for 10 seconds. The possibilities are endless.*

2½ pounds russet or Yukon Gold potatoes, peeled, cut into 1-inch chunks

water to cover

fine sea salt

3 tablespoons wasabi powder

¼ cup soy milk

4 tablespoons margarine

1. Place the potatoes into a large pot. Cover with water. Sprinkle in 1½ teaspoons salt. Bring to a boil. Cook for 30-35 minutes, until potatoes are fork tender. Dissolve the wasabi powder in the soy milk. Stir and allow it to sit for 10 minutes.

2. When the potatoes are soft, drain them. Mash with a hand masher, potato ricer, or electric mixer until fluffy and smooth. Immediately add the margarine so it melts into the potatoes. Stir in the wasabi mixture.

*Yield: 6 servings*

# mushroom mashed potatoes

*Mashed potatoes can be prepared 2 hours ahead. Cover and keep at room temperature. Rewarm over low heat, stirring frequently. Never use a food processor to mash potatoes; it destroys the starch granules and turns them to paste. If you must make them more in advance, cover tightly with foil and heat in a 325°F oven for 1½ hours, to thoroughly heat through so they will stay hot.*

*Yukon Gold potatoes will yield a creamier result; russet potatoes will give you a fluffier one.*

2½ pounds Yukon Gold or russet potatoes, peeled, cut into 1-inch chunks

fine sea salt

3 tablespoons canola oil

5 shallots, thinly sliced

1 small onion, chopped

3.5 ounces shiitake mushrooms, cut into ½-inch dice, stems discarded

3.5 ounces cremini mushrooms, cut into ½-inch dice

4 tablespoons margarine

1. Place the potatoes into a large pot. Cover with water. Sprinkle in 2 teaspoons salt. Bring to a boil. Cook for 30-35 minutes until potatoes are fork-tender.

2. Meanwhile, heat the oil in a medium skillet. Add the shallots, onion, and mushrooms. Turn the heat to medium-low and sauté for 25-30 minutes, stirring with a wooden spoon every few minutes to make sure the shallots are not sticking to the pan. The mushrooms will be nicely browned.

3. When potatoes are soft, drain. Mash with a hand masher, potato ricer, or electric mixer until fluffy and smooth. Immediately add the margarine so it melts into the potatoes. Season with salt and black pepper to taste. Add the mushroom-shallot mixture with the oil they cooked in. Serve warm.

*Yield: 6 servings*

# whipped root vegetables with caramelized onions

Dairy or Parve

3 medium parsnips, peeled, cut into ½-inch dice

1 large Idaho potato, peeled, cut into ½-inch dice

2 medium turnips, peeled, cut into ½-inch dice

coarse sea salt or kosher salt

water to cover

canola oil

1 large onion, cut into ½-inch dice

¼ cup dairy or non-dairy sour cream

3 tablespoons butter or margarine

½-1 teaspoon ground white pepper

1. Place the parsnips, potato, and turnips into a pot with enough salted water to cover. Bring to a boil and cook until vegetables are very tender, about 30–40 minutes.

2. Meanwhile, pour ¼-inch of canola oil into a large pan and place over medium heat. When the oil shimmers, add the onion. Allow to slowly cook until caramelized and brown, about 30 minutes.

3. When the vegetables are done, drain them well and place into the bowl of a mixer with a whisk attachment. Pour off all but 1 tablespoon of the oil and add the onions with the 1 tablespoon of oil into the bowl. Whip all the vegetables until mashed and creamy.

4. Add the sour cream, butter, 1 teaspoon salt, and pepper. Whip until combined.

*Yield: 6 servings*

# oven-roasted asparagus

*This simple preparation brings out the natural essence of this wonderful vegetable. The cooking time will vary based on the thickness of the spears.*

*You can also grill the asparagus on an outdoor grill. For a pretty presentation, lay 5–6 asparagus spears horizontally on the grill. Soak wooden skewers in water to prevent burning, then skewer the asparagus vertically, using 3 skewers for each "asparagus raft." Season both sides with the olive oil, salt, and pepper and then grill, turning once. The skewers will also make it easy to turn the asparagus during the cooking process.*

1½ pounds fresh asparagus

extra-virgin olive oil

Fleur de Sel, coarse sea salt, or kosher salt

freshly ground black pepper

1. Preheat oven to 400°F.
2. Trim off the very bottom of the spears, leaving as much of the length as possible. Using a vegetable peeler, slice down the sides of the spears to trim off the thorns.
3. Lay the spears on a baking sheet. Drizzle with olive oil. Sprinkle with salt and pepper.
4. Roast for 15–20 minutes, until fork-tender and bright green in color. Cooking time will depend on the thickness of the asparagus. Do not overcook or the asparagus will burn and shrivel.

*Yield: 4-6 servings*

# sweet potato wedges with vanilla rum sauce
Dairy or Parve

6 medium sweet potatoes, unpeeled

½ cup (1 stick) butter or margarine

½ cup dark brown sugar

1 tablespoon pure vanilla extract

1 tablespoon dark rum

1. Preheat oven to 375°F.
2. Cover a large jelly-roll pan with parchment paper.
3. Cut the sweet potatoes in half lengthwise. Cut each half in half again lengthwise. You will have long wedges. Place into a bowl.
4. In a small saucepan, melt the butter and brown sugar. Stir in the vanilla and rum. Simmer for 1 minute. Pour over the sweet potatoes and toss to combine.
5. Arrange the wedges in a single layer on the prepared pan.
6. Bake, uncovered, for 45 minutes–1 hour, checking at the 45-minute mark, until potatoes are soft and caramelized.

Yield: 8-10 servings

# carrot and snap pea bundles

*This is a beautiful, healthy, two-toned vegetable presentation. Be patient when tying the bundles; they are worth the effort. Keep extra chives on hand in case they snap when tying.*

1 tablespoon canola oil

2 tablespoons sugar

1 pound carrots (about 5 large), peeled, cut into 3- by ⅛-inch matchsticks

4 ounces snap peas, cut into matchsticks

20-25 fresh chives

1. Heat the oil in a large skillet over medium heat. Add the sugar and carrots. Sauté 4–6 minutes, until carrots begin to soften. Add the snap peas. Sauté 2 minutes longer. Remove from heat.

2. Place the chives in a pot of hot water; let them soften for 30 seconds. Quickly remove chives to a paper towel.

3. Take a small pile of the carrots and snap peas and place them in the center of 1 chive. Tie the chive into a knot, securing the matchsticks into a bundle. Repeat until all the vegetables are used.

*Yield: 15-18 bundles*

# strawberry-apple kugel

Parve

*I have really enjoyed getting to visit so many different Jewish communities that have hosted me for cooking demonstrations over this past year. While they have all been wonderful, one I will never forget took place in Baltimore, Maryland. The setting was a beautiful home in a woodsy neighborhood. My gracious hostess, Gilah Spero, had commandeered some friends to help me prepare, since I had just a few hours before the event. As I laid out the ingredients and gave each woman her marching orders, the entire block went black. We lost all lights and power. After waiting a short while, it was becoming clear that the electricity was not returning and I would soon be out of preparation time, with 50 women arriving shortly, expecting dinner and a class. This was a seasoned group that had suffered through a 5-day blackout the previous summer. They kicked it into gear, mobilized husbands to lug over generators, and, in the interim, broke out yahrtzeit candles to cook by. As we worked in the candlelight I spotted an ace helper, a ringer in the crowd, who it turns out was a cook for the local girls' seminary. As we chopped, diced, and talked food, Ida Glenner was kind enough to share this recipe, her most requested at the seminary, and the Sweet Noodle Kugel Roulade on page 204.*

*Enjoy these sweet side dishes; they are the kind that you keep going back to the baking dish and spooning out just one last taste.*

3 cups all-purpose flour

1¼ cups sugar

1 teaspoon vanilla

¾ cup canola oil

1 large egg

1 teaspoon baking powder

3 Granny Smith apples, peeled, cut into small cubes

ground cinnamon

1 (21-ounce) can strawberry pie filling

1. Preheat oven to 350°F.

2. In a large bowl, prepare the streusel crumbs: Combine the flour, sugar, vanilla, oil, egg, and baking powder. Mix with the tips of your fingers until crumbs form.

3. Sprinkle one-third of the crumbs into the bottom of a 9- by 13-inch baking pan. Top with the cubed apples. Sprinkle with cinnamon.

4. Top with another third of the crumbs.

5. Pour the strawberry filling over the crumb layer.

6. Top with the rest of the crumbs.

7. Bake, uncovered, for 1 hour.

*Yield: 10 servings*

# orzo with ratatouille vegetables

*Don't just dump in all the veggies — the eggplant is porous and the zucchinis are hard and need longer cooking times.*

1½ cups orzo, uncooked

olive oil

1 small red onion,
cut into tiny dice

½ zucchini, unpeeled,
cut into tiny dice

½ yellow squash, unpeeled,
cut into tiny dice

fine sea salt

freshly ground black pepper

¼ teaspoon dry oregano

½ small eggplant, unpeeled,
cut into tiny dice

6–7 fresh basil leaves,
chiffonade

½ cup jarred roasted red
peppers, cut into tiny dice

¼ cup Merlot or other red wine

1 tablespoon tomato paste

1. Cook orzo al denté according to package directions; drain and set aside.

2. Place 2–3 tablespoons olive oil into a large skillet over medium heat. Add the onion and sauté for 3 minutes, until shiny but not brown. Add the zucchini and squash and sauté for another 3–4 minutes until soft but not mushy. Season with salt and pepper. Sprinkle in the oregano.

3. Add 1 tablespoon olive oil. Add the eggplant and sauté for 3–4 minutes. Season with more salt and pepper. Add the basil leaves and red peppers. Sauté 1 minute.

4. Add the wine and tomato paste. Stir to coat all the vegetables and cook for 1 minute. Add the orzo to the frying pan. Toss and remove from heat.

*Yields: 10 servings*

# zucchini-carrot bread

*A sure winner for kids and adults. This one works great at room temperature. It is just as useful as an accompaniment to soup, salad, your main dish, or on a brunch table.*

## Zucchini Carrot Bread:

3 cups all-purpose flour

2 teaspoons ground cinnamon

1 teaspoon baking soda

½ teaspoon fine sea salt

½ teaspoon baking powder

1½ cups sugar

2 medium carrots, peeled, grated, using the biggest holes on a box grater

2 medium zucchini, unpeeled, grated, using the biggest holes on a box grater

½ cup canola oil

2 large eggs

## Streusel Topping:

½ cup dark brown sugar

¼ cup rolled oats or old-fashioned oats (not quick or 1-minute type)

¼ cup Grape Nuts cereal

⅓ cup all-purpose flour

⅛ teaspoon fine sea salt

¼ cup (½ stick) margarine, cut into 4 pieces, at room temperature

1. Preheat oven to 350°F. Lightly grease the bottom and halfway up the sides of a 9- by 13-inch baking pan or 2 loaf pans. Set aside.

2. In a medium bowl, combine the flour, cinnamon, baking soda, salt, and baking powder. Set aside.

3. In a separate bowl, combine the sugar, carrots, zucchini, oil, and eggs. Stir.

4. Add the flour mixture. Stir until combined.

5. Pour mixture into prepared pan or pans.

6. Prepare the topping: In a small bowl, mix the brown sugar, oats, Grape Nuts, flour, and salt. With the tips of your fingers or a spoon, mix in the margarine until combined.

7. Sprinkle the topping over the batter.

8. Bake, uncovered, for 1 hour.

9. Serve and store at room temperature.

*Yield: 10-12 sevings*

# cauliflower popcorn

Parve

*You will pop these gorgeous golden carb-friendly treats into your mouth like popcorn. The simple high-heat roasting method brings out the natural sugars of the vegetable, and the spice combination works great in both flavor and color. Don't cut florets too small because they shrink while cooking.*

2 heads cauliflower, cut into medium sized florets, stems discarded

1 teaspoon fine sea salt

2 teaspoons sugar

¼ teaspoon onion powder

¼ teaspoon garlic powder

½ teaspoon paprika

¼-½ teaspoon turmeric

6–8 tablespoon olive oil

1. Preheat oven to 450°F.

2. Line a jelly-roll pan or baking sheet with parchment paper.

3. In a large bowl, combine the salt, sugar, onion powder, garlic powder, paprika, turmeric, and oil. Add cauliflower florets and toss to evenly coat.

4. Place in a single layer on the prepared sheet.

5. Roast, uncovered, for 30–35 minutes, until the largest pieces can be pierced with a fork. If the tops begin to become too brown, toss the cauliflower during the baking process.

*Yield: 8 servings*

# champagne green beans

Parve

1 tablespoon extra-virgin olive oil

1 pound haricot verts or green beans, root ends trimmed

1 shallot, finely minced

1 clove garlic, minced

fine sea salt

freshly ground black pepper

¾ cup champagne or sparkling white wine

1 tablespoon margarine

1. In a large pan, heat the olive oil over medium heat. Add the green beans and shallot. Cook for 1 minute until shiny, don't let them brown. Add the garlic. Season with salt and pepper. Sauté 2 minutes longer for haricot verts, 4 minutes for green beans. Remove the pan from the flame. Add the champagne. Return to the flame, cover, and steam the green beans for 2–3 minutes. You will notice the beans are a gorgeous green color.

2. Turn off the heat. Add the margarine to the pan and swirl the pan until the margarine is melted and coats the beans.

*Yield: 4-6 servings*

# graham cracker-crusted squash pie

Parve

*The reason for partially baking the dish before adding the topping is that the batter is very runny and the topping will sink if added at the beginning, so follow the directions as written.*

## Squash Pie:

1½ cups graham cracker crumbs

¾ cup margarine, melted

1 (12-ounce) box puréed butternut squash, defrosted

4 large eggs

¾ cup soy milk

½ cup firmly packed dark brown sugar

½ cup all-purpose flour

1 teaspoon ground cinnamon

½ teaspoon fine sea salt

## Topping:

½ cup all-purpose flour

½ cup dark brown sugar

1 teaspoon ground cinnamon

4 tablespoons chilled margarine, cut into small chunks

1. Preheat oven to 350°F.

2. Combine graham cracker crumbs and melted margarine in a small bowl. Press into the bottom and slightly up the sides of a 9-inch springform pan.

3. In the bowl of a mixer, combine squash, eggs, soy milk, brown sugar, flour, cinnamon, and salt. Beat at a medium speed until all combined.

4. Pour into the prepared crust.

5. Bake for 35 minutes.

6. Prepare the topping: In a small bowl, mix the flour, brown sugar, and cinnamon with a fork. Sprinkle in the chunks of margarine and use your fingers to knead the mixture together to make coarse crumbs.

7. Sprinkle the topping over the squash. Return to oven, uncovered, for another 25 minutes.

*Yield: 8-10 servings*

# pineapple challah kugel

*This dish is a combination of a bread pudding and a kugel. It is delicious and pretty. The sweetness appeals to both young and old, and the 5-minute preparation will appeal to you.*

1 large challah

1 cup sugar

1 cup (2 sticks) margarine

7 large eggs

1 (20-ounce can) crushed pineapple, drained

¼ cup soy milk or non-dairy creamer

1 teaspoon vanilla

1 teaspoon ground cinnamon

1 tablespoon sugar

1. Preheat oven to 425°F.

2. Cut most of the crust off the challah and discard. Cut the challah into cubes. Set aside.

3. In the bowl of a mixer, at medium speed, cream the sugar and margarine. Add the eggs and mix.

4. Add the pineapple, soymilk, and vanilla. Mix to combine; the batter will not be smooth.

5. Add the challah cubes and toss the mixture with a spoon until combined.

6. Pour into a pretty oven-to-table baking dish. I like a rectangular shape but you can do this dish in any shape.

6. In a small bowl, mix the cinnamon and sugar. Sprinkle the top with cinnamon/sugar.

7. Bake, uncovered, 40 minutes. The top will be golden brown.

*Yield: 8-10 servings*

# tapas potatoes

Parve

*Tapas is a Spanish word for "little dishes." In Spain, what we call the appetizer course is usually served as a series of small dishes that are passed around at a gathering, served on a buffet, or placed out at a bar. As for their versatility, these potatoes would go great with a simple grilled chicken breast, a steak, or even a good omelette. You can adjust the heat by cutting the hot sauce. Delicioso!*

5 tablespoons olive oil

5 medium russet potatoes, peeled, cut into ½-inch cubes

1 (14-ounce) can diced tomatoes

4 cloves fresh garlic, chopped

juice of ½ lime

1 tablespoon fresh cilantro leaves

½ teaspoon ground cumin

1 teaspoon sugar

½ teaspoon crushed red pepper flakes

8 dashes hot sauce, such as Tabasco

½ teaspoon fine sea salt

1. In a large skillet, heat olive oil over medium-low heat until it shimmers.

2. Add the potatoes in a single layer and cook until the edges are beginning to brown, about 10–15 minutes.

3. Meanwhile, place the tomatoes with their juices, garlic, lime juice, cilantro, cumin, sugar, red pepper flakes, hot sauce, and salt into the bowl of a food processor fitted with a metal blade. Pulse 2–3 times, until just combined, not puréed.

4. Add the tomato mixture to the potatoes and cook for 8–10 minutes, stirring occasionally. Check to make sure potatoes are cooked through.

*Yield: 8-10 servings*

# asparagus shiitake loaf

4 tablespoons margarine

6 ounces shiitake mushroom caps, sliced, stems discarded

2 shallots, sliced

2 tablespoons all-purpose flour

2 tablespoons Merlot, Madeira wine, or other full-bodied red wine

½ cup chicken broth or vegetable broth, divided

1 bunch thin asparagus, bottom 3 inches discarded, the rest cut into 1-inch pieces

1 sheet puff pastry dough (from a 17.3-ounce box)

1 egg yolk

1 tablespoon water

1. Preheat oven to 375°F.

2. Cover a cookie sheet with parchment paper. Set aside.

3. Melt the margarine in a saucepan over medium heat. Add the sliced shiitake mushrooms and shallots. Sauté 4–5 minutes, until beginning to soften. Whisk in the flour; it will be sticky. Add the wine and ¼ cup stock. Cook until liquid is cooked out and the mixture has thickened, about 15 minutes; stir often.

4. Add the sliced asparagus and remaining ¼ cup stock. Cook for 6–8 minutes. You want the liquid to cook out and the asparagus to still look crisp.

5. On a piece of parchment or wax paper, roll out the sheet of puff pastry into a large rectangle. Cut 2 (½-inch wide) strips from the top of the sheet. Set aside.

6. Place the asparagus filling down the center of the pastry sheet. Using the parchment or waxed paper to assist you, bring both long ends into the center and pinch to close the roll. Seal the ends.

7. Invert the roll, seam-side-down, onto the prepared cookie sheet.

8. Cut each piece of trimmed puff pastry in half and drape over the top of the loaf to make 2 criss-cross shapes. Tuck the ends under the loaf.

9. Beat the egg yolk with 1 tablespoon water. Brush a heavy coating of egg wash all over the top and sides of the loaf.

10. Place it into the oven and bake, uncovered, for 20–25 minutes, until puffed and golden brown. Turn the cookie sheet in the oven after 15 minutes so all sides brown evenly.

*Yield: 8-10 servings*

## Tips on Using Puff Pastry:

Remove the puff pastry sheets from the package and allow to sit, covered, at room temperature for 15 minutes. Open up the flaps to make a tent and let sit for 5 minutes longer. Put the sides down and pinch the seams together. Proceed with your recipe.

# parsnip and spinach gratin

*Combine creamed spinach and parsnips, and you get smooth, creamy vegetable perfection. Dig into this side dish with both forks.*

*Look for large-diameter parsnips — they will slice into larger circles. This will make layering them easier than narrower parsnips, which yield smaller circles.*

4 tablespoons margarine

2 large onions, cut into ½-inch dice

1 (10-ounce) box frozen chopped spinach, defrosted, squeezed dry

½ cup flour

¼ cup non-dairy sour cream, such as Sour Supreme

¼ cup mayonnaise

¼ teaspoon freshly ground black pepper

¼ teaspoon fine sea salt

28 ounces chicken broth

3 pounds large parsnips, peeled, thinly sliced into ¼-inch rounds

paprika

1. Preheat oven to 350°F. Spray a 9- by 13-inch oven-to-table ceramic baking dish with nonstick cooking spray. Set aside.

2. Melt the margarine in a large pot over medium heat. Add the onions and sauté for 6–7 minutes, until wilted and beginning to turn golden. Add the spinach and sauté for 3 minutes longer, until most of the liquid has evaporated.

3. Add the flour to make a roux that will thicken the sauce. Stir until the flour is mixed into the other ingredients. Add the sour cream, mayonnaise, salt, and pepper. Stir to combine.

4. Add the broth, stirring until smooth. Bring to a simmer. The sauce will thicken slightly.

5. Ladle a layer of spinach sauce into the bottom of the prepared pan. Spread a layer of tightly overlapping parsnips rounds. Top with a layer of sauce. Repeat, alternating parsnips and spinach sauce. There should be a total of 3 layers of sauce and 2 layers of parsnips, with the sauce on the top.

6. Sprinkle the top with paprika. Bake, uncovered, for 1½ hours.

*Yield: 10-12 servings*

housewarming party

# housewarming party
## buffet format

## Menu

❧

**Wild Mushroom Velouté Soup**
page 67

❧

**Blackened Steak and Asparagus Salad**
page 86

❧

**Mashed Potato Bar**
page 216-217

❧

**Moroccan Short Ribs**
page 151

❧

**Pineapple Chicken Piccata**
page 136

❧

**Graham Cracker-Crusted Squash Pie**
page 226

❧

**Cauliflower Popcorn**
page 225

❧

**Apple Crunch Galette**
page 270

Whether it's your first home or a relocation, settling into a new place is always something to celebrate. Open your doors and invite your friends and family to share this milestone.

We set up our housewarming as a buffet with stations. A buffet is a feast for the eyes. Groupings of foods with varied flavors and colors are set out together. Elegant and effortless, it permits you to entertain without being a slave to the stove. Everything was done before the guests arrived, so that the buffet could be mostly set. Practically speaking, we needed the kitchen as one of our buffet spaces. The foods that needed to be hot were fully cooked and left in the oven set to a low warming temperature. The fragrance from that food filled the air and made everyone feel welcome.

Pineapple Chicken Piccata

The first step in setting up a buffet meal is to find a convenient place for the majority of the food, such as a table, sideboard, or in our case, a kitchen island. We set up smaller stations in other parts of the kitchen and around the house to keep people moving. One of these stations was for covered crocks of Wild Mushroom Velouté Soup, another for most of the side dishes, and yet another for drinks. The object of these stations is to a create an easy flow, to keep people in different parts of the house at different times. The dining room was the location for our Mashed Potato Bar, where we had beautiful martini glasses filled with two kinds of mashed potatoes, and even included a lower-carb look-alike option in our Whipped Root Vegetables.

Plates were placed with the main dishes; silverware and napkins were waiting on the dining table. Our guests walked around filling their plates and mingling, without waiting on line or being stuck in one area. This made for a lively party and gave people a chance to see different parts of the house.

At dessert time, to accompany our Apple Crunch Galette, we set out a coffee bar. We used two thermal carafes that can keep coffee hot for almost two hours — one for decaf, one for regular coffee. Our espresso machine was not only sleek-looking, but was also a very popular attraction. We set out shakers of cinnamon, cocoa, and nutmeg. We included sugar cubes and sugar substitutes and a bowl of parve whipped cream. We laid coffee beans into an oval platter and set in small jugs to hold plenty of spoons. Flavored syrups or liquors to add to the coffee go nicely as well.

As our guests left, and our new house was "warmed up," our parting gift to them was an address book with our new address preprinted into the page.

# berry-filled mini noodle kugels

2½ cups Rice Krispies cereal

4 tablespoons sugar

1 teaspoon cinnamon

3 tablespoons butter, cut into 12 pieces

4 large eggs

¾ cup sugar

1 (8-ounce) block cream cheese, not whipped, at room temperature for 20 minutes

1 cup milk

½ cup sour cream

6 ounces fine or medium egg noodles, cooked al denté, according to package directions, drained

strawberry preserves or seedless raspberry preserves

fresh blueberries, plus more for garnish

ground cinnamon

1. Heat oven to 350°F. Spray 1 (12-muffin) or 2 (6-muffin) large capacity muffin tray(s), or mini bunt pan tray with nonstick baking spray. This can also be done in mini loaf pans, yielding 10 mini kugels.

2. Place the Rice Krispies into a small bowl. Using a spoon or your fingertips, coarsely crush the cereal. Mix in the sugar and the cinnamon.

3. Place a piece of butter into each of the 12 muffin cups and place into the hot oven to melt, about 2 minutes.

4. Remove from oven and spoon the cereal mixture evenly into the bottom of each of the muffin cups.

5. In the bowl of a mixer, beat the eggs and sugar until light and fluffy. Beat in the cream cheese, milk, and sour cream. Stir in the prepared noodles.

6. Ladle the noodle batter evenly into the prepared muffin tins to fill half-full.

7. Add 1 teaspoon jelly and 3-4 fresh blueberries to the center of each muffin. Fill muffin cups full with remaining batter.

8. Sprinkle with cinnamon.

9. Bake for 45 minutes.

10. Allow to cool for 5 minutes. Remove from pan. Repeat as necessary with remaining batter. If you don't have enough to fill all the compartments, fill the empty ones with a little bit of water to prevent the empty cups from scorching.

11. The mini kugels can be served warm or at room temperature. Garnish with fresh bluberries.

*Yield: 10-14 mini-kugels, depending on shape*

# upscale sandwiches

*My husband and father-in-law worked together for many years. A few times a month their work would take them on long travel days that would culminate in a light dinner at my house. With my father-in-law supplying the bread, we often shared interesting sandwiches on those visits. These are some of our favorite combinations.*

Arrange thinly sliced Bosc or Anjou pears with brie and thick honey mustard (such as Honeycup brand) on Italian or French bread. Wrap in foil and warm for 10 minutes in 350°F oven.

Slice fresh hand-rolled mozzarella and arrange with oven roasted tomatoes (see box, page 101), roasted red peppers (see box, page 195), and pesto (see box, page 57) on Italian bread, French bread, or focaccia.

Arrange thinly sliced cucumber and watercress on a dark crusty raisin-walnut or pumpernickel bread that has been spread with whipped cream cheese.

Arrange grilled portobello mushrooms, fresh basil leaves, and thinly sliced tomato on a kaiser roll that has been spread with thick honey mustard.

# spinach calzones

*I pick up the dough fresh from my local pizza store, but you can make your own, or buy frozen. Just have it thawed and defrosted before beginning the recipe.*

1 (10-ounce) box frozen chopped spinach, thawed, squeezed dry

1¼ cups ricotta cheese

1 large egg

8 ounces shredded mozzarella

4 cloves fresh garlic, minced

½ teaspoon fine sea salt

½ teaspoon freshly ground black pepper

2 pounds pizza dough

2 tablespoons whole milk

2 cups jarred marinara sauce

1. Preheat oven to 425°F. Line two cookie sheets with foil or parchment paper.

2. In a medium bowl, mix the spinach, ricotta, egg, mozzarella, garlic, salt, and pepper.

3. With a rolling pin, roll the dough into a large square. Cut into 4 squares. Roll each square very thin into 10- by 10-inch squares. Cut each square on the diagonal to form 2 triangles. Place a large scoop of the filling to the left of center of each triangle. Fold the triangle in half to form a smaller triangle. Seal the edges by pulling and pressing the dough together. Transfer the calzones to the prepared cookie sheets. Cut 2 slits in the top of each calzone to allow the steam to escape. Brush the tops of each one with the milk. Bake until golden brown, about 15-18 minutes. Serve hot. Heat the marinara and serve with the calzones.

*Yield: 8 calzones*

# stuffed challah french toast

*I first demonstrated this recipe at Career Day in my daughter Jodi's nursery school class. It got a standing ovation from the little cuties and my phone rang all day from Moms wanting to know what I had served their kids.*

3 large strawberries, hulled, chopped

½ medium banana, peeled, chopped

7 (1-inch thick) slices challah

5 large eggs

¼ cup heavy cream

freshly ground black pepper

pinch of cinnamon

4-5 tablespoons butter

pancake or maple syrup

1. Mix the chopped strawberries and chopped bananas in a small bowl. Cut each slice of challah in half down the center. Into the exposed cut side of each slice, create a pocket by inserting a sharp knife into the center and working the knife in both directions. Make sure to just cut a pocket and not cut through to the top or through either end. Use a small spoon to stuff some of the strawberry-banana mixture into each slice. Don't overstuff.

2. In a medium or large bowl whisk the eggs, cream, pepper, and cinnamon. Dip each slice of stuffed challah into the egg mixture, soaking each side, and shaking off the excess.

3. Melt the butter in a large skillet set over medium heat. Add the stuffed challah and sauté, turning each piece once until golden on both sides, about 2-3 minutes per side. Serve two to a plate with pancake or maple syrup.

*Yield: 7 servings*

# smoothies

*These smoothies were taught to me by my daughter Kate, the smoothie queen. She wows her sisters and friends by using all different fruits, and switches her flavors and combinations throughout the year based on what fruits are fresh and in season. Try the recipe with blueberries, raspberries, peaches, pineapple, or any combination of these fruits.*

*These smoothies are quick, colorful, and delicious. They are a great focal point at a brunch or breakfast where you would make them with lowfat vanilla yogurt. They are also great as a dessert or snack, where you would make them with the vanilla ice-cream or frozen yogurt option. This makes the smoothies shakelike. If you need a non-dairy option, they are great with orange juice instead of the dairy ingredients.*

*When partially freezing the fruit, there is no need to cut up blueberries, raspberries, or any other small berry. They can go into the blender whole. If using frozen berries, partially defrost them.*

## Mango Smoothies:

1-2 ripe mango, peeled, pitted, cut into ½-inch dice (about 1½ cups)

1 ripe banana, sliced

1 cup lowfat vanilla yogurt, vanilla ice-cream, frozen yogurt, or orange juice

1-2 tablespoons sugar or honey (add lesser amount if fruit is very sweet)

1 cup ice cubes, allow to thaw for 10 minutes at room temperature

## Strawberry Smoothies:

1 pound strawberries, hulled, halved (about 1 quart)

1 ripe banana, sliced

1 cup lowfat vanilla yogurt, vanilla ice-cream, frozen yogurt, or orange juice

1-2 tablespoons sugar or honey (add lesser amount if fruit is very sweet)

1 cup ice cubes, allow to thaw for 10 minutes at room temperature

1. Place the fruits with the bananas on a baking tray and partially freeze them for 30 minutes. This will boost their flavor and add good texture to the smoothie. Place the partially frozen fruits of choice and banana into the blender. Add the yogurt, frozen yogurt, ice-cream, or orange juice. Add the sugar or honey. Place the ice cubes on the top. Blend until smooth. Stop to stir as needed.

2. For the two-tone option, make two different batches of smoothies, transferring the first batch to a pitcher or a container and rinsing out the blender in between. Using two measuring cups or teacups, scoop out some of each flavor. Slowly pour the smoothies at the same time into opposite sides of the glass.

*Yield: each batch makes 4-5 smoothies, the two-tone option makes 8-10*

# dutch apple pancake

*If your skillet is not ovenproof, you can prepare the apples in the butter, cinnamon, and brown sugar in a pan. Meanwhile, place 1 tablespoon butter into a 9-inch deep-dish pie plate and place into the hot oven. When the apples are tender, remove the pie plate from the oven, swirl the butter around it, and transfer the sautéed apples into the pie plate. Pour the batter into the pie plate and bake in the oven as directed.*

2 tablespoons butter

1 Granny Smith apple, peeled, cored, thinly sliced

½ teaspoon cinnamon

2 tablespoons dark brown sugar

2 large eggs

½ cup milk (2% or whole)

½ cup all-purpose flour

1 tablespoon sugar

¼ teaspoon pure vanilla extract

confectioner's sugar

maple or pancake syrup

1. Preheat oven to 400°F.

2. Heat the butter in a 10- or 11-inch ovenproof skillet over medium heat. Add the apple slices, cinnamon, and brown sugar. Cook, mixing occasionally, until the apple slices are tender, 5-6 minutes. Spread them out evenly in the pan.

3. While the apples are cooking, in a small bowl whisk the eggs, milk, flour, sugar, and vanilla until combined.

4. Pour over the apples. Immediately, while the pan is still hot, place into the hot oven.

5. Bake until pancake is puffed and golden, 20-25 minutes. Dust with confectioner's sugar and serve immediately with syrup.

*Yield: 4 servings*

# pumpkin praline cream cheese muffins

*A crunchy praline topping crowns this moist muffin. With its creamy surprise filling, get used to making these — they will be requested over and over.*

## Praline Topping:

⅓ cup light or dark brown sugar

2 tablespoons sour cream

⅔ cup chopped pecans

## Cream Cheese Filling:

1 (3-ounce) bar cream cheese (not whipped), softened at room temperature for 15 minutes

1 tablespoon sugar

1 tablespoon milk

## Muffins:

2 cups all-purpose flour

2 teaspoons baking powder

1 teaspoon ground cinnamon

½ teaspoon baking soda

¼ teaspoon fine sea salt

¼ teaspoon ground nutmeg

1 large egg

¾ cup buttermilk

¾ cup canned pumpkin purée (not pumpkin pie filling)

⅔ cup light or dark brown sugar

⅓ cup butter, melted

1. Preheat oven to 375°F. Grease 12 (2½-inch) muffin cups, or line them with paper baking cups. Set aside.

2. Prepare the topping: In a small bowl, combine the brown sugar, sour cream, and pecans. Stir with a spoon to combine. Set aside.

3. Prepare the cream cheese filling: In a small bowl, with a spoon, mix the cream cheese, sugar and milk. Set aside.

4. Prepare the muffins: In a medium bowl, stir together the flour, baking powder, cinnamon, baking soda, salt, and nutmeg. Make a well in the center of these dry ingredients and set aside.

5. In another bowl, whisk the egg, buttermilk, pumpkin, brown sugar, and melted butter.

6. Add the pumpkin mixture all at once to the flour mixture. Stir until just moistened and combined; the batter will be lumpy.

7. Fill the muffin cups ⅓ full. Place a rounded teaspoon of cream cheese filling on batter in each muffin cup. Top with remaining batter. Spread 2 teaspoons praline mixture on top of each muffin.

8. Bake 20-25 minutes or until golden brown. Cool for 5 minutes, serve warm or at room temperature.

*Yield: 12 muffins*

# popovers with strawberry and cinnamon honey butter Dairy

*Popovers are fun puffy breads that have a crisp brown crust, and a hollow but moist interior. They "pop over" the tops of their baking container, hence the name. The batter is simple and made with just a few ingredients that most people have on hand all the time. The key is in the tricks and techniques, so follow them and don't take shortcuts.*

*If you don't have a popover pan or Pyrex custard cups you can use a regular muffin tin, the popovers just won't rise as perfectly. If you have more muffin cups than batter, pour water halfway up the sides of any empty muffin cup. The steam the water creates will help the popovers rise. Popovers rise 3-4 inches so make sure your racks are spaced appropriately. Popovers do not freeze well.*

## Popovers:

2 large eggs, at room temperature

1 cup whole milk (not lowfat)

1 tablespoon melted butter or warmed olive oil

1 cup all-purpose flour

½ teaspoon fine sea salt

canola oil

popover pan or 6-ounce glass or Pyrex custard cups

1. In a large bowl, whisk the eggs, milk, and butter. In a small bowl mix the flour and salt. Add into the egg mixture, stirring with a spatula, just until the flour is incorporated; the batter will be lumpy, like pancake batter. Allow the batter to stand at room temperature for 30 minutes.

2. Meanwhile, pour ½ teaspoon canola oil into the bottom of each popover cup or ramekin. Place the pans into the oven. Preheat the oven with the pans to 450°F.

3. After the batter has stood for the 30 minutes and the oven is at 450°F, quickly and carefully remove the pans from the oven and close the oven door. Fill each cup ⅔ full of batter. Return the pans to the oven for 20 minutes. Without opening the door, reduce heat to 350°F and bake for 16-18 minutes longer, until puffed and golden.

4. Don't open the door during baking; the cool air rushing in will cause the popovers to collapse. Serve hot with flavored butters (see box on facing page).

*Yield: 6 popovers*

### Strawberry Butter:

6 tablespoons unsalted butter, at room temperature

¼ cup strawberry preserves or jelly

### Cinnamon Honey Butter:

6 tablespoons butter, at room temperature

3 tablespoons honey

½ teaspoon cinnamon

½ teaspoon pure vanilla extract

### Strawberry Butter:

Place the butter into the bowl of an electric mixer. Beat until light and fluffy. Add the strawberry preserves and beat 1 minute longer. Spoon or pipe into pretty small dishes, ramekins, or butter molds. Refrigerate until firm. Can be made 2-3 days ahead.

### Cinnamon Honey Butter:

Place the butter into the bowl of an electric mixer. Beat until light and fluffy. Add the honey, cinnamon, and vanilla and beat 1 minute longer. Spoon or pipe into pretty small dishes, ramekins, or butter molds. Refrigerate until firm. Can be made 2-3 days in advance.

# capellini frittata

6 ounces capellini or angel hair pasta

4 tablespoons olive oil, divided

1 tablespoon butter

1 scallion, thinly sliced

2 button mushrooms, sliced

1 large tomato, seeded, cut into ½-inch dice

2 tablespoons jarred roasted red peppers, chopped

4 cloves fresh garlic, minced

¼ teaspoon freshly ground black pepper

⅛ teaspoon fine sea salt

⅛ teaspoon dried oregano

¼ teaspoon dried basil

4 large eggs

1 cup grated Parmesan cheese

1. Preheat the broiler.

2. Cook the capellini until cooked al denté, according to package directions

3. Heat 2 tablespoons olive oil and butter in a medium skillet over medium heat. Add the scallion and mushrooms. Sauté for 3 minutes. Add the tomato, red peppers, garlic, pepper, salt, oregano, and basil. Sauté for 3 minutes longer. Remove from heat and set aside.

4. Beat the eggs in a medium bowl with the Parmesan cheese. Mix in the capellini, coating the pasta with the egg mixture. Add the vegetable mixture. Wipe out the pan.

5. Place remaining 2 tablespoons olive oil into the pan. Heat over medium heat. Pour the pasta/egg mixture evenly into the pan. Cook until it begins to set, about 3 minutes. Place into the oven and cook under the broiler for 2 minutes. With a thin metal spatula, loosen the edges and try to slip your spatula under as far as it can go to loosen the center as well. Hold a plate over the pan and invert to flip the frittata out of the pan. Cut into wedges.

*Yield: 4-6 servings*

# eggplant lasagna

*As a shortcut, feel free to use your favorite jarred sauce, but nothing tastes like homemade. There are some supermarkets that sell breaded eggplant as well; you can also substitute these. This dish freezes very well. Assemble all the parts and just don't bake it. Freeze it and then place it from the freezer into a preheated oven.*

nonstick cooking spray

1 (16-ounce) box lasagna
noodles

### Eggplant Layer:

1 medium eggplant

fine sea salt

2 large eggs, lightly beaten

1 cup unflavored breadcrumbs

olive oil

### Sauce Layer:

2 tablespoons olive oil,
plus more for frying

3 cloves fresh garlic, chopped

1 medium onion, finely
chopped

1 (28-ounce) can chopped
tomatoes, undrained

1 (28-ounce) can crushed
tomatoes

½ teaspoon freshly ground
black pepper

1 tablespoon dark brown sugar

½ teaspoon crushed red
pepper flakes

1 teaspoon dried oregano

### Cheese Layer:

2 cups ricotta cheese

8 ounces shredded Muenster
cheese

16 ounces shredded
mozzarella cheese

1. Lightly grease a 9- by 13-inch rectangular baking dish with nonstick cooking spray. Set aside.

2. Bring a pot of salted water to a boil. Cook the lasagna noodles until still slightly hard, a minute less than al denté. Drain and set aside.

3. Meanwhile prepare the eggplant: The first step is to salt the eggplant to draw out the bitterness from the seeds. Peel the eggplant. Slice into ⅓-inch slices. Place slices on a paper towel. Sprinkle with salt on both sides. Top with a second paper towel. Place a weight, such as a heavy can, on top and allow to sit for 20 minutes. Preheat oven to 350°F.

4. Meanwhile, prepare the sauce: Heat the 2 tablespoons olive oil in a large pot over medium heat. Add the garlic and onion. Sauté for 5-6 minutes, making sure not to brown the garlic; just cook until the onions are soft and fragrant. Add the chopped tomatoes and the crushed tomatoes. Season with the pepper, brown sugar, red pepper flakes, and oregano. Simmer on low for 20 minutes.

5. Heat about an inch of oil in a large skillet on medium heat. Place the beaten egg and breadcrumbs in two shallow bowls or plates side by side. Dip the eggplant slices in the egg, dredge in the breadcrumbs and place into the hot oil. Brown on both sides. Remove from pan and drain the eggplant on paper towels. Discard the oil.

6. In a medium bowl, combine the ricotta and Muenster cheese.

7. Assemble the lasagna: Ladle 1 cup of sauce into the bottom of the prepared pan. Top with a layer of lasagna noodles. Add a single layer of the eggplant. Spread the ricotta mixture over the eggplant. Add a layer of lasagna noodles. Pour an even layer of sauce over the noodles and sprinkle with 8 ounces of mozzarella cheese. Top with a final layer of lasagna noodles. Cover with remaining sauce, allowing it to drip down the sides. Top with remaining mozzarella. You may have extra noodles.

8. Cover with foil and bake for 1 hour. Remove foil and bake, uncovered, for 10 minutes, until cheese is all melted.

*Yield: 12 servings*

# gemelli with broccoli agli olio

*Agli olio is a traditional Italian pasta sauce that simply calls for garlic and olive oil.*

1 pound gemelli or spaghetti pasta

½ cup best-quality extra-virgin olive oil

8 cloves fresh garlic, peeled, thinly sliced

2 teaspoons fresh parsley

1 cup broccoli florets, cut into ½ inch pieces, lightly steamed

¼ teaspoon freshly ground black pepper

2-3 tablespoons Italian breadcrumbs, or grated Parmesan

1. Bring a large pot of salted water to a boil. Add the pasta and cook until al denté, according to package directions.

2. Meanwhile, heat the oil in a large skillet over medium heat. Add the garlic and parsley.

3. Sauté for 5 minutes, until the garlic turns golden. Mix in the pasta and broccoli, tossing to coat. Season with pepper and salt to taste. Serve with a sprinkle of breadcrumbs or Parmesan.

*Yield: 4-6 servings*

## Soup/Pasta Pot with Strainer Insert:

The strainer insert sits in the pot while the soup or pasta cooks. All you do is lift the insert and you are left with crystal clear chicken soup or drained pasta.

# ravioli with four-cheese sauce

2 tablespoons extra-virgin olive oil

3 cloves fresh garlic, minced

1 teaspoon dried minced onion

1/8 teaspoon crushed red pepper flakes

1/4 teaspoon onion powder

1 teaspoon dried oregano

1 teaspoon sugar

1/4 teaspoon fine sea salt

1 (28-ounce) can crushed tomatoes

1/4 cup grated Parmesan or Romano cheese

3/4 cup shredded mozzarella cheese

1/2 cup shredded cheddar cheese

3 tablespoons ricotta cheese

1 pound cheese ravioli or tortellini, cooked according to package directions

1. Heat the olive oil in a medium pot over medium-low heat. Add the garlic, minced onion, red pepper, onion powder, oregano, sugar, and salt. Cook for 3-4 minutes, until fragrant. Add the crushed tomatoes. Simmer for 10 minutes.

2. Add the Parmesan, mozzarella, cheddar, and ricotta cheeses. Cook until melted and thick.

3. Serve hot over ravioli or tortellini.

*Yield: 6 servings*

---

### Pasta Tips:

To keep pasta from sticking together, stir during the first two minutes of cooking.

Don't add oil to the water; this will make the pasta oily and sauce won't cling to it.

Generously salt the pasta water with 1-2 tablespoons for a large pot of water.

Make sure your pasta and sauce are both hot when tossing together. Do not rinse the pasta; this cools off the pasta and washes away any starch residue that helps the sauce thicken and stick to it.

# spinach linguine with walnut cream sauce

Dairy

1 pound spinach linguine
or spinach fettuccine

2 cups walnut halves

1 cup heavy cream

½ cup fresh baby spinach
leaves, minced

1 clove fresh garlic, minced

fine sea salt

freshly ground black pepper

¼ cup grated Parmesan

fresh parsley, chopped,
for garnish

1. Preheat oven to 350°F.

2. Cook pasta; when ready, drain and set aside.

3. While pasta is cooking, spread the walnuts on a parchment-lined baking sheet; toast for 8-10 minutes until fragrant. Remove from oven.

4. Place 1 cup of the walnut halves into the bowl of a food processor fitted with a metal blade and process until finely chopped but not ground. Transfer to a large pot. Add the cream, spinach, and garlic. Place over low heat and bring to a simmer. Add the cooked pasta and toss to coat. Mix in the remaining cup of walnuts, reserving a few for garnish. Season with salt and pepper.

5. Remove to a platter or bowl. Sprinkle with the Parmesan and chopped parsley. Garnish with reserved walnut halves.

*Yield: 6 servings*

# capellini and peas in pink sauce

Dairy

*Capellini or angel hair pasta cooks very quickly, usually in 2-3 minutes. If left out, it gets sticky. So, put your water up to boil when you start preparing the sauce but don't drop your pasta in until your sauce is simmering.*

4 tablespoons butter

1 small onion, minced

2 cloves fresh garlic, chopped

½ teaspoon crushed red
pepper flakes

1 teaspoon dried basil

1 (28-ounce) can crushed
tomatoes

½ cup frozen green peas

1 cup heavy whipping cream

fine sea salt

freshly ground black pepper

water as needed

16 ounces capellini pasta

1. Melt the butter in a large pot over medium heat. Add the onion and sauté until soft but not brown, about 4-5 minutes. Add the garlic, crushed red pepper, and basil. Sauté 3 minutes, until fragrant. Add the crushed tomatoes. Bring to a simmer and cook for 3-4 minutes. Reduce heat to low and add the peas and cream. Cook for 3-4 minutes. Season generously with salt and pepper.

2. Meanwhile, fill a large pot with salted water and bring to a boil. When sauce is ready, cook your pasta. Drain.

3. Toss the drained capellini or angel hair, coating with the sauce. Remove to a platter or large bowl. Serve immediately.

*Yield: 6-8 servings*

# shells with romesco sauce

Parve

*The nice thing about this dish is that it contains no butter or cream. The taste is complex and wonderful over any shape pasta and can be made in advance; just reheat before serving.*

16 ounces medium pasta shells, cooked al denté, according to package directions

3 tablespoons olive oil, divided

2 cloves fresh garlic, divided

1 slice white bread

¼ cup blanched almonds

1 (14.5-ounce) can diced tomatoes, undrained

1 teaspoon paprika

½ teaspoon crushed red pepper flakes

3 red bell peppers, roasted and seeded (see box, p. 195), can use 24-ounce jarred roasted red peppers, not in vinegar, drained

1 tablespoon balsamic vinegar

fine sea salt

freshly ground black pepper

fresh parsley, for garnish

1. Heat 1 tablespoon olive oil in a medium skillet over medium heat. Mince one garlic clove and add to the pan. Sauté for 1 minute. Add the slice of bread and fry, turning so that both sides become golden brown. Transfer the bread to the bowl of a food processor fitted with metal blade. Add remaining garlic clove, almonds, tomatoes with their liquid, paprika, red pepper flakes, and roasted red peppers. Pulse to purée.

2. Pour this puréed mixture into a medium pot. Add the vinegar and remaining 2 tablespoons olive oil. Stir to combine and bring to a simmer over medium heat for 10 minutes. Season with salt and pepper to taste.

3. Toss with pasta. Garnish with parsley leaves.

*Yield: 6-8 servings*

# summer celebration
## outdoor entertaining

The sun is shining. It could be a graduation, block party, or a family get-together before relatives scatter for the season. But when the weather is perfect, is there really an occasion necessary? The warmth beckons us outdoors to enjoy a feast for the senses!

At our outdoor celebration, small bowls of Edamame with Dipping Sauce awaited our guests. It gave them something to nibble on while they grabbed a drink. Mason Ball jars were filled with ice-water. A large galvanized tub loaded with a variety of micro-brewed beers was placed in a corner of the deck. These small-batch-brewed specialty beers are great conversation starters. They have fun labels and quirky names, and come in so many varieties. We even tossed in some bottles of root beer for the children.

The tabletop was a riot of color and texture, with an outdoor theme. Bird cages, grapevine balls, nests with bird's eggs, and faux butterflies, all easily available at craft stores, adorned the table. The napkins were bandanas in shades of blue and were set into a whimsical duck that is really a CD holder. The silverware was haphazardly tossed into jars. The dishes were a simple white with blue band, but could have easily been pretty disposable paper.

The flowers complemented our color scheme: white stock, blue delphinium, love-in-a-mist, bachelor's buttons, and dahlias. Some were picked right out of our garden. Pots of flowers on the deck brought even more color to the scene.

Summertime is the time to savor nature's produce. We served fresh corn, grilled to perfection, and a healthy Mexican Turkey and Portobello Salad set up on a tall footed stand. Both were bursting with color and flavor.

The casual setting called for a casual atmosphere. Most of the food was prepared in advance and the last-minute cooking was limited primarily to the main course. The Tri-Colored Pasta Salad and the Hasselback Potatoes beautifully complemented the grilled food. To allow the guests to see all their choices, the food was set out on different heights in various baskets and platters.

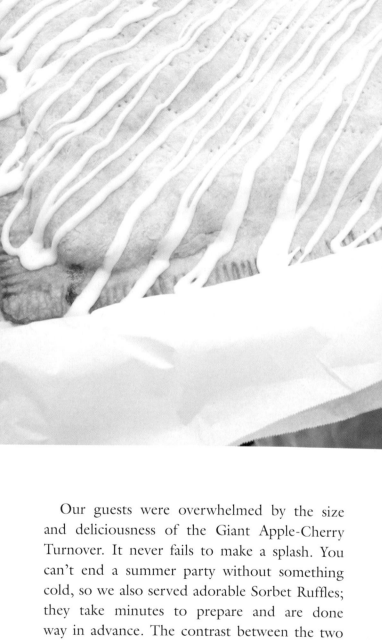

Our guests were overwhelmed by the size and deliciousness of the Giant Apple-Cherry Turnover. It never fails to make a splash. You can't end a summer party without something cold, so we also served adorable Sorbet Ruffles; they take minutes to prepare and are done way in advance. The contrast between the two desserts left something for everyone.

# chocolate mint dalmatian cookies

Dairy or Parve

*Warn the neighborhood Girl Scouts, there's a new thin mint cookie in town! The dotted dalmatian effect is just precious. If you are making the cookies parve and can't find the parve white chips, you can substitute regular chocolate chips, but you will lose the polka-dotted look.*

1½ cups all-purpose flour

¾ cup unsweetened Dutch processed cocoa powder

¼ teaspoon fine sea salt

¾ cup (1½ sticks) butter or margarine, room temperature

1 cup sugar

¾ teaspoon peppermint extract

½ teaspoon pure vanilla extract

1 large egg

½ cup white chocolate chips

1. In a medium bowl, whisk the flour, cocoa powder and salt. Set aside.

2. In the bowl of a stand mixer at medium speed, cream the butter or margarine, and sugar until light and fluffy. Beat in the peppermint extract, vanilla extract, and the egg. Add the dry ingredients in three additions and beat until just blended, scraping down the sides with a spatula as needed. The dough will be a little sticky.

3. Divide the dough into two. Place each piece on a sheet of parchment paper or plastic wrap. Using the parchment or plastic as an aid, roll each piece into a 2-inch diameter log, about 9 inches long. Chill for 2 hours in the freezer or make a day in advance and keep in the refrigerator.

4. Preheat oven to 350°F. Line two jelly-roll pans or cookie sheets with parchment paper. Unwrap the cookie dough. Try to roll the logs to make them as round as possible, because when you slice the cookies, the shape will be what it is — the cookies don't spread or rise when baked.

5. Cut into ¼-inch slices. If necessary, pat around the edges to smooth them and make them perfectly round. Place the sliced cookies onto the prepared pans. Stick 4-5 white chocolate chips into each cookie, upside-down, and press into the dough to make the polka dots. Bake the cookies for 12-14 minutes, until dry to the touch. Remove to a rack and cool completely.

6. Cookies an be made 4-5 days ahead and kept in an airtight container.

*Yield: 36-40 cookies*

# mrs. friedler's jelly strips

*I grew up in Oceanside, New York, among a very tight-knit group of families. My mother and her friends were all so close that not only did they swap their own best recipes, but they shared cherished family recipes as well. Many of these became enmeshed in my family's holidays. These cookies came from our neighbor Hannah Fischberger's mother, "Ma" Friedler. They can always be found in my own mother's house. I love them straight from the freezer.*

⅔ cup sugar

¾ cup pure vegetable shortening, such as Crisco

1 large egg

2 teaspoons pure vanilla extract

2 cups all-purpose flour

1 teaspoon baking powder

seedless raspberry preserves or apricot preserves

1. Preheat oven to 325°F.

2. Cover two cookie sheets with parchment paper. Set aside.

3. In the bowl of a mixer at medium speed, cream the sugar, shortening, and egg. Add the vanilla. Sprinkle in the flour and baking powder. Mix until dough forms.

4. Divide the dough into four equal pieces. Place two rolls on each of the prepared sheets, leaving room between them for spreading. With a rolling pin, roll each piece into a flattened log shape, 2 inches wide and ¼-inch thick. With the back of a wooden spoon or your index finger, form a shallow indentation down the length of each log. Spoon preserves into this indentation; don't use too much or the weight of the preserves will make the cookies break when you lift them to eat.

5. Bake the logs, switching the pans halfway through for even browning. Bake until golden, 40-45 minutes. Slice into 1-inch-wide strips while warm.

*Yield: 40 cookies*

---

**Parchment Paper:**

Parchment paper is a baker's best friend. It turns every pan into a nonstick pan and makes cleanup a snap. It can withstand temperatures up to 425°F without burning. It also cuts preparation time. While one batch of cookies is in the oven, load up the next on a second sheet of parchment. Don't re-use parchment; it will burn.

# plum crumble cake

Parve

*This recipe was the third ArtScroll recipe contest winner. It was submitted by Leah Goldman of Queens, NY. Whenever someone does something nice for her, she makes them this cake. She loves making it at the end of August when the small purple/black plums are at their best. In the summer, when the plums are in season, by all means use the fresh. They are larger than the canned, so the cake will be plummier than when made with the canned, which yield a cakier result. I love it both ways.*

10 tablespoons unsalted margarine, at room temperature for 15 minutes

⅔ cup sugar

4 large egg yolks

1½ teaspoons pure vanilla extract

1¼ cups all-purpose flour

1 teaspoon baking powder

1 (15-ounce) can purple plums, drained well, or 10 fresh purple plums, halved, pits discarded

## Crumbs:

8 tablespoons unsalted margarine

⅔ cup light or dark brown sugar

1 cup all-purpose flour

confectioner's sugar

1. Preheat oven to 350°F. Spray a 10-inch springform or 10-inch round baking pan with nonstick cooking spray. If using a round cake pan with sides that don't release, cut out a circle of parchment paper and line the bottom with it. Set aside.

2. In the bowl of a stand mixer, at medium-high speed, beat the margarine and sugar until fluffy and light. Add the yolks one at a time, beating after each addition. Add the vanilla and beat until smooth.

3. Place the flour and baking powder into a small bowl. Mix with a fork. Stir into the cake batter. Beat to just combine. Spread the batter evenly into the prepared pan. Starting at the center, arrange the plums, in concentric circles, cut-side-down, on the batter, packed closely together.

4. Prepare the crumbs: In the bowl of a mixer, at medium-high speed, beat the margarine and brown sugar until soft and light. Stir in the flour and, with your fingers or a fork, rub the mixture into coarse crumbs. Sprinkle evenly over the cake to cover the plums and batter.

5. Bake for 45 minutes until center is firm and the crumbs are a deep golden color. Cool in pan.

6. Release the sides of the springform pan. Dust top of the cake with confectioner's sugar.

*Yield: 10-12 servings*

# chocolate-dipped almond horns

*I love almond horn cookies. While they are a staple of bakeries and caterers, it took me a long while to find and perfect a homemade version of the classic treat. Bakery box and string not included.*

16 ounces almond paste, at room temperature

¾ cup sifted confectioner's sugar

¾ cup granulated sugar

¼ teaspoon fine sea salt

4 large egg whites, at room temperature

½ teaspoon almond extract

1 cup sliced almonds

¼ cup (½ stick) margarine

3 ounces semi-sweet chocolate

1. In the bowl of a mixer, combine the almond paste with the confectioner's sugar and granulated sugar. Mix on low speed for 6-8 minutes.

2. Add the salt, egg whites, and almond extract. Continue to mix for 30 seconds. The batter will be gooey. Freeze for 2 hours.

3. Preheat oven to 300°F.

4. Cover cookie sheets with parchment paper.

5. Fill a container with cold water.

6. Place the sliced almonds on a plate.

7. Remove the dough from the freezer and roll into 1½-inch balls. Wet your hands with the cold water if the dough starts sticking. Roll the balls into the sliced almonds. Shape into crescent shapes. Place 2 inches apart on prepared cookie sheets. Re-freeze dough if it becomes too soft to handle.

8. Bake 35 minutes or until light brown on bottom. Do not overbake; the centers should be chewy.

9. Remove from oven and cool.

10. Prepare the glaze: In a small saucepan over low heat, melt the margarine and chocolate. Stir to combine.

11. When cookies are cool enough to handle, dip both ends of each cookie into the glaze and place on sheet of waxed or parchment paper. Let stand until chocolate is set, about 1 hour.

*Yield: 24 cookies*

# chocolate berry tart

*This recipe is a variation of a wonderful tart that was sort of sent to me by Arline Heimlich, a woman I don't know. I found it at the very end of a long e-mail chain on a subject matter totally unrelated to food. I don't know what made me read all the way to the bottom, but I came to a comment that said, "Girls, here is the recipe for those tarts we were devouring." That was all I needed to read. I whipped up a batch and loved the results. By tracing back through the e-mail recipient list I found someone who put me in touch with Arline, who was happy to share the recipe.*

*You can freeze these tarts before adding the berry garnish. You can also make them in miniature tart pans, as pictured below.*

3 cups pecan halves

⅔ cup light brown sugar

½ teaspoon ground cinnamon

6 tablespoons unsalted butter or margarine, melted

10 ounces semi-sweet or bittersweet chocolate

2 cups heavy or whipping cream; if using parve, I like Rich's whipped topping

2 pints raspberries, blueberries, or sliced strawberries

½ cup seedless red raspberry, blueberry, or seedless strawberry preserves

1. Preheat oven to 325°F.

2. Cut out a 10-inch circle of parchment paper and place it into a 10-inch tart pan with removable bottom or into 8 (4-inch) mini tart pans with removable bottoms. Set aside.

3. Place the pecans on a parchment-lined baking sheet. Toast the pecans for 10 minutes, until fragrant. Check toward the end to make sure they are not burning; shake the pan occasionally.

4. Remove the pecans from the oven and transfer them to the bowl of a food processor fitted with a metal blade. Add the brown sugar and cinnamon. Process until finely ground. Add the melted butter or margarine and process until moist clumps form.

5. Press the dough into the bottom and up the sides of the prepared pan or pans. You may need to let it cool for a few minutes until it can be touched.

6. Bake until the crust is golden brown and firm to the touch, 28-30 minutes. Remove from oven and cool completely.

7. Chop the chocolate into small pieces. Place into a medium bowl.

8. Bring the cream to a simmer in a medium-sized heavy saucepan over low heat. Pour the hot cream over the chocolate. Gently stir until smooth. Pour mixture into crust and chill until set, about 1 hour. This can be made up to 2 days in advance.

9. Before serving, arrange the berries of your choice over the top of the tart in overlapping concentric circles.

10. Place the jam into a small heavy saucepan over low heat until melted. Brush melted jam over the berries.

*Yield: 10 servings*

# apple crunch galette

*To tell you the truth, I am awful at rolling two-crusted pie dough. I know all the techniques in my head but somehow they don't transfer well to my rolling pin. Necessity being the mother of invention, I bring you the galette, the free form, no top crust, no lattice work needed, yummy, flaky, crunchy, easiest apple pie you will ever make.*

## Crust:

2½ cups all-purpose flour

1¼ teaspoons fine sea salt

2 tablespoons sugar

8 tablespoons unsalted butter or margarine, at room temperature, cut into 7 pieces

8 tablespoons pure vegetable shortening, cut into 7 pieces

4-4½ tablespoons ice water

## Crunch:

¾ cup all-purpose flour

¾ cup dark brown sugar

½ cup old-fashioned oats (not quick cooking or 1-minute type)

6 tablespoons butter or margarine, melted

## Apple Filling:

3 McIntosh or Braeburn apples

2 Granny Smith apples

½ cup sugar

3 tablespoons all-purpose flour

1 teaspoon cinnamon

⅛ teaspoon fine sea salt

3 tablespoons apricot preserves

1 egg yolk, beaten with 1 teaspoon water

1. In the bowl of a stand mixer fitted with a dough or batter hook, or in the bowl of a food processor fitted with a metal blade, mix the flour, salt, and sugar. Cut the butter or margarine and shortening into the flour and mix until mixture resembles baby peas. Sprinkle the ice water over the dough, 1 tablespoon at a time, and blend in with the mixer or with a fork. Repeat until the dough is moist enough to come together. Gather the dough and knead just to form into a ball. Flatten the ball slightly and shape into a disc. Wrap in parchment or plastic wrap and chill for 30 minutes in the refrigerator.

2. Prepare the crunch topping: In a medium bowl, combine the flour, brown sugar, oats, and melted butter or margarine. Stir to combine. Set aside.

3. Prepare the apple filling: Peel, seed, and slice the apples. In a large bowl, combine the sugar, flour, cinnamon, and salt. Add the apple slices and toss to coat.

4. Preheat oven to 375°F.

5. Remove dough from refrigerator. On a lightly floured piece of parchment paper, roll the dough into a large (14-15 inch) circle. Leaving a 3-4-inch border, brush the apricot preserves over the center of the dough. Place ¾ of the crunchy oat mixture over the preserves, still leaving the border of dough uncovered. Starting at the outer edge of the preserves, and working your way toward the center, lay the apple slices in concentric circles, going around and adding layers until all the apples are used. Sprinkle remaining crunch topping over the apples. Using the parchment to help, fold the dough border over the apples, turning the galette as needed. The dough will cover 2-3 inches of the filling. Carefully peel back parchment and slide the parchment with the galette on to a rimless baking sheet. Brush the exposed dough with the beaten egg yolk.

6. Bake for 25 minutes. Remove from oven and carefully cover the dough with foil to prevent burning. Return to oven and bake 30 minutes longer. The galette is great served warm or at room temperature with a scoop of ice-cream or caramel flavored ice-cream topping.

*Yield: 10-12 servings*

# chocolate peanut butter diamonds

*If you like those famous peanut butter cups, you will love this grown-up version. Cut them small — they are very rich.*

2 cup (4 sticks) butter or margarine, divided

4 cups confectioner's sugar

1 (18-ounce) jar reduced-fat creamy peanut butter

1½ cups graham cracker crumbs

6 ounces chocolate chips (about 1¼ cups)

1. Line a jelly-roll pan with parchment paper. Set aside.

2. In a medium saucepan over low heat, melt 1 cup of butter or margarine. Remove from heat and add the sugar, peanut butter, and graham cracker crumbs. Stir to combine.

3. Spread into prepared pan. Place a piece of waxed paper or parchment paper over the peanut butter and use a kid-sized rolling pin or your palm to pat evenly into the pan.

4. In a small saucepan over low heat, melt remaining 1 cup butter or margarine and chocolate chips. Stir to combine. Pour over the peanut butter layer. Tilt the pan to spread the chocolate into a thin layer that evenly coats the peanut butter. Try not to manipulate the chocolate too much. Refrigerate ½ hour.

5. Cut into diamond shapes. If your jelly-roll pan sides are in the way, use the parchment paper to slide the whole cake out of the pan and onto a flat surface before cutting.

6. Hold the long side of the cake in front of you, and use a warm knife to make horizontal cut lines every 1-inch. Starting at the bottom left corner, make diagonal cuts every 1½ inches to form diamond shapes.

*Yield: 36-40 diamonds*

## Baking Pans:

If the pan has 4 sides with rims, it is called a jelly-roll pan, half-sheet pan or full sheet pan, depending on its size. If it has at least 1 rimless side it is a cookie sheet or a baking sheet.

Buy the largest sheet that will fit in your oven, to put a dent in baking time.

Heavy-duty pans are the best; they heat quickly and evenly. Stay away from black metal pans — they burn dough quickly.

# melon granitas

*The sugar water that you make for this recipe is really a simple syrup. It is wonderful to flavor teas or as the base for lemonade. The ratio is always 2:1, so feel free to make a larger batch than specified below and store the remainder in your refrigerator. Serve granitas in clear glasses so you can see the beautiful glittering ice crystals.*

*You can also make espresso granitas by following the same procedure and substituting 3 cups cooled espresso or coffee for the watermelon juice and garnishing with a dollop of whipped cream.*

1 cup sugar

½ cup water

3-4 pounds ripe seedless watermelon, honeydew, or cantaloupe

½ bunch mint leaves, stems discarded

fresh mint leaves, for garnish

1. Place the sugar and water into a small pot. Bring to a boil and cook for 2 minutes. Remove from heat and cool completely to room temperature.

2. Remove the rind from the watermelon or other melon and discard. Chop the flesh into 1½-inch chunks. Purée the melon in a blender, in batches if necessary, until smooth. Strain through a mesh sieve into a large bowl and discard the pulp. You should have 4 cups melon juice. Add ⅓ cup of the prepared sugar water to the melon juice. You will have extra sugar water for another use.

3. Pour the mixture into a large, shallow, non-reactive pan, such as glass or stainless steel; aluminum will react with the fruit acids and leave a metallic taste in the granita. The larger and shallower the pan, the larger the surface area will be and the granita will freeze more quickly. Just make sure it fits comfortably in your freezer so the mixture doesn't spill. Cover with plastic wrap. Place into the freezer. Stir and scrape with a fork every 30 minutes. Be sure to scrape ice crystals off the sides and into the middle of the pan, until too frozen to stir, between 3-4 hours.

4. Put mint and ¼ cup of the remaining sugar water into blender and purée until smooth.

5. When mixture is frozen solid, scrape with the tines of a fork, pulling the mixture in rows toward you to make the mixture fluffy, with large ice crystals. If too frozen to scrape, leave at room temperature for 10 minutes. Place into serving glasses. Garnish the granitas with a drizzle of the mint syrup and a fresh mint leaf.

*Yield: 10-12 servings*

# sorbet ruffles

*No time too bake? Too hot to be in your kitchen? Here's the perfect answer. A gorgeous little layered ruffle of sorbet and ice-cream. A perfect light end to a summer meal. My favorite parve sorbet is Sharon's Sorbet, as it is so creamy, but any brand will do.*

*One of my favorite food finds was a gift from Barbara Strashun. She was my wonderful tour guide when I did a cooking show at the Viking Culinary Arts Center for her school in St. Louis. On our way to the airport, we detoured to a food warehouse for this goodie — squeeze bottles of incredible parve dessert sauces in chocolate, vanilla, kiwi, mango, and raspberry. See the resource guide, page 315, for buying information. If you don't have these, parve chocolate syrup such as Bosco works fine too.*

1 pint raspberry sorbet

1 pint vanilla ice cream,
can be parve

1 pint mango, passion fruit,
or lemon sorbet

16 (2½-inch) pleated paper
baking cups (muffin size)

dessert sauces (see note above)
or chocolate syrup, such as Bosco

16 red or black raspberries

1. Let the sorbets and the ice cream sit at room temperature for 15 minutes to soften. Transfer the sorbets and ice cream to bowls to better stir them and make them spreadable.

2. Place the muffin cups into metal muffin tins. If you don't have muffin tins, create a double thickness of the paper muffin cups and place them into a metal baking pan so that they support each other.

3. Spread an even layer of raspberry sorbet into the bottom third of each cup. Place into the freezer for 15 minutes. Remove from freezer and spread dollops of vanilla ice-cream to evenly cover the raspberry layer and come up to the second third of the cup. Return to the freezer for 15 minutes. Repeat procedure with the mango sorbet. Cover the pan with plastic wrap. Freeze overnight. Can be made 4 days ahead; keep frozen.

4. When ready to serve, invert each sorbet cup onto a dessert plate. Remove muffin cup. Decorate plate with desired sauce. Top each with a fresh raspberry.

*Yield: 16 servings*

# marbled pistachio chocolate cake

3 cups all-purpose flour

2 cups sugar

1 tablespoon baking powder

½ teaspoon coarse sea salt or kosher salt

1 (3.4-ounce) box pistachio pudding mix

1 cup vegetable oil

1 cup orange juice

1 teaspoon vanilla extract

4 large eggs

chocolate syrup, such as Bosco

## Glaze:

1½ cups confectioner's sugar

4 tablespoons orange juice

¼ cup raw (not roasted or salted) pistachio nuts, chopped

1. Preheat oven to 350°F. Grease and flour a bundt pan or 10-inch tube pan.

2. Combine flour, sugar, baking powder, salt, and pudding mix. Stir until blended

3. Add oil, orange juice, vanilla, and eggs. Beat at medium speed with an electric mixer until well blended, scraping down sides of the bowl.

4. Pour ½ the mixture into the prepared pan. Add a few squeezes of chocolate syrup into the remaining batter. Mix until it is a nice chocolate color. Pour it into the pan. Using the tip of a knife, make swirls to marbleize the green and brown batters.

5. Bake for 1 hour. Let cool for 10 minutes. Remove from pan and cool completely.

6. Prepare the glaze: Place the confectioner's sugar into a small bowl. Add the orange juice and mix with a spoon until it becomes a thick white glaze.

7. Drizzle over the top of the cake. Toss the chopped pistachios over the top of the cake and into the glaze.

*Yield: 10 servings*

## Chocolate Lattice:

An impressive base for any dessert, from a simple slice of cake to a scoop of whipped cream and berries, is a chocolate lattice. Melt chocolate in a bowl set over a pot of simmering water, stirring every 20 seconds to prevent burning. Let cool. Place in a heavy-duty ziplock bag. Snip the tip off a corner of the bag. Pipe the chocolate in a freeform lattice pattern, zigzagging the chocolate in thin streams crisscrossing over itself, onto a piece of waxed paper. Place into the refrigerator to set. Remove and use as desired.

# homemade milano sandwich cookies

1 cup (2 sticks) butter
or margarine, at room
temperature

¾ cup light brown sugar

2 teaspoons pure vanilla extract

2 cups all-purpose flour

## Filling:

7 ounces good-quality
semi-sweet chocolate,
broken into small pieces

2 tablespoons butter or
margarine

1. Preheat oven to 325°F. Line 2 cookie sheets with parchment paper. Set aside.

2. In the bowl of an electric mixer, cream the butter or margarine and sugar. Add the vanilla and flour, mixing until smooth.

3. Using a teaspoon measure, remove a level teaspoon of dough. Roll between your palms into a log. Place the dough log on the inside of your middle finger of the hand that is not your strong hand (I am right-handed, so for me, this is my left hand). Your middle finger serves as a guide. Using your thumb and middle finger of your other hand, (for me this would be my right hand) shape the dough into a log shape that extends from the tip of your finger to the line of your knuckle. This will ensure that all of the cookies are of uniform size and shape.

4. Place the formed cookies on the prepared cookie sheets, leaving about 1 inch for spreading.

5. Bake for 17-18 minutes, or until golden brown. Remove from the sheet to cool.

6. Prepare the filling: Place the chocolate and butter or margarine into a microwave-safe dish, and microwave at 70% for 1 minute. Stir until smooth and completely melted.

7. Spread about ½ teaspoon chocolate on the flat side of one cookie. Top with another and push the cookies slightly askew, so the chocolate shows between the cookies.

*Yields: 30-36 cookies*

# fresh fruit lollipops

*Your guests will love and appreciate this beautiful and lowfat dessert option. When presented in such a pretty way, your guests won't feel that they are sacrificing if they only go for the fruit. This recipe is more of a concept than a recipe. Use whatever fruits you have on hand that are just ripe. If your fruit is overripe you will have a hard time threading it. Be creative with your shapes. There are thousands of cookie cutters out there in all shapes and sizes, so the only limit is your imagination. If you want to display them upright, as pictured on page 112 in a lollipop stand, you will need wooden lollipop sticks; the standard white paper ones collapse from the wetness and weight after a short while. They are fine, however, and look very cute if you want to lay the lollipops out on a platter.*

blueberries

raspberries

green and red grapes

honeydew, peeled, cut into ¾-inch thick slices

cantaloupe, peeled, cut into ¾-inch thick slices

watermelon, peeled, cut into ¾-inch slices

kiwi, sliced into ¾-inch slices

lollipop sticks (see resource guide, p. 318)

medium round cookie cutters

miniature assorted cookie cutters

1. Thread the skewers with blueberries, raspberries, or grapes, or alternate any two or three of these, leaving the top 4 inches bare.

2. Using the medium round cookie cutter, cut out the desired shape from any of the honeydew, cantaloupe, or watermelon slices. Using the mini cookie cutters, cut a hole in the center of each shape. Using the same mini cookie cutter, cut that shape from a different melon or a kiwi. Set that shape into the hole in the outer circle. Thread the lollipop stick or skewer through both, making sure it goes through both fruits and back into the top of the first fruit for stability.

3. Continue until all of the fruit is used.

*Yield: depends on amount of fruit used*

# peanut brittle

*This recipe was inspired by a longtime favorite of my Aunt Malva. It gives Mr. Peanut a run for his money.*

1 cup sugar

1 cup water

½ cup light corn syrup

⅛ teaspoon fine sea salt

2 tablespoons butter or margarine, plus extra for greasing the pot

1 teaspoon baking soda

1 cup shelled raw peanuts

1. Place a jelly-roll pan into the oven and set the oven to 350°F. Heating the pan will help the brittle spread when it is poured into the pan.

2. Using butter or margarine, grease the sides of a large heavy pot or saucepan. Place the sugar, water, corn syrup, salt, and 2 tablespoons margarine into the pan. Cook over medium-low heat, stirring constantly, until mixture starts to boil. Allow it to boil until the color turns a light golden amber color, about 25-30 minutes, until a candy thermometer reads 280°F. Heat can vary so the time is less important than the temperature; make sure to refer to the thermometer. You can brush down the sides of the pan with a wet pastry brush as necessary. Do not overcook or the sugar will burn. Don't stir too much or too vigorously or the sugar will stick to the sides of the pot.

3. Remove the hot pan from the oven. Lay a sheet of parchment paper into the jelly-roll pan.

4. Remove the sugar mixture from heat. Stir in the baking soda. The mixture may bubble up the side of the pot, so be careful. Add the peanuts. Mix well. Working quickly, drizzle the mixture evenly and thinly into prepared pan. It may not fill the whole pan. Spread with the back of an oiled metal spoon or spatula. Allow the peanut brittle to cool and harden for 20 minutes. Break into shards and pieces. Store in an airtight container to keep it crisp and crunchy. Keep it out of humidity.

5. Any caramel remaining on the spoon, brush, or pot will easily dissolve if you run hot water over it.

*Yield: 1 pound*

# fudge-covered brownie cheesecake

**Brownie Layer:**

4 ounces good-quality semi-sweet or bittersweet chocolate, chopped

2 ounces unsweetened chocolate, chopped

½ cup (1 stick) unsalted butter

1¼ cups sugar

3 large eggs

1½ teaspoons vanilla

¾ teaspoons fine sea salt

¾ cup all-purpose flour

**Cheesecake Layer:**

2 (8-ounce) blocks cream cheese, not whipped, softened at room temperature for 20 minutes

½ cup plus 2 tablespoons sugar

juice of 1 fresh lemon

2 large eggs

½ teaspoon pure vanilla extract

¼ teaspoon fine sea salt

2 tablespoons all-purpose flour

**Fudge Layer:**

6 ounces good-quality milk chocolate chips

¾ cup heavy cream

1 tablespoon light corn syrup

1 teaspoon pure vanilla extract

1. Preheat oven to 350°F.

2. Butter and flour a 9½-inch springform pan. Set a metal bowl over a pot of simmering water. Place the semi-sweet and unsweetened chocolates and butter into the bowl and allow them to melt. Carefully remove from heat, as bowl will be hot. Whisk in the sugar. Whisk in the eggs, one at a time. Whisk in the vanilla and salt. Whisk in the flour until just combined and spread into prepared pan.

3. Prepare the cheesecake layer: In a bowl of an electric mixer, cream the cream cheese and sugar until light and fluffy. Beat in the lemon juice, eggs, vanilla, and salt. Beat in the flour. Spread evenly over the brownie layer.

4. Bake for 55 minutes-1 hour. The top should be golden and puffed.

5. Prepare the fudge layer: Place the milk chocolate into a medium bowl. Pour the cream and corn syrup into a small pot. Over low heat, heat the mixture until it comes to a simmer. Immediately pour it over the chocolate. Let the chocolate stand for 1 minute so it begins to melt. Add the vanilla and whisk until melted. Place into the refrigerator for 10 minutes.

6. Pour over the cheesecake layer. Tilt to cover the cake. Let cool to room temperature and then refrigerate at least 6 hours or overnight. Can be made 3-4 days in advance.

*Yield: 12 servings*

# stained-glass cookies

Dairy or Parve

*This is a beautiful cookie. The crushed candy melts to give a stained-glass effect. Tailor the shape of the stained glass to your occasion. I have made the cutouts with hearts or my childrens initials for their birthdays. To tie two cookies together, just poke a hole in the top of each cookie with a drinking straw before baking. When completely cooled, tie together with a pretty ribbon.*

1 cup (2 sticks) butter or margarine, softened at room temperature for 10 minutes

1¼ cups sugar or superfine sugar

2 large egg yolks

2 teaspoons pure vanilla extract

3 cups all-purpose flour

¼ teaspoon fine sea salt

2 tablespoons milk or soy milk

6 ounces hard candies, such as sour balls, butterscotch, or lollipops (assorted colors)

sparkling white or colored sugar

medium 3-inch round or heart-shaped cookie cutter

smaller cookie cutters in any shape, such as heart, star, round, letters, numbers, etc.

1. Preheat oven to 375°F. Line 2 baking sheets with parchment paper. Set aside.

2. In the bowl of a mixer, beat the butter or margarine and sugar until smooth and creamy. Add the egg yolks and vanilla. Mix for 1 minute, scraping down the sides.

3. Into a medium bowl, with a sifter or a strainer, sift the flour and salt together.

4. Add half the flour mixture to the butter/margarine mixture. Add the milk or soymilk and then the remaining flour mixture. Mix until just combined. Set aside.

5. Prepare the candies: Unwrap them and separate by color. Place each color into a heavy-duty ziplock bag (a thinner bag will tear). Seal each bag. Wrap one or two bags at a time in a kitchen towel. Use a rolling pin to break and crush the candies. Repeat until all the candies are crushed.

6. Tear off a piece of dough and place on the prepared baking sheets. Roll it to ¼-inch thickness. Using the larger round cookie cutter, cut out cookies, and, without removing the cookie cutter, use the small cookie cutter to cut out the center of the cookie. Place this inside piece alongside the cookies to make their own smaller cookies. Pick up any dough outside the larger cookie cutter and re-roll these scraps into another mound of dough for another cookie.

7. Continue until all of the dough is used. If the dough becomes too soft to handle, put it back in the refrigerator to firm up.

8. Spoon ½-1 teaspoon of crushed candy into the center of each cookie. The amount will depend on the size of the cutout. You can sprinkle the smaller cookies with pretty colored or plain sparkling white sugar. Bake for 13 minutes.

9. Remove from oven and let cool for 8-10 minutes. Using a spatula, transfer the cookies to a plate or container. Keep covered at room temperature.

*Yield: 25 stained glass cookies and 25 mini cut-out cookies*

282    KOSHER BY DESIGN ENTERTAINS

# pineapple truffles

*Two years before I was asked to teach a class at De Gustibus Cooking School, in Macy's Times Square, I did the backroom kitchen work for two different chef friends who were teaching there. The head assistant, Amaral Ozeias, who during his long tenure has seen every great chef and TV personality pass through the doors of that kitchen, quietly motioned for me to come into his office. He pulled out the prettiest little yellow truffle and proceeded to recite the recipe, one of his all-time favorites. This kind gesture was the most delicious favor he could have done for me.*

1¼ cup firmly packed sweetened flaked coconut, divided

¾ cup sugar, divided

1 medium ripe pineapple

¾ cup confectioner's sugar

4 large egg yolks

1. In a blender or food processor fitted with a metal blade, process ¼ cup coconut with ¼ cup sugar. Remove to a bowl or ziplock bag. Set aside.

2. Cut the pineapple out of the shell. Discard core and cut the flesh into chunks. Purée pineapple in blender or food processor. Transfer the puréed pineapple to a medium pot. Mix in 1 cup coconut, ½ cup sugar, and the confectioner's sugar. Bring to a boil over medium heat. Cook until all the liquid evaporates, about 30-35 minutes, stirring often to make sure the mixture is not browning on the bottom. If the mixture starts to brown, lower heat slightly and stir more often. The mixture will turn a dark golden color. Turn off the heat.

3. Remove ½ cup of the pineapple mixture and mix it into the egg yolks to temper them. Add the tempered yolks into the pot and mix back on heat until dry and pulling away from the sides of the pot, about 5 minutes.

4. Place the pot in the freezer and chill completely.

5. Remove the pineapple mixture from the freezer. Using a tiny melon baller or ¼ teaspoon measure, make balls. Roll in the coconut/sugar that was blended in the first step. If the truffles become too sticky to roll, place the mixture back into the freezer for a few minutes.

6. Place on parchment-lined baking sheets and place into freezer. Once frozen, remove and store in an airtight container in layers separated by parchment paper. Return truffles to freezer.

7. Serve right from the freezer or place in little paper candy cups or on a platter 10 minutes before serving.

*Yield: 50-60 truffles*

# cookie crunch brownies

*My husband teases me that I married him for his brownie recipe. As he was growing up, Purim in his house meant a brownie assembly line. His family would churn out dozens of batches, and heard rumors that there were neighbors who gave Shalach Manot to his family just to get the brownies in return! His family's heirloom uses unsweetened chocolate. The brand we always used became dairy and I could not find a replacement brand so I set out to create an equally fabulous brownie using other kinds of chocolates. Much to my family's happiness, many batches of brownies later, I think we have a winner, and yes, to my husband's amazement, a real contender for best brownie recipe. It is the basis for both this recipe and Peanut Butter Swirl Brownies that follow. If you use cookie cutters to make fun-shaped brownies, as we did on the facing page, save the scraps. Mix them into chocolate ice cream for a delicious fudge brownie flavor.*

1 tablespoon all-purpose flour

12 ounces semi-sweet chocolate, broken up

1½ cups sugar

¾ cup (12 tablespoons) butter or margarine

1 cup all-purpose flour

¼ cup Dutch processed cocoa, sifted

2 teaspoons baking powder

¼ teaspoon fine sea salt

4 large eggs, at room temperature

2 teaspoons instant coffee granules or espresso powder

1 tablespoon pure vanilla extract

15 Oreo cookies, or parve chocolate sandwich cookies, broken into chunks

4-5 extra Oreo or parve chocolate sandwich cookies, broken in half, for garnish

1. Arrange a rack in the middle of your oven and preheat to 350°F. Spray an 11-by 7-by 1 ½ inch brownie pan with nonstick cooking spray. Place the tablespoon of flour into the pan. Shake it all around and tap it over a sink or garbage can to discard excess.

2. In a heatproof medium bowl set over a saucepan of simmering water, heat the chocolate, sugar, and butter or margarine. Whisk until melted and smooth. Remove bowl from heat and set aside to cool to room temperature, about 15-20 minutes.

3. In a small bowl, mix the flour, sifted cocoa, baking powder, and salt.

4. In a medium bowl, with a mixer at medium speed, beat the eggs, coffee granules, and vanilla until foamy. If your stand mixer has a whisk attachment, it will work well here.

5. Blend the cooled chocolate mixture into the egg mixture.

6. Sprinkle all but four tablespoons of the flour/cocoa mixture into the chocolate mixture. Place the 15 broken Oreos into the remaining flour/cocoa mixture and toss to combine. Add the Oreo mixture into the chocolate mixture, stirring gently to combine; try not to crush the cookies. Pour batter into prepared pan. Place the extra broken cookies on top of the batter for garnish.

7. Bake 35 minutes; do not overbake. Allow to cool. Refrigerate, tightly wrapped, until cold. Cut into squares. Store, tightly wrapped, in refrigerator. Serve chilled.

*Yield: 15-18 brownies*

# peanut butter swirl brownies

## Brownies:

1 tablespoon all-purpose flour

12 ounces semi-sweet chocolate, broken up

1½ cups sugar

¾ cup (12 tablespoons) butter or margarine

1 cup all-purpose flour

¼ cup Dutch processed cocoa, sifted

2 teaspoons baking powder

¼ teaspoon fine sea salt

4 large eggs, at room temperature

2 teaspoons instant coffee granules or espresso powder

1 tablespoon pure vanilla extract

## Peanut Butter Filling:

4 tablespoons butter or margarine, melted

½ cup confectioner's sugar

¾ cup smooth peanut butter

¼ teaspoon fine sea salt

½ teaspoon vanilla extract

1. Arrange a rack in the middle of your oven and preheat to 350°F. Spray an 11-by 7-by 1½ inch brownie pan with nonstick cooking spray. Place the tablespoon of flour into the pan. Shake it all around and tap it over a sink or garbage can to discard excess.

2. In a heatproof medium bowl set over a saucepan of simmering water, heat the chocolate, sugar, and butter or margarine. Whisk until melted and smooth. Remove bowl from heat and set aside to cool to room temperature, about 15-20 minutes.

3. In a small bowl, mix the flour, sifted cocoa, baking powder, and salt.

4. In a medium bowl, with a mixer at medium speed, beat the eggs, coffee granules, and vanilla until foamy. If your stand mixer has a whisk attachment, it will work well here.

5. Blend the cooled chocolate mixture into the egg mixture.

6. Add the flour/cocoa mixture into the chocolate mixture, stirring gently to combine.

7. Prepare the filling: Stir together the butter or margarine, confectioner's sugar, peanut butter, salt, and vanilla in a bowl until smooth.

8. Pour ⅓ of the batter into prepared pan, and spread evenly with a rubber spatula. Place tablespoon dollops of filling about 1-inch apart on top of batter, reserving about 4 tablespoons of filling. Drizzle remaining batter on top and gently spread to fill the pan. Place dollops of remaining filling on top.

9. With a knife, gently swirl the filling into the batter, running the knife lengthwise and crosswise across the layers to create a swirled effect.

10. Bake 35-40 minutes, or until a toothpick inserted 3 inches from the center comes out clean; do not overbake. Allow to cool. Refrigerate, tightly wrapped, until cold. Cut into squares. Store, tightly wrapped in plastic wrap, in refrigerator and serve chilled.

*Yield: 15-18 brownies*

# double chocolate cookies

*Usually a crisp, flat cookie lover myself, these cookies win me over to the other side.*

1 cup (2 sticks) butter or margarine, at room temperature

1½ cups sugar

2 large eggs

2 teaspoons pure vanilla extract

2 cups all-purpose flour

⅔ cup Dutch processed cocoa powder

¾ teaspoons baking soda

¼ teaspoons fine sea salt

2 cups semi-sweet chocolate chips

1. Preheat oven to 350°F.

2. Line 2 cookie sheets with parchment paper. Set aside.

3. In the bowl of a mixer, at medium speed, beat the butter or margarine with the sugar until fluffy.

4. Scape down the sides of the bowl. Mix well. Add the eggs and vanilla. Beat until mixed.

5. In a separate bowl mix the flour, cocoa, baking soda, and salt. Toss with a fork.

6. Add the flour mixture into the butter mixture, beating until incorporated.

7. Mix in the chocolate chips.

8. Scoop up by rounded teaspoons and roll each into a ball. Place 1½ inches apart on prepared sheets and flatten each dough ball slightly.

9. Bake 10-12 minutes, until they no longer look wet in the center.

10. Cool for 5 minutes on cookie sheets, then transfer to a rack to cool completely.

*Yield: 75 medium-sized cookies*

---

### Freezing Cookies:

Freeze cookie dough rather than cookies. For round cookies, just partially thaw, slice, and bake. For shaped cookies, thaw, roll, and cut into shapes. Cookie dough keeps for about 1 month in the freezer.

# giant apple-cherry turnover

*This dessert is fabulous, like a giant pop tart! It is delicious and serves an army! My best trick for rolling the dough for this recipe is on a sheet of parchment paper. The width is the exact width that the dough needs. For the length, I place the parchment into the jelly-roll pan, and crease both ends to show me how long to roll the dough. I use a knife to slice off any jagged edges and then I just slide the parchment paper right into the jelly-roll pan, perfect and professional-looking every time. And yes, you can halve the recipe or even make individual turnovers.*

6½ cups all-purpose flour

2 teaspoons fine sea salt

2 cups vegetable shortening, such as Crisco, cut into chunks

3 large egg yolks

soy milk

1 cup sugar

6 tablespoons cornstarch

2 (16-ounce) cans pitted sweet dark red cherries, drained

6 Granny Smith apples, peeled, cored, cut into ½-inch pieces

1½ cups confectioner's sugar, sifted

½ teaspoon pure vanilla extract

7 teaspoons very hot water

1. Preheat oven to 375°F.

2. For the pastry, in a large mixing bowl, stir together the flour and salt. Using a pastry blender or the tips of your fingers, cut in the shortening until mixture resembles coarse crumbs.

3. Place the egg yolks into a large measuring cup. Lightly beat. Add enough soymilk to total 1½ cups liquid; mix well. Stir egg yolk mixture into flour mixture. Start the mixing with a wooden spoon or spatula. When it gets less sticky you can use your hands. Divide the dough in half.

4. On a piece of parchment paper or lightly floured surface, roll out half the dough into an 18- by 12-inch rectangle. Make sure it is thin, around ¼-inch thickness. You may have excess dough, just trim it off and discard it. It's always easier to have too much than too little dough.

5. In a large bowl, combine the sugar, cornstarch, cherries and apples; toss to combine. Spoon onto the prepared crust, leaving an inch-wide border on all sides.

6. Roll the remaining dough into an 19- by 13- by ¼-inch rectangle. Trim and discard excess dough. Place over the fruit. Seal the edges with the tines of a fork. Prick pastry all over with the tines of a fork. Slide onto a large cookie sheet or inverted jelly-roll pan. Bake about 45-50 minutes, until lightly golden. Cool in pan.

7. Prepare the glaze: In a small bowl, combine the confectioner's sugar, vanilla, and water. Stir to a smooth drizzling consistency. Drizzle in thin criss-crossing lines over the pie.

*Yield: 25 servings*

---

### Coring Apples and Pears:

To easily cut the seed packet out of an apple or pear, forget a corer, use a melon baller; in one scoop it gets all the seeds.

# triple chocolate explosion

*Smooth, dense, chocolate perfection. A small slice with a dollop of whipped cream or a few berries ... the things that dreams are made of.*

## Cake:

24 ounces good-quality semi-sweet or bittersweet chocolate, cut into small pieces

¾ cup butter or margarine

6 eggs, separated, at room temperature

2 tablespoons sugar

2 tablespoons all-purpose flour

## Ganache:

¾ cup dairy heavy cream or non-dairy whipping cream

1 tablespoon light corn syrup

6 ounces good-quality semi-sweet or bittersweet chocolate, chopped into small pieces

½ teaspoon pure vanilla extract

## Glaze:

½ cup (1 stick) butter or margarine

6 ounces good-quality semi-sweet chocolate chips

## Garnish:

edible glitter (see resource guide, p. 313)

1. Preheat oven to 375°F. Lightly grease a springform pan. Heat the chocolate over a double boiler until melted and smooth. Stir in butter or margarine and set aside.

2. Beat egg whites at high speed with an electric mixer until stiff peaks form; set aside.

3. Beat the egg yolks at high speed until thick and pale yellow. Turn down speed and gradually add sugar, beating constantly. Return to high speed and beat 1 minute. Add flour to the yolk mixture and beat until just blended. Stir in chocolate mixture.

4. Fold the chocolate mixture into the egg whites with a wire whisk. Spoon into prepared pan.

5. Place in oven and immediately reduce heat to 350°F. Bake for 35 minutes. Cool completely. Place in refrigerator.

6. Prepare the chocolate ganache layer: In a small saucepan over low heat, heat the cream and corn syrup together until it comes to a simmer. Immediately add the chocolate and turn off the heat. Let stand for 1 minute so that the chocolate begins to melt. Add the vanilla and stir until chocolate has melted.

7. Allow this ganache to stand for 10 minutes to thicken. Spread over the cake. Smooth with a spatula. Return to the refrigerator for 1 hour or to freezer for 20 minutes.

8. Prepare the glaze: In a small saucepan over low heat, heat the margarine and chocolate chips. Stir until the mixture melts.

9. Release and remove the sides of the springform pan. Set the cake on a platter. Slide strips of waxed paper, parchment, or foil under the bottom of the cake to catch drippings. Pour the glaze over the cake, tilting the cake to help it run down the sides. Refrigerate 3 hours or overnight.

10. Remove from refrigerator 20 minutes before serving. Remove and discard the strips that caught the drippings. Garnish with edible glitter.

*Yield: 12 servings*

# lemon chocolate chip pound cake

*Over a long Shabbat at my Mom's house, I went digging into her old organizational cookbooks, the really old tattered ones from the 60's and 70's. It was a walk down memory lane as my Mom, like many, got her recipes and ideas from these treasured collections, and I recalled dishes that she used to make but had dropped from her repertoire. I dug out this recipe, which had a lot of smudges near it, meaning my family liked it at some point, and updated it.*

1 cup (2 sticks) butter or margarine, at room temperature

½ cup pure vegetable shortening, such as Crisco

2 cups sugar

4 large eggs

¼ teaspoon fine sea salt

1 teaspoon pure vanilla extract

1 teaspoon lemon extract

2 teaspoons baking powder

3 cups all-purpose flour, sifted

1 (8-ounce) can lemon-lime soda, such as Sprite or 7-Up

1 (3-ounce) good-quality bittersweet chocolate bar, I like the Noblesse brand but any good Belgian or Israeli eating chocolate bar will do

confectioner's sugar

1. Preheat oven to 350°F.

2. Spray a 10-inch tube pan or bundt pan with nonstick cooking spray. Set aside.

3. In the bowl of a stand mixer, cream the butter or margarine with the shortening. Gradually add the sugar; beat until fluffy. Scrape down bowl as needed.

4. Add the eggs and beat to combine. Add the salt, vanilla, and lemon extracts. Mix. Sprinkle in the baking powder. Add the flour alternately with the soda, beating after each addition.

5. On a cutting board, chop the chocolate into small pieces, and fold the chocolate, along with any shavings that flaked off, into the batter.

6. Pour into prepared pan.

7. Bake for 1 hour. Cool for 10 minutes. Remove from pan. Cool completely.

8. Use a sifter or colander to sprinkle generously with confectioner's sugar.

*Yield: 10-12 servings*

---

### Downsizing Desserts:

Making your desserts miniature makes for a great presentation when plated individually or grouped on a platter. Take your favorite recipes and bake them in baby tube pans, mini muffin tins, mini springforms, reducing the baking time by half to three-quarters.

# glazed cinnamon chocolate ribbon cake

**Cake:**

4 ounces good-quality semi-sweet chocolate, chopped

3 cups minus 6 tablespoons all-purpose flour

6 tablespoons cornstarch

1½ teaspoons baking powder

½ teaspoon fine sea salt

3 large eggs

2 cups sugar

1 cup canola oil

1 cup whole milk or soy milk

1 teaspoon pure vanilla extract

4 teaspoons ground cinnamon

**Glaze:**

6 tablespoons unsalted butter or margarine

6 tablespoons heavy cream or non-dairy whipping cream

6 ounces semi-sweet chocolate; or milk chocolate, chopped

1⅓ cups confectioner's sugar

1 teaspoon vanilla extract

1. Prepare the cake: Arrange a rack in the middle of your oven and preheat to 325°F. Spray a 10-inch angel-food-cake or bundt pan with nonstick cooking spray. Place 1 tablespoon of flour into the pan. Shake it all around and tap it over a sink or garbage can to discard excess.

2. In a heatproof medium bowl set over a saucepan of simmering water, heat the chocolate. Stir and remove from heat when melted and smooth. Set aside.

3. Sift the flour, cornstarch, baking powder, and salt into a large bowl.

4. Place the eggs into the bowl of a mixer. Beat the eggs for 30 seconds. Add the sugar and beat for a full 3 minutes; it will become thick and fluffy. Gradually beat in the oil, milk or soy milk, and vanilla. Add the flour mixture to the eggs and beat until just blended.

5. Transfer 1½ cups of the batter to the melted chocolate and mix to combine. Mix the cinnamon into the remaining batter.

6. Spread half of the cinnamon batter into the prepared pan. Spoon chocolate batter over. Top with remaining cinnamon batter. With the tip of a knife make swirls to marbleize the two batters.

7. Bake about 1 hour and 10-15 minutes, until a toothpick inserted near the center comes out clean.

8. Allow cake to cool for 15 minutes before turning it out of the pan. Cool completely before glazing.

9. Prepare the glaze: Combine the butter or margarine, cream, chocolate, sugar, and vanilla in a heavy saucepan over low heat. Cook, whisking constantly, until smooth. Cool slightly. Pour over cake, letting it run over the sides. Try not to manipulate the glaze too much; let set. Cake can be kept covered at room temperature.

*Yield: 12 servings*

# blueberry lemon crème brûlée tart

## Crust:

13 tablespoons unsalted butter or margarine, at room temperature for 15 minutes

⅓ cup confectioner's sugar

1 large egg yolk

1½ cups unbleached all-purpose flour

1 tablespoon heavy cream or soy milk

1 egg white, whisked, for brushing after tart is baked

## Blueberry Lemon Filling:

1 cup sugar

grated zest of 1 lemon, preferable a Meyer lemon

½ cup freshly squeezed lemon juice, from about 4-5 lemons

1 large egg yolk

4 large eggs

¾ cup heavy cream or soy milk

3 tablespoons unsalted butter or margarine, melted

½ cup fresh blueberries

2-3 tablespoons sugar

1. Place the butter or margarine and confectioner's sugar into the bowl of a stand mixer. Cream the mixture at medium speed until no sugar is visible. Scrape down the sides of the bowl with a spatula. Add the egg yolk and beat until blended. Scrape down the sides of the bowl again. Add half the flour and beat until dough becomes crumbly. Add remaining flour and cream or soy milk. Beat until dough forms a sticky mass. Scrape the dough onto a piece of parchment or waxed paper. Flatten into a disc and place in refrigerator until firm, about 2 hours.

2. Remove from the refrigerator and press into the bottom and up the sides of a 10-inch tart pan with removable bottom. The dough will be sticky, so don't bother with a rolling pin. Just flour your hands and use the heel of your palm and the side of your thumb to work it evenly into the pan. Place this shell into the freezer for 30 minutes.

3. Preheat oven to 375°F. Prick the bottom of the tart all over with a fork. Place tart pan on a baking sheet; the heat it conducts will help brown the crust evenly. Bake the tart shell for 18-20 minutes, until pastry is golden and the interior is dry. Remove tart from oven and evenly brush the egg white over the entire surface of the tart. Reduce oven temperature to 350°F.

4. Prepare the filling: Place the sugar and lemon zest into a medium bowl. Rub the sugar and zest together between the palms of your hands. Add the lemon juice, egg yolk, eggs, cream or soy milk, and melted butter or margarine. Whisk to combine. Pour filling into crust. Sprinkle in the fresh blueberries, scattering them evenly in the tart filling. Bake until filling is slightly puffed at edges and set in center, about 30 minutes. Cool completely, about 1 hour.

5. If you have a hand-held blow torch, it is a snap to caramelize the top. Sprinkle the sugar evenly over the tart, then, with the torch nozzle 4 inches from the top, circle the flame until the sugar has melted and caramelizes. If you don't have a torch, preheat the oven to broil. Carefully wrap the exposed tart dough with aluminum foil, or it will turn black. Place the tart on a rack 4-6 inches from broiler coil. Sprinkle the sugar evenly over the filling. Place under the broiler for 2-5 minutes, watching the entire time to make sure the sugar turns golden brown and caramelizes but doesn't burn. Turn the pan for even browning.

6. Store at room temperature.

*Yield: 10-12 servings*

# chocolate layer cake with creamy coconut glaze Parve

**Chocolate Layer Cake:**

1 cup canola oil

2½ cups sugar

4 large eggs

2 teaspoons pure vanilla extract

2 teaspoons instant coffee or espresso powder, dissolved in 2 cups hot water

1 cup Dutch processed cocoa

3 cups all-purpose flour

1 teaspoon fine sea salt

1 teaspoon baking powder

1 teaspoon baking soda

**Creamy Coconut Glaze:**

1 cup soy milk

½ cup light brown sugar, firmly packed

½ cup sugar

8 tablespoons margarine

1 teaspoon pure vanilla extract

3 large egg yolks, lightly whisked

2 cups sweetened flaked coconut

½ cup chopped almonds, optional, for garnish

fresh coconut ruffles, made from ½ fresh coconut, optional, for garnish

1. Preheat oven to 350°F.

2. Lightly grease and flour the bottoms and sides of two 9-inch round baking pans.

3. In the bowl of a mixer, at medium speed, beat the oil, sugar, eggs, and vanilla. When all combined, turn the mixer to low and add the coffee. Beat to combine.

4. In a medium bowl, combine the cocoa, flour, salt, baking powder, and baking soda. Stir to combine. Slowly add flour mixture into the egg mixture. Beat on low until incorporated.

5. Pour batter into prepared pans. Bake 25-30 minutes, until toothpick inserted in center comes out mostly clean.

6. Meanwhile, prepare the coconut glaze: Place the soymilk into a medium saucepan. Bring to a boil over medium heat. Turn down to a simmer and allow to cook for 5-6 minutes. Add the brown sugar, sugar, margarine, and vanilla. Bring to a full boil, stirring constantly. Turn heat down slightly and cook for 5 minutes. Remove from heat. In a small bowl whisk the 3 egg yolks. Quickly stir ½ cup of the hot liquid into the beaten egg yolks to temper them. Return egg yolk mixture to the saucepan. Blend well. Return to a boil, stirring constantly and cook for 5-6 minutes. Remove from heat and add the coconut. Stir well. Cool to spreading consistency.

7. When cakes are done, remove from oven and cool for ten minutes. With a spatula, loosen the cakes from the edges of the pan. Invert onto a rack and cool completely. When cool, carefully trim the uneven surfaces, using a serrated knife.

8. Spread a little more than half the coconut glaze on one layer of cake. Top with the second layer. Spread remaining coconut glaze on top of the cake as well, leaving a 1-inch border of cake peeking out around the edges.

9. You can sprinkle the top with chopped almonds or fresh, wafer-thin coconut ruffles made by scraping a fresh coconut with a vegetable peeler.

*Yield: 8-10 servings*

# angel food cake

*The ultimate in light desserts; angel food cake is light in color, texture, calories, and fat. It can be the perfect ending to a meal and one of the simplest cakes around. Serve with fresh berries or a squirt of chocolate or fruit sauce (see resource guide, p. 315)*

*Just a few angel food cake tips: Make sure you start with a perfectly clean bowl and beaters; even a trace of grease will keep the whites from whipping to a high volume. Separate the eggs while they are still cold; they will be firmer and separate easier. Then allow the whites to come to room temperature. (This would be a good time to make the bread machine challah recipe from **Kosher By Design**, as it calls for just egg yolks.) Do not allow any yolk to mix into the whites; it will keep them from whipping up nicely. For a chocolate variation, just add ¼ cup sifted unsweetened cocoa powder to the flour mixture.*

1 cup all-purpose flour

1½ cups sugar, divided

12 large egg whites, at room temperature

½ teaspoon fine sea salt

1 teaspoon pure vanilla extract

½ teaspoon almond extract

1½ teaspoons cream of tartar

1. Preheat oven to 325°F.

2. In a large bowl, whisk the flour and ¾ cup sugar. Set aside.

3. In a large mixing bowl or the bowl of your stand mixer, combine the egg whites, salt, vanilla, and almond extracts. If your mixer has a whisk attachment or copper bowl, here's the time to use it.

4. Beat the mixture until just frothy. Sprinkle the cream of tartar on top and continue beating until the whites form stiff, glossy peaks. Sprinkle in the remaining sugar, ¼ cup at a time, making sure each addition is dissolved before adding the next. The whites should look shiny, moist, and almost like snow drifts. The peaks should hold high when you lift the beater. Do not overbeat or the cake will be tough.

5. Using a spatula, with large sweeping motions, gradually fold in the flour mixture; this will ensure that the flour will get mixed in without deflating the whites.

6. Spoon the batter into an ungreased 10-inch angel food pan. Use a knife to run through the batter and break up any air pockets that may have formed when pouring in the batter. Smooth the top of the batter. Bake for 45 minutes in the center of the oven or until golden brown and the top springs back when lightly touched. Do not open the oven door while baking or your cake may deflate.

7. Remove the cake from the oven. If your pan has "feet," just invert the pan. If not, place it upside down on the neck of a wine or grape juice bottle to keep from crushing the top. Let the cake cool this way for 1½ hours. This will maintain the cake's structure and keep it from collapsing.

8. Loosen the edges with a knife or spatula, including the center tube, and remove it from the pan. Cut with a serrated knife or bread knife, using gentle sawing motions. Store, covered, at room temperature for 2 days or freeze for up to a month.

*Yield: 12 servings*

# streusel-topped chocolate chunk banana cake

Parve

Cake:

4 ripe bananas, mashed

1 cup (2 sticks) margarine, melted

2 cups sugar

2 large eggs

½ cup lowfat mayonnaise

½ cup soy milk

1 teaspoon baking soda

3 cups all-purpose flour

⅛ teaspoon fine sea salt

1 teaspoon vanilla

Streusel Topping:

1¼ cups all-purpose flour

1 cup sugar

2 tablespoons ground cinnamon

½ cup margarine, melted

1½ teaspoons vanilla

7 ounces good-quality bittersweet chocolate, coarsely chopped with a knife

1. Preheat oven to 350°F.

2. Grease a 13- by 9-inch baking dish. Set aside.

3. In the bowl of an electric mixer, place the mashed banana. Add the melted margarine, sugar, eggs, mayonnaise, soymilk, baking soda, flour, salt, and vanilla. Beat until combined.

4. In a separate bowl, prepare the topping: Combine the flour, sugar and cinnamon. Add the melted margarine and vanilla. Mix by hand until the mixture resembles coarse crumbs. Stir in the chocolate and any shavings that came off the chocolate when you were chopping it.

5. Pour half the cake batter into the prepared pan. Sprinkle with half the streusel. Top with remaining batter. Sprinkle the rest of the streusel over the top of the cake.

6. Bake for 1 hour.

*Yield: 14-16 servings*

# peach and berry crisp

*In my town there is a farmer's market every Thursday. It is such a treat to get fresh-from-the-farm, amazing, ripe produce right in my neighborhood's Walgreen's parking lot! That part always makes me laugh, but in the summer there is no beating the peaches and fresh berries for this dessert. In the winter, when these fruits are no longer in season, substitute a combination of Macintosh and Granny Smith apples with fresh or frozen blueberries. For one party I threw, I used very small ramekins and made 3 different versions of this crisp recipe; peach, apple, and one with pears and raspberries. I arranged them on a three-tiered cake plate. My guests loved the chance to sample all three without feeling too indulgent and the cute tiny size made them irresistible. Just watch your baking time; the smaller amounts in each ramekin cook faster than the larger size.*

4-5 large ripe peaches
(2 pounds), peeled (see box),
pitted, chopped

10 ounces blueberries

10 ounces raspberries, can be
combination of red and black
raspberries

juice of ½ lemon

⅓ cup plus 2 tablespoons
sugar

2 tablespoons all-purpose flour

## Topping:

1¼ cup all-purpose flour

¾ cup dark brown sugar

¼ cup finely chopped pecans

1 teaspoon ground cinnamon

½ teaspoon ground ginger

½ teaspoon fine sea salt

8 tablespoons cold butter or
margarine, cut into 16 pieces

1. Preheat oven to 350°F.

2. Line a baking sheet with parchment paper.

3. Spray 14 (½-cup) ramekins, 7 (1-cup ramekins) or 1 large (4-quart) baking dish, any shape, with nonstick cooking spray. Arrange on the prepared sheet to avoid oven spills and for ease in removing from oven.

4. Place the peaches, blueberries, and raspberries into a large bowl. Toss with lemon juice, sugar, and 2 tablespoons flour. Combine. Transfer to prepared ramekins or baking dish.

5. Bake fruit for 20 minutes.

6. Remove from oven. Increase oven temperature to 400°F.

7. While fruit is baking, prepare the topping: Whisk flour with brown sugar, pecans, cinnamon, ginger, and salt. Add butter or margarine. Rub in with fingertips until small moist clumps form. Sprinkle generously and evenly over the hot fruit. Return to oven and bake until crisp and golden brown, about 20 minutes.

8. Serve warm or at room temperature. Can be re-warmed if made in advance.

*Yield: 14 servings*

---

## Just Peachy:

To find a ripe peach look for well-colored fruit that yields slightly when pressed. Sniff the bottom, not the stem end of your peach; if it is very fragrant it is ripe. If it has little or no aroma, it is not. To peel, cut a small x into the bottom of each peach. Drop into a pot of boiling water for 45-60 seconds. Run under cold water and slip the skins off with your fingertips.

# cupcakes

Dairy or Parve

1½ cups sugar

½ cup (1 stick) butter or margarine

2 large eggs

1 tablespoon pure vanilla extract

1½ cups all-purpose flour

½ teaspoon fine sea salt

1¾ teaspoons baking powder

¾ cup milk or soy milk

1 tablespoon orange juice

Frosting:

2 large egg whites

3½ cups confectioner's sugar

1-2 drops glycerin (see resource guide p. 313)

1 tablespoon orange juice

pastel food colorings

pastel lustre dragées and assorted sprinkles (see resource guide, p. 313)

1. Preheat oven to 350°F.

2. Line muffin pans with 18 paper liners.

3. In a medium bowl with mixer at medium speed, beat the sugar and the butter or margarine until creamy. Beat in the eggs and vanilla.

4. In a medium bowl, combine the flour, salt, and baking powder. Stir with a fork. Add into the creamed mixture. Stir in the soy milk or milk and orange juice. Mix until batter is smooth.

5. Fill each muffin cup two-thirds full with batter. Fill any empty cups halfway with water. Bake 25-30 minutes, until toothpick inserted in center comes out clean and the tops are golden. Remove from pans to cool.

6. Meanwhile, prepare the frosting: Beat the egg whites until stiff but not dry. Slowly add the sugar, glycerin, and orange juice. Beat for 1 minute at medium speed. Thin with water if too thick to spread or add more confectioner's sugar if too thin.

7. Divide the frosting into several bowls. Tint each bowl with a few drops of food coloring. Stir to combine until you get an even shade in each bowl. Frost the cooled cupcakes. Decorate with sprinkles and candies.

*Yield: 18 cupcakes*

# strudel bites

*My Mom's life-long Williamsburg friend, Janet Pernick, is such a good cook she used to have her own home catering business. I remembered my Mom telling me years ago about these strudels, which were Janet's most requested item. She must have made thousands of them over the years. I was kind of surprised when I called Janet for the recipe and she couldn't really recall how to make them. She dug up the recipe and sent it to me. When I was testing the recipe I called her with questions and again she was a little hazy. I couldn't help myself, I had to ask her, how could she not really remember what to do if this is her signature recipe? Doesn't she still make them? She replied that when she closed the business she kind of hid the recipe ... from herself, because she couldn't make the strudels and not eat all of them herself. I wasn't laughing so hard 1 hour after my first batch came out of the oven. My friend and I polished off the ENTIRE batch. After I type this recipe, I think I will hide my recipe card ... from myself.*

2 cups all-purpose flour, sifted

8 ounces cream cheese, at room temperature for 20 minutes, cut into 8 pieces

8 ounces butter, at room temperature for 20 minutes, cut into 8 pieces

⅛ teaspoon fine sea salt

6 tablespoons apricot preserves, divided

6 tablespoons seedless raspberry preserves, divided

cinnamon

sugar

6 tablespoons chopped walnuts, divided

6 tablespoons raisins, divided

6 tablespoons sweetened, shredded coconut, divided

6 teaspoons sour cream, divided

1. In a medium bowl, mix the sifted flour, cream cheese, butter, and salt. With your fingertips, mix and knead until it forms a dough. Roll into a ball and cover with plastic wrap or parchment paper. Refrigerate overnight.

2. Preheat oven to 375°F.

3. Cover a baking sheet with parchment paper. Set aside.

4. Remove dough from refrigerator and allow to soften for 10 minutes. Divide the dough into 6 equal parts. On a piece of parchment paper, roll each piece into a long rectangle, rolling as thin as possible. If the dough is sticky, sprinkle your rolling pin with as little flour as you can in order to roll the dough. Spread 2 tablespoons preserves on each of the pieces of dough. Half of the strudels will be apricot and half will be raspberry. Sprinkle each with cinnamon and sugar. Toss 1 tablespoon of walnuts, 1 tablespoon raisins, and 1 tablespoon coconut evenly over each piece of dough. Roll up one of the pieces of dough lengthwise, using the parchment to help. Peel back the parchment as you roll. Seal the edges. Repeat with remaining five pieces of dough.

5. Transfer the 6 rolls to the prepared baking sheet. Brush the top of each roll with 1 teaspoon sour cream.

6. Bake 30-35 minutes until golden. Allow to cool for 10 minutes and then slice into bite-sized strudels.

*Yield: 36-42 strudels*

# pumpkin doodles

Dairy or Parve

*Like snickerdoodles, my childhood favorite, only with an updated twist.*

1 cup (2 sticks) butter or margarine

1½ cups sugar

½ cup canned pumpkin purée (not pumpkin pie filling)

1 large egg

2 teaspoons pure vanilla extract

1 teaspoon cream of tartar

½ teaspoon baking soda

½ teaspoon fine sea salt

2⅔ cup all-purpose flour

½ cup sugar

1 tablespoon ground cinnamon

1. In the bowl of a mixer at medium speed, cream the butter or margarine with the sugar. Add the pumpkin and beat until combined.

2. Blend in the egg and vanilla.

3. In a separate bowl, with a fork, mix the cream of tartar, baking soda, salt, and flour.

4. Slowly add it into the batter; you will have a sticky, light-orange batter.

5. Cover the bowl and place it in the refrigerator for an hour. If you are pressed for time, place it in the freezer for 15 minutes.

6. Preheat the oven to 350°F.

7. Line 2 baking sheets with parchment paper.

8. In a small bowl, mix the ½ cup sugar with the cinnamon.

9. Using a small spoon, scoop up a spoonful of batter. Roll it into a ball between your hands.

10. Roll the ball in the cinnamon/sugar mixture and place on the prepared cookie sheets, 2 inches apart.

11. Bake 12-15 minutes

*Serves: 48-58 cookies*

---

Vanilla:

You can add a vanilla bean to a bottle of vanilla extract to infuse it with more vanilla flavor or make vanilla sugar by burying 2 vanilla beans in a pound of sugar for a week or two.

# pistachio cranberry biscotti

Dairy or Parve

*This recipe is adaptable to many variations. I've used cashew nuts with chocolate chips. I've used hazelnuts with white chocolate chips. I've even used chocolate-covered raisins and chocolate-covered peanuts. Let your imagination run with this one.*

1¾ cup all-purpose flour

¼ teaspoon fine sea salt

1 teaspoon baking powder

6 tablespoons butter
or margarine, at room
temperature

¾ cup sugar

2 large eggs

2 teaspoons pure vanilla
extract

½ teaspoon almond extract

1 cup shelled, natural,
unsalted pistachio nuts

1 cup sweetened dried
cranberries, such as Craisins

1. Preheat oven to 325°F.

2. Cover 2 cookie sheets with parchment paper. Set aside.

3. Sift the flour, salt, and baking powder into a medium bowl. Set aside.

4. Using an electric mixer, beat the butter or margarine with the sugar. Beat in the eggs, vanilla, and almond extract. Slowly mix in the flour mixture. Beat until all combined into a sticky dough.

5. With a sharp knife, on a large cutting board, chop ⅔ of the pistachio nuts into small pieces. Add the chopped pistachios, remaining whole pistachios, and the cranberries to the dough. Fold in with a spatula.

6. Divide the dough in half. Form two logs (12 inches long by 2 inches wide) on one of the prepared cookie sheets. You will need to wet your hands to handle and shape the dough. When you have shapped the logs into loaf shapes, run a moistened silicone or rubber spatula across the top of each log to smooth any rough spots.

7. Bake the logs until almost firm to the touch but still pale in color, about 28-30 minutes.

8. Cool logs on the cookie sheet for 10 minutes, maintaining oven temperature.

9. Carefully remove the logs with the parchment paper to a cutting board. Using a serrated knife and a gentle sawing motion, cut the logs crosswise, on the diagonal, into ¾-inch-thick slices. Lay the biscotti on their sides on the second prepared cookie sheet. Return to the oven for 9-10 minutes, until firm and pale golden. Turn onto the other cut side and bake an additional 10 minutes. Transfer to a rack to cool.

*Yield: 28-30 biscotti*

# caramelized apple cheesecake

*Lorye Weiss of Valley Village California and her Mom get together to bake for the holidays. This recipe, based on their **Kosher by Design** recipe contest winner, is the result of crossed wires. Lorye showed up for one of their baking dates prepared to make an apple pie and her Mom showed up the same day prepared to make a cheesecake. Like all good collaborations, both moved off their stance and combined their efforts to create something wonderful in this cheesecake.*

### Crust:

1½ cups graham cracker crumbs

¼ cup sugar

1 teaspoon vanilla

4 tablespoons melted butter

### Filling:

3 (8-ounce) blocks cream cheese, not whipped, softened for 20 minutes at room temperature

½ cup sugar

3 large eggs

1 cup heavy cream

juice of ½ lemon

1 cup applesauce

1 teaspoon ground cinnamon

¼ cup dark brown sugar

1 tablespoon butter

### Topping:

1 (21-ounce) can apple pie filling

½ teaspoon ground cinnamon

¼ cup dark brown sugar

1 tablespoon butter

1. Preheat oven to 350°F.

2. Spray a 9½-inch springform pan with nonstick cooking spray. Set aside.

3. In a medium bowl, combine the graham cracker crumbs, sugar, vanilla, and melted butter. Press into the pan. Use your palm to press it a little up the sides. Set aside.

4. Prepare the cheesecake filling: With an electric mixer, beat the cream cheese and sugar until very smooth. Add the eggs and beat to combine. Beat in the cream and lemon juice. Fold in the applesauce and cinnamon. Mix until well blended.

5. Place the brown sugar and butter into a small saucepan or skillet. Heat over medium until the sugar is just melted, stirring often. Drizzle into the filling in a swirl pattern. Pour into prepared crust. Bake 1 hour and 20 minutes, until the top feels firm to the touch. Remove from oven to cool.

6. Raise oven temperature to 400°F.

7. Prepare the topping: Spread the apple pie filling evenly over the cheesecake, starting at the center, leaving a tiny border of the cheesecake visible. Sift the cinnamon over the top. Place the brown sugar and butter into a small saucepan or skillet. Heat over medium until the sugar is melted, stirring often.

8. Drizzle over the apples. Return to oven and bake 15 minutes.

9. Cool completely and refrigerate at least overnight.

*Yield: 10 servings*

# chocolate truffles

12 ounces good-quality semi-sweet or bittersweet chocolate

⅔ cup heavy cream, or non-dairy whipping cream, I like Rich's whipped topping for parve

2 tablespoons Dutch processed cocoa powder

2 tablespoons confectioner's sugar

3 tablespoons finely chopped unsalted pistachios, almonds, or hazelnuts

1. Finely chop the chocolate by hand or in a food processor and place in a medium bowl. Pour the cream into a small heavy saucepan. Bring to a rolling boil over medium heat. Pour the cream over the chocolate. With a wooden spoon, gently stir to melt the chocolate. Don't whisk or stir too strongly or you will incorporate air. Cover. Chill until firm, about 2 hours.

2. Line a baking sheet with parchment or waxed paper. With a small melon baller or ice-cream scoop, drop mixture by rounded teaspoonfuls onto prepared sheet. Freeze until firm, about 20 minutes.

3. Place the cocoa, confectioner's sugar, and chopped nuts into 3 separate shallow bowls.

4. Roll ⅓ of the balls in the cocoa mixture, ⅓ in the confectioner's sugar, and ⅓ in the chopped nuts. Quickly roll between your palms to get them into a perfect round shape. You may need to re-roll in the nuts or sugar if too much falls off. Return to parchment-lined baking sheet or other parchment-lined container, in a single layer. Cover with plastic and chill until ready to serve. Can be made 10 days ahead; keep refrigerated.

*Yield: 30-36 truffles*

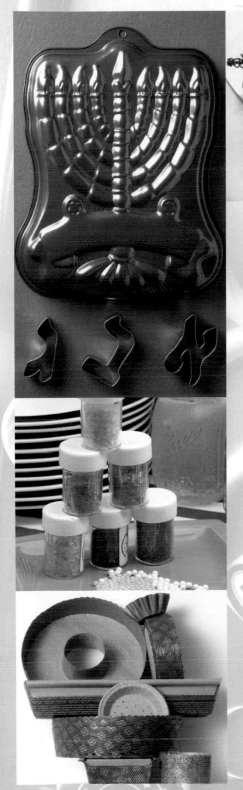

*Please note: At the time of original publication, each of the products listed was available with kosher certification. Before purchasing any of these products — or before purchasing any food item, for that matter — you must always make certain that the product carries reliable kosher certification which is indicated on the label. When in doubt, please contact a knowledgeable, competent rabbinic authority. Not all items on the mentioned websites are kosher.

resource guide

From oyster, to chanterelle, to morels, dried mushrooms are great to keep on hand when some varieties are hard to find fresh. They can be used to enhance risotto, soups, and sauces. White truffle oil is another hard-to find kosher gourmet product. Use this rare finishing oil to enhance fish dishes, salads, or even egg dishes. Available at The Peppermill, (866-871-4022) or (718-871-4022)
www.thepeppermillinc.com

Pomegranate juice, molasses and paste are wonderful ingredients that I call for in a number of recipes. Look for them in the Middle Eastern section of the supermarket or try www.sadaf.com

I love these heavy paper baking molds. No greasing or washing necessary. They are freestanding, although I use a supporting cookie sheet. They are oven-and microwave-safe up to 450°F. The pretty gold overlay make sthem ideal for gift-giving; no need to get your dish back. And they come in a huge selection of shapes and sizes. Available at Novacart. (877-896-6682)
www.novacartusa.com

This is a candy version of sand art. The colored sugar comes in 30 colors and flavors with assorted sized straws. It will keep your kids busy for hours. (877-643-8922) www.esandycandy.com

A great selection of gourmet honey and honey straws are available at www.moonshinetrading.com

One of my favorite food finds was this collection of designer dessert sauces by Lyons Magnus. With a simple squeeze you can decorate your dessert plates like a professional pastry chef. They come in assorted flavors and are parve. www.tenajanutrition.com (800-452-5067) or www.lyonsmagnus.com

From Sol Danablu (French Blue cheese) to Edam, Havarti, and Tavor, this website is a great resource for kosher Chalav Yisrael cheeses that can be hard to find. Do a search for kosher cheese in the website's search bar. www.igourmet.com

Get everything you need for authentic sushi at home, including sushi rice, pickled ginger, and wasabi powder. Sushi mats, chopsticks, and instruction books are available as well. Available at The Peppermill, (866-871-4022) or (718-871-4022)
www.thepeppermillinc.com

The Kosher Cook is an innovative company that makes products to help organize a kosher kitchen. They carry color-coordinated items to help separate meat, dairy, and parve. Baking sheets, labels, and wooden spoons embossed with the categories, as well as metal medallions for pots and pot covers, really help keep it all straight.          www.thekoshercook.com

Jewish-themed baking molds and aleph-bet cookie cutters are a great touch to a Shabbat or holiday table. Use the baking molds for cakes, jello, tuna fish, and more. The cookie cutters are great for cookie dough and brownies.
www.thekoshercook.com

In the world of spices and spice blends, Spice House International has no match for high-quality spices and hard to find products like kosher panko breadcrumbs. They sell over 400 spices, including blends that I call for in my books. Instead of blending your own, you can purchase Hickory Spice blends, Moroccan blends, Cajun blends, specialty salts, and more.

(516-942-7248)

www.spicehouseint.com

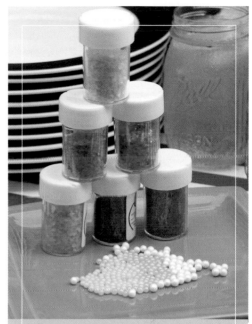

This company imports British and French pastry supplies. They are one of the few suppliers of kosher dragées, holiday sprinkles, and edible glitter.

www.beryls.safeshopper.com

Silpat nonstick, ovenproof baking mats, embossed rolling pins, kosher unflavored gelatin, Scharfenberger parve good-quality chocolates, chocolate transfer sheets, Nielson Massey Madagascar Vanilla Extract and beans, kosher glycerin, Dulce De Leche Chalav Yisrael caramel and parve butterscotch, peanut butter, cinnamon, and white chocolate chips. All available at The Peppermill, the only kosher gourmet kitchenware store in the world.

(866-871-4022) or (718-871-4022)

www.thepeppermillinc.com

*Unless otherwise indicated, tableware shown in the photographs is privately owned.*

## COVER:

Jean Louis Coquet Limoges Samoa 8½-inch gold fluted salad plate/Richard Ginoiri Rapallo dinner plate/ Richard Ginoiri Impero charger/Wainwright Pottery gold-rimmed charger/Ottagonale drinkware/ Carrs Sheffield English silverware/all from **Avventura** (212)769-2510 www.forthatspecialgift.com rhinestone placecard holder/ribbons from **Kate's Paperie**; calligraphy from **Lee's Art Studio**

## COCKTAIL ENGAGEMENT PARTY:

Ricky 4-ounce cordial cups/Lemongrass Sauce Dish/assorted cocktail glasses/Seasons Leaf Plates/and tablecloth from **Crate & Barrel** www.crateandbarrel.com; knot skewers from **Broadway Panhandler** (212-966-3434)

## JUST FOR GUYS:

Placemats/chicken casserole/enamel jug/napkin rings/cups/plates/and saucers from **MacKenzie Childs** www.Mackenzie-childs.com; Swerve Black Bowl centerpiece bowl/Carlson pilsner/Oliver beer mug/ Quinn pilsner/Carved pillar candleholder all from **Crate & Barrel** www.crateandbarrel.com; pillar candles from **Bed Bath and Beyond** www.bedbathandbeyond.com; shepard's pie ramekins from **Chef Central**; cigars from **Dunhill**; Reed & Barton silverware from **Michael C. Fina** (800-289-3462)

## LADIES' LUNCH:

Shoes/boots/and hat boxes from **Daffy's**; Herend plates from **Neiman Marcus**; flatware from **Gorham**; hats from **Hedy's Hat Rack** (718-376-7695); ribbons from **Artistic Ribbon** (212-255-4224); popover pans from **Williams Sonoma** www.williams-sonoma.com; little shoes and hats from **Party City**; all bath bar items, including soaps, powders, brushes, potpourri, from **Crabtree and Evelyn** www.crabtree-evelyn.com

## WELCOME BABY DESSERT BUFFET:

Lollipop rack/8-inch wooden candyapple sticks/from www.candylandcrafts.com; ribbons from **Michael's Arts & Crafts**; Ice Cream Cone Holder from **Bridge Kitchenware** (212-688-4220); baby tags/block charms/pacifier elastics all from **Party City**; assorted candy from **Candy Land** (718-436-9308); silver candy scoops from **Metropolitan Deluxe** (919-572-2677); oversized martini glasses from **Planter Resource** (212-206-7687) www.potteryking.com; rectangular ice trays from **Broadway Panhandler** (212-966-3434)

## DINNER FOR TWO:

White paint marker from **Michael's Arts and Crafts**; country onion soup crocks/tealight holder (truffle tray)/Baranthal Carving Set/boat sauce dish/all from **Crate & Barrel** www.crateandbarrel.com; Nichinan Paris White china from **Replacements Ltd.** www.replacements.com; Grand Baroque Sterling flatware from **Michael C. Fina** (800-289-3462); napkin cording from **M & J Trimmings**

## FAMILY OUTING PICNIC:

Wicker items/trays/picnic basket/all from **United Basket Company** (718-894-5454) www. unitedbasket.com; clothes pins from **Bed Bath & Beyond**; quilt/pillows/and silverware from **Sears**; candy sand art from Sandy Candy (877-643-8922) www.esandycandy.com

buying guide

## FORMAL ANNIVERSARY DINNER:

Heart confetti from **Photo Confetti (419-396-1787)** www.photoconfetti.com; silver calendar from **Michael Strauss Silversmith** (212-744-8500); Richard Ginoiri Palermo Yellow china from **Michael C. Fina** (800-289-3462); tablecloths from **Atlas Florists** (718-457-4900); menus from **ArtScroll Printing**

## HOUSEWARMING BUFFET:

Covered cake stand from **The Grey Dove** (973-994-2266); silverware from **Target**; mahogany flower boxes from **TJ Maxx**; oven-to-table casserole dish from **Harriet Eisenberg** (973-994-7117); covered onion soup crocks from **Kitchen Kapers** (800-455-5567) www.kitchenkapers.com; Medici ceramic dishes from **Fortunoff's**; metal shelf/brown glittered platter/and martini glasses from **Marshalls**; espresso machine from **Starbucks**; espresso cups and Trophy mugs from **Williams Sonoma** www.williams-sonoma.com; cream pitchers/small jugs from **Fishs Eddy** www. fishseddy.com

## SUMMER CELEBRATION OUTDOOR ENTERTAINING:

Eggs/nests/birds/bandanas/butterflies/from **Michael's Arts and Crafts**; bird cages/Gray Wire CD napkin holder from **United Basket Company** (718-894-5454) www.unitedbasket.com; grapevine balls from **Frank's Arts and Crafts**; Ball Mason Jars from **Shoprite**; blue rim plates and other platters from **Fishs Eddy** www. fishseddy.com; 3-tiered Honeymoon Sweet Stand from **MacKenzie Childs** www.Mackenzie-childs.com

## ASSORTED PICTURES:

(p. 30) JL Coquet Limoge Aile Orange salad plate, Bernardaud Poudre Citron dinner plate
      **Michael C. Fina** (800-289-3462)
(p. 35) Haviland Limoges plate from **Avventura** (212-769-2510) www.forthatspecialgift.com
(p. 41) skewers and Lemongrass Sauce Dish from **Crate & Barrel** www.crateandbarrel.com
(p. 42) square dish set from **Crate & Barrel** www.crateandbarrel.com
(p. 51) Herend footed soup bowl and dish from **Neiman Marcus**
(p. 67) covered onion soup crocks from Kitchen Kapers (800-455-5567) www.kitchenkapers.com
(p. 85) JL Coquet Limoge Aile Green salad plate from **Michael C. Fina** (800-289-3462)
(p. 92) Holland Wood Bowl from **Crate & Barrel** www.crateanbarrel.com
(p. 120) Switzer Silvestri plate **Avventura** (212-769-2510) www.forthatspecialgift.com
(p. 130) Chicken Casserole from **MacKenzie Childs** www.Mackenzie-childs.com
(p. 152) Bronze peppermill from **Manhattan Center for Kitchen & Bath** (212-995-0500)
(p. 165) fluted ramekin from **Chef Central**
(p. 173) Kate Spade Irving Place bowl **Michael C. Fina** (800-289-3462)
(p. 174) Global knives
(p. 189) Celadon plate from **Avventura** (212-769-2510) www.forthatspecialgift.com
(p. 212) Oval Carved Wood Bowl from **Crate & Barrel** www.crateandbarrel.com
(p. 224) Emile Henry handled casserole from **Williams Sonoma** www.williams-sonoma.com
(p. 249) Herend plate and butter dish from **Neiman Marcus**
(p. 273) All-Clad bakeware
(p. 295) JL Coquet Limoge Decor Hemisphere plate from **Michael C. Fina** (800-289-3462)

*To make this book more user-friendly for Passover, I have highlighted those recipes from every section that can be used as is or with minor adjustments for the holiday.*

*To ensure that ingredients are kosher for Passover, it is advisable to use only new packages and to check each package for Passover certification.*

| RECIPE | PAGE | CLASS* | ADJUSTMENT |
|---|---|---|---|
| Mexican Gefilte Fish | 32 | P | Substitute vegetable oil for canola oil |
| Roasted Pepper, Artichoke & Caramelized Onion Fritatta | 38 | P | Substitute nondairy creamer for soy milk |
| Moussaka | 39 | M** | Substitute nondairy creamer for soymilk, potato starch for flour, and matzo meal for breadcrumbs |
| Lamb Kabobs on Eggplant Purée | 40 | M | Omit tahini |
| Broccoli and Almond Bisque | 52 | M/D/P** | Substitute nondairy creamer for soy milk and use Passover imitation Dijon mustard |
| Sweet and Sour Cabbage Soup | 54 | M | None |
| Root Vegetable Soup | 55 | M/D/P | None, but use sour cream for dairy meals |
| Winter White Soup | 56 | M/P | Substitute nondairy creamer for soy milk |
| Roasted Cauliflower Soup | 58 | M/D/P | Substitute nondairy creamer for soy milk |
| Porcini Celery Soup | 58 | M/P | Substitute nondairy creamer for soy milk |
| Yukon Gold and Caramelized Leek Soup | 59 | M/P | None in the soup but leave off the garnish |
| Carrot and Spinach Soup | 62 | M/P | None |
| Cream of Sweet Potato Soup | 63 | M/D/P | Substitute nondairy creamer for soy milk |
| Carrot Coconut Vichyssoise | 64 | M/D/P | Substitute nondairy creamer for soy milk |
| Roasted Eggplant Soup | 66 | M/D/P | None |
| Wild Mushroom Veloute Soup | 67 | M/D/P | Substitute potato starch for flour |
| Tri-colored Matzo Balls | 68-69 | M/P** | None |
| Yellow Tomato Basil Bisque | 70 | M/D/P | None |
| Orange Fennel Salad | 80 | P | None |
| Hearts and Flowers Salad | 83 | M/P | None |
| Grilled Peach Salad | 84 | M/D/P | None |
| Blackened Steak and Asparagus Salad | 86 | M | None |
| Watermelon and Heirloom Tomato Salad | 90 | M | None |
| Mexican Turkey and Portobello Salad | 92 | M** | Use Passover imitation Dijon mustard and vegetable oil. |
| Mizuna, Fig, and Honey Salad | 95 | P | Use clover honey. |
| Chicken Salad with Cherry Balsamic Vinaigrette | 96 | M** | Use Passover imitation mustard |
| Seared Duck Salad | 98 | M | None |
| Mediterranean Fatoush Salad | 99 | P | Omit the spiced pita chips |
| Mango Tuna Salad | 100 | D | Omit vanilla bean and use vegetable oil |
| Roasted Beet Salad | 106 | D/P** | Use Passover imitation Dijon mustard |

*\* Class = meat, dairy, or parve*                    *\*\* This recipe is gebrokts.*

| RECIPE | PAGE | CLASS* | ADJUSTMENT |
|---|---|---|---|
| Marinated Spring Chicken Breast | 114 | M | Omit the techina |
| Ratatouille Chicken Stew | 115 | M | None |
| Roasted Garlic Chicken Stuffed with Dried Fruits and Nuts | 116 | M | None |
| Mushroom Stuffed Chicken | 118 | M | None |
| Cornish Hen with Pistachio Paste | 121 | M | None |
| Chicken Tagine | 122 | M | Omit couscous |
| Coq au Vin | 123 | M | Substitute potato starch for cornstarch |
| Glazed Chicken Breast with Strawberry Salsa | 124 | M | Subsitute potato starch for cornstarch |
| Pastrami-Stuffed Turkey Roast | 128 | M | None |
| Citrus-and-Garlic-Crusted Duck Breasts | 129 | M | None |
| Slow-Roasted Rotisserie Chicken | 133 | M | None |
| Whole Roasted Autumn Chicken | 134 | M | None |
| Homestyle Roasted Chicken | 139 | M | None |
| Chicken Curry | 140 | M | None |
| Moroccan Short Ribs | 151 | M | Omit dried mustard powder and cardomom |
| Barbecue Beef | 153 | M | None |
| Balsamic Braised Brisket with Shallots and Potatoes | 154 | M | None |
| Braised Rib Roast with Melted Tomatoes | 155 | M | None |
| Juniper Berry and Peppercorn Crusted Skirt Steak with Spiced Onions | 156 | M | None |
| Shepherd's Pie | 164 | M | Use non-dairy creamer for soy milk |
| Braised Roasted Veal Provençal | 166 | M | None |
| Hazelnut-and-Honey-Crusted Veal Chop | 169 | M | Use regular honey |
| Fillet Split with Mushroom Wine Reduction | 174 | M | None |
| Tuna with Pico de Gallo Sauce | 186 | P | None |
| Pesce Arrabbiata | 187 | P | Omit the pasta |
| Cod, Potatoes, and Sun-dried Tomatoes | 188 | P | Substitute potato starch for flour |
| Halibut with Zucchini Confit | 192 | P | Substitute potato starch for flour |
| Pecan Crusted Grouper over Amaretto Whipped Potatoes | 194 | D | None |
| Poached Salmon with Roasted Red Pepper Sauce | 195 | P | None |
| Oranges Stuffed with Cranberry-Cherry Relish | 206 | P | None |
| Hasselback Potatoes | 207 | P | None |
| Two-Tone Potatoes with Pesto Sauce | 212 | P | None |

* *Class = meat, dairy, or parve*

** *This recipe is gebrokts.*

| RECIPE | PAGE | CLASS* | ADJUSTMENT |
|---|---|---|---|
| Mushroom Mashed Potatoes | 216 | P | Substitute vegetable oil for canola oil |
| Whipped Root Vegetables with Caramelized Onions | 217 | D/P | Omit non-dairy sour cream |
| Oven Roasted Asparagus | 219 | P | None |
| Sweet Potato Wedges with Vanilla Rum Sauce | 219 | D/P | Use imitation vanilla |
| Cauliflower Popcorn | 225 | P | None |
| Tapas Potatoes | 229 | P | None |
| Smoothies | 244 | D/P | None |
| Melon Granitas | 274 | P | None |
| Sorbet Ruffles | 275 | D/P | None |
| Fresh Fruit Lollipops | 279 | P | None |
| Pineapple Truffles | 285 | P | Use kosher for passover confectioner's sugar |
| Triple Chocolate Explosion | 293 | D/P | Substitute passover cake meal for flour, omit corn syrup, and use imitation vanilla |
| Chocolate Truffles | 312 | D/P | Use kosher for passover confectioner's sugar |

## Suggested holiday menus

### Shabbat Lunch
Challah (see *Kosher by Design*, pp. 15-19)
Thai Beef in Cucumber Cups
Mexican Turkey and Portobello Salad
Cornish Hen with Pistachio Paste
Cholent (see *Kosher by Design*, p. 146)
Cranberry Relish
Pineapple Challah Kugel
Tri-Colored Pasta Salad
Cookie Crunch Brownies or
Marbled Pistachio Chocolate Cake

### Rosh Hashanah Dinner
Salmon Mousse
Chicken Soup with 3-Colored Matzo Balls
Mizuna, Fig, & Honey Salad
Hazelnut-and-Honey-Crusted Veal Chop
Roasted Garlic Chicken Stuffed with
Dried Fruits and Nuts
Strawberry Apple Kugel
Oven-Roasted Asparagus
Giant Apple-Cherry Turnover

### Sukkot
Root Vegetable Soup
Mini Chicken Wellingtons
Chicken Osso Buco
Moussaka
Moroccan Sweet Potato Stew
Apple Kugel
Chocolate Layer Cake
with Creamy Coconut Glaze

### Chanukah
Cajun Sweet Potato Latkes &
Guacamole Latkes
Roasted Tomato Bread Soup
Peking Duck Wontons
Moroccan Short Ribs
Mushroom Mashed Potatoes
Champagne Roasted Green Beans
Glazed Cinnamon Chocolate Ribbon Cake

### Purim
Chicken Dumplings in Ginger Broth
Standing Rib Roast with Melted Tomatoes
Coq au Vin
Hasselback Potatoes
Broccolini in Mustard Vinaigrette
Hamantach (see *Kosher by Design* p. 263)
Triple Chocolate Explosion

### Shavuot
Yellow Tomato Basil Bisque
Roasted Beet Salad with Blue Cheese
Berry Filled Mini Noodle Kugels
Salmon Primavera
Multi-Grain Chick Pea Pilaf
Fudge-Covered Brownie Cheesecake

# index

# Also available in the
# the kosher by design®
### cookbook series

### KOSHER BY DESIGN

- Over 250 luscious recipes
- 120 stunning color photographs
- Holiday menus with complementary wine lists
- Tips on food preparation, table decorations, floral arrangements, and more

ISBN: 978-1-57819-707-1

### KOSHER BY DESIGN
### SHORT ON TIME

- 140 fabulous brand-new recipes
- Large full-color photo featured with every recipe
- Prep time and cooking time
- Innovative ideas for quick and easy table décor

ISBN: 978-1-57819-072-0

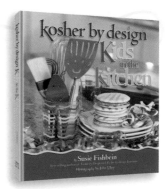

### KOSHER BY DESIGN
### KIDS IN THE KITCHEN

- 80 kid-friendly recipes
- Large full-color photo featured with every recipe
- Equipment lists
- Ingredient lists
- Helpful tips
- Easy-to-follow instructions

ISBN: 978-1-57819-071-3

### PASSOVER BY DESIGN

- Over 30 brand-new recipes, many developed with kosher catering star, Moshe David
- Over 100 *Kosher by Design* favorites reformulated and retested for Passover
- Over 140 full-color images throughout, with over 40 brand-new photos
- Table décor and entertaining ideas

ISBN: 978-1-57819-073-7

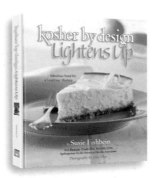

### KOSHER BY DESIGN
### LIGHTENS UP

- Over 145 brand new recipes
- Over 160 full color photos
- Over 320 pages
- Creative entertaining ideas, including olive oil tasting, a party spritzer station and more!
- Simple, healthy approaches to: cooking oils, sweeteners, whole grains, superfoods, smarter shopping, and efficient kitchen gadgets.

ISBN: 978-157819-117-8

### KOSHER BY DESIGN
### TEENS AND 20-SOMETHINGS

- 100 easy-to-prepare brand new recipes
- Large Full-color photo featured with every recipe
- Icons to indicate vegetarian, nut-free, dairy-free, and gluten-free recipes
- Unforgettable party ideas

ISBN: 978-142260-998-9